JUST ONE RIOT

EPISODES OF
TEXAS RANGERS
IN THE 20th CENTURY

JUST ONE RIOT

BEN PROCTER

EAKIN PRESS ★ Austin, Texas

Published in the United States of America
By Eakin Press
An Imprint of Sunbelt Media, Inc.
P.O. Drawer 90159   ★   Austin, TX 78709-0159

ISBN 0-89015-806-1

2 3 4 5 6 7 8 9

Library of Congress Cataloging-in-Publication Data

Procter, Ben H.
  Just one riot : Texas Rangers in the 20th century / by Ben Procter
    p. cm.
  Includes bibliographical references (p.   )
  ISBN 0-89015-806-1 : $17.95
  1. Texas Rangers — History — 20th century. I. Title.
F391.P94   1991
976.4 — dc20   90-24104
                                                                   CIP

To the Hoyts — Peggy and Dirk
for providing an atmosphere for writing some of these chapters.
And to Phoebe Procter, who knows the reason why.

Contents

Foreword

A decade or more ago, much of the time I spent at annual meetings of the Western History Association was occupied in explaining the presence of three historians — Donald Worcester, John Alexander Carroll, and Ben Procter — to first-time attendees. The trio, all members of the Texas Christian University history department, would sweep through the lobby — tall, dressed in flashy Western style (except for Procter), and particularly wearing outsized Stetsons. No one had to ask whether they came from the state of Texas — they looked like Texans, they swaggered like Texans, and they talked like Texans. Procter was the only Texan in the group. Many people wondered whether they were young Texas Rangers (we were all younger then!). They looked like Texas Rangers historically are supposed to look, whereas many Texas Rangers looked like most of us non-noticeable types.

I had only one brush with a Texas Ranger. Del Mar College invited me down to Corpus Christi to give a public talk on the American cowboy. After I finished, a tall straight man, looking as if he might be kin to Worcester, Carroll, and Procter, cornered me and suggested we eat in the campus lunch room. Cowed by his size, I readily assented. He turned out to be Bill Sterling, former adjutant general of the Texas Rangers and author of a better-than-usual autobiography. He talked as if he were yelling into a hurricane, and soon we were surrounded by a gawking and almost adulatory congregation of college students and faculty. Adulatory toward Sterling, not toward me.

Since I had talked about cowboys, he didn't want to talk about Rangers, but about cowboys. A man on horseback, he opined, had to be put on the back of a horse when his bones and shape were still forming. Otherwise he would never make a proper horseman. As a Ranger, he knew. Your two lower cheeks had to lie equally on either side of the horse's backbone, like saddlebags, and gradually assume the shape of a horse's upper sides and rise and fall in rhythm with the horse's flanks.

"You take Roy Rogers," Sterling shouted. "He makes a million dollars, but you can tell he was born in Ohio or somewhere. He has two little round balls for a behind, and they just bounce along as though he and the horse don't know each other yet! Yet he's been making movies for thirty years or more. It's because he didn't grow up on a horse."

I nodded approvingly, and was glad he couldn't analyze my rhythms on the back of a horse. Our little claque whistled with approval. I wished I were somewhere else.

Walter Webb, frequently quoted in the following book, often told me he wished he could rewrite his landmark book on *The Texas Rangers* because he had swallowed whole their distrust of anyone who might have crossed the Rio Grande into Texas anywhere in the past 375 years. To a Ranger, he said, anyone with an olive skin, black eyes, black hair, and a hint of a Mexican accent must be guilty of something illegal, preferably murder, robbery, cattle-rustling, or invasion. Webb had listened to the Rangers while he supped with them at night, and had absorbed some of their prejudices into the pages that ensued.

He also liked to tell the story of Frank Hamer, famous for his tracking and ambush of Bonnie and Clyde after his Ranger days. Hamer told Webb that as a young man, barely adult, he had been stationed in San Angelo with the Rangers, his first post. He and another Ranger, equally youthful, devised a plan to hold up the San Angelo bank. They arranged for fresh mounts to be stashed at convenient spots between San Angelo and the Rio Grande, so they could dash like old Pony Express boys across into Mexico before their Ranger buddies could catch up with them.

"We never thought of the money," said Hamer. "We were young men full of being young, and we just wanted to see if we could pull it off. Most of all, we didn't like the teller in the bank, and we really wanted to see the look of surprise on that s.o.b.'s face when we stuck two pistols in his face and told him to reach for the money!"

But at the last moment they were ordered out on a look-see at another problem area, and the plans were abandoned. And so the Rangers avoided a scandal, of which few have seen the light. Then

Hamer would look off into the distance and say again, "But oh how I'd have liked to have seen that s.o.b.'s face!"

The point of these personal notes is to indicate that Rangers were human beings, young and impulsive and careless, as well as, like Sterling, down-to-earth philosophers and observers. The movies and novels have portrayed them as some sort of other-worldly figures, hard-eyed and cold, almost grim and godlike in their search for justice and retribution.

Ben Procter's book shows the Texas Rangers as human beings and brings them out of the stern shadows into vivid life. The manuscript reads like a succession of Hollywood or TV action scripts, each chapter focusing on a dramatic incident or a Texas Ranger who will not be faced down, no matter how great the trouble or the guns facing him. I can see half-a-dozen movies being made from this book. The story is there, and Procter has told it vividly. He reminds me of Leander McNelly's definition of courage — "a man who just keeps on coming on." Procter has kept on coming on with this story of the modern Texas Ranger, and it's going to be a difficult book to put down. Whether the Rangers have outlived their time is problematical and political, but they will **live** again through the following pages.

— JOE B. FRANTZ

Preface

In 1965 Steve Schuster, a graduate student at Texas Christian University, wrote a master's thesis, under my direction, entitled "The Modernization of the Texas Rangers, 1930–1936." His study piqued my curiosity in law enforcement, especially concerning the men who made up the statewide organization. As a result, I encouraged two graduates, James Ward of San Angelo State University and John McClung of Pepperdine University, to do dissertations on the twentieth-century Texas Rangers, and I began conducting taped oral history interviews with the most outstanding and revered Ranger officers. Periodically over the next ten years, I interviewed such men as Red Burton, Leo Bishop, Bob Crowder, Manuel T. "Lone Wolf" Gonzaullas, A. Y. Allee, Bill Wilson, Clint Peoples, Jim Riddles, Dogie Wright, Trenton Horton, Charlie Miller, and Lewis Rigler, as well as Colonel Wilson Speir and Lieutenant Colonel Leo Gossett, the director and assistant director of the Texas Department of Public Safety. In the summer of 1974, after the hostage crisis at the Huntsville prison, I interviewed a number of participants in that ordeal: Texas Department of Corrections Director Jim Estelle, Ranger Captain G. W. Burks, and hostages Linda Woodman and Novella Pollard. This book is based largely on those taped interviews, together with accompanying evidence from newspapers, memoirs, theses, dissertations, and Ranger scrapbooks and documentary records.

The writing of any work enlists the talents and skills of many individuals. No better proof of this statement can be found than in *Just One Riot*. Besides the Rangers who spent hours with me recalling the past on tape, I am indebted to Roger Conger of Waco, who gained me an audience with Red Burton as well as with Mr. and Mrs. Tilley Buchanan, Margrett Curton, and Mary Dollins, the children of former Sheriff Bob Buchanan. Arlan Hayes, editor of the *San Augustine Tribune*, Judge Wardlow Lane, former Lieutenant Governor Ben Ramsey, and former Ambassador to Australia Edward Clark helped corroborate the history pertaining to Leo Bishop. Inspector J. L. Rogers of the DPS and Ranger Trenton Horton, both active participants at Thornton with Ranger Captain Clint Peoples, were invaluable sources of information. Emmett Whitehead, editor and publisher of the *Rusk Cherokeean*, not only recounted the events at the Rusk State Hospital and his specific participation but also provided newspapers and scrapbooks about Bob Crowder and the other participants. TDC Director Jim Estelle, Ranger Captain G. W. Burks, Mrs. Pete Rogers, and former hostages Linda Woodman and Novella Pollard helped me piece together the "Fred Gomez Carrasco vs. Texas Law Enforcement" chapter. And former Senior Ranger Captain Bill Wilson, Colonel James B. Adams (director of the DPS), Senior Captain H. R. "Lefty" Block, and Assistant Supervisor Maurice Cook provided the facts in the recent history of the Rangers. I am grateful to acting curator Tom Burks and librarian Janice Reece of the Texas Ranger Hall of Fame Museum, as well as former FBI agent Bob Wiatt, who is head of security and university police at Texas A&M, for helping secure a number of photographs. But, above all, I am most grateful to James Ward, John McClung, and Steve Schuster, who did excellent work on the Rangers in two dissertations and a thesis. I am especially appreciative of Janet Schmelzer, Ron Law, Vista McCroskey, and Schuster — professors and former graduates — who helped me prepare this manuscript. Finally, I am most grateful to Dr. Larry Adams and the TCU Research Foundation, who provided two grants to assist my study of the Rangers, and to Margaret Farmer of Fort Worth, who was most helpful in typing the manuscript.

Ben Procter
Texas Christian University
June 1991

I.

The Texas Rangers: Into the Twentieth Century

The land from which the Texas Rangers arose was a primitive frontier, fraught with danger and the disquieting struggles of nature. Far from civilization, the Anglos who settled Texas early in the 1820s found themselves in an abundant, yet inhospitable, country. In certain areas the soil was rich, capable of producing bountiful crops of cotton and corn; yet, fearsome climatic conditions were rampant — blue northers, tornadoes, sleet and hail, torrential rain, and blistering heat. Partly because of the Spanish influence, many Indian tribes were relatively peaceful, but in August and September a "full Comanche moon," signifying the most propitious time for brutal raids, illuminated lonely frontier settlements and outposts.

So in this raw land the Rangers pooled past knowledge and experience. Out of necessity they used whatever means at hand to survive. From the Mexican they learned horsemanship, the importance of a good mount on the open prairies, the spirit of the *vaquero*. From the Indian they acquired an understanding of plainscraft, of tracking and relentless pursuit, of savagery in fighting. And from their own background they inherited a rugged stubbornness for frontier living and an ability to adapt to a new environment. In fact, through this combination of cultures, they became an awesome force of men, prompting John Salmon "Rip" Ford to remark: "They ride like Mexicans; trail like Indians; shoot like Tennesseans; and fight like the devil."[1]

In looks and manner the Rangers were quite distinguishable

1

from such fighting units as the militia or regular army. Recruited at first from the craftiest frontier fighters, and later from leather-faced cowboys and hard-bitten lawmen, they were not concerned with clothes and personal appearance but rather with performance. During the Mexican War — and, for that matter, during most of the nineteenth century — they had a "ferocious and outlaw look" about them, usually "dressed in every variety of garment" and "armed to the teeth" with knives, rifles, and at least a brace of pistols. In fact, the only well-groomed "critters" among them were their horses, magnificent animals that the Rangers cared for meticulously. Nowhere was there evidence of the military — no flags or pennants, no insignias or indications of rank, no furnishing of equipment or medical supplies, no formality between officers and enlisted men.[2]

Yet no one would mistake a Ranger captain. He had a charismatic quality that set him apart from his men. Although not necessarily large or powerful physically, he exuded a quiet confidence. In a time of crisis he knew almost instinctively what to do, possessing that rare combination of boldness and judgment that allowed him, as historian Walter Prescott Webb observed, "to lead rather than direct his men." For him retreat was unpardonable, defeat unbearable; his reputation and prestige demanded success, for in any situation he still had to prove himself capable of leadership before his men.[3]

So for a century, beginning informally as early as 1823 and officially in 1835, the Rangers protected Anglo settlers in a personalized manner. Along the Rio Grande or on the northern and western frontiers they conducted investigations in man-to-man confrontations, relentless in their performance of duty and oftentimes pitiless in their administration of the law. After all, nothing about frontier justice was complex. The only criteria for law-enforcement officers seemed to be: Could they ride? Could they shoot? Did they have the guts and skills to enforce Anglo-American law?

Because of their special aptitude for survival, the Rangers achieved an awesome reputation as frontier fighters. In the Mexican War — with Captains John Coffee "Jack" Hays, Ben McCulloch, and Samuel Walker as leaders — they were "the eyes and ears" for General Zachary Taylor as well as "the cutting edge" for the American army that conquered Mexico City. During the late 1850s, under Senior Captain "Rip" Ford, they fought the formidable Comanches to a standstill, then confronted Juan Cortina, the "Red Robber of the Rio Grande," routing his forces in a series of encounters. After the Civil War and Reconstruction, they once again became the scourge of the outlaw population, with brutally efficient Captain Leander "Lee" McNelly administering primitive six-gun protection for Anglos along the Rio Grande and with highly organized Captain John B. Jones effectively directing the Frontier Battalion on the northwestern frontier.[4]

Because of their incredible deeds, these captains fashioned traditions which affected all future Rangers. For each new member they created an aura of invincibility, a course of action requiring dedication and perseverance, toughness and endurance. No Ranger could escape such legendary exploits as Jack Hays in 1841 single-handedly fighting off a hundred Indians and braves at Enchanted Rock (in Gillespie County); Ben McCulloch in 1847 risking torture and death at Encarnación to obtain accurate information for General Zachary Taylor; Lee McNelly in the 1870s telling his men that "you can't lick a man who just keeps on coming on"; Bill McDonald in 1906 successfully backing down twenty armed black soldiers at Fort Brown and later disdainfully telling an angry mob that they "looked like fifteen cents in Mexican money." These captains fixed an image of personal toughness, indifferent cruelty, and six-gun justice — a reputation helpful to them in frontier Texas, but a source of considerable difficulty for the force in modern times.[5]

Although Rangers cherished these hard-won and impressive traditions, in the twentieth century they would no longer have the luxury of unrestrained action and limited accountability. The frontier had largely disappeared, and with civilization came publicity, politics (local, state, and national), diplomacy and international relations, prohibition, crime waves, two world wars, labor disputes, civil rights, and a communications revolution, all of which imposed limitations on rugged individualism and frontier justice. Nineteenth-century traditions would linger, but twentieth-century realities would require numerous changes and considerable adaptations.

Even so, in the late nineteenth and early twentieth centuries, Texas was still a frontier west of the 100th meridian. And those who lived along the Rio Grande especially recognized the deadliness of that area and the vulnerability of their position. Although the Mexican government was conscientiously striving to maintain order on

its side of the border, violence was an expected commonplace oc-
currence. Time and again Rangers and local Texas lawmen participated in bloody brush fights with Mexican nationals, killing those
who were crossing the river illegally or who had entered Texas and
were fleeing southward with stolen cattle or other ill-gotten booty.
After 1910 such savagery and brutality increased; the floodgates
were open and all restraints gone as revolution once again engulfed
Mexico.[6]

For the next ten years, therefore, the Rangers focused specifically on the border country, dealing with problems that became increasingly difficult and complex. Besides trying to ward off the de-
structive forces unleashed by revolution, they had to contend with
conditions created by World War I: German intrigue and sabotage,
Mexican nationalism and a growing hatred for the *gringo,* draft
dodgers attempting to escape across the border. Then, after 1919,
they had to enforce "the Noble Experiment" — the Eighteenth
Amendment — patrolling approximately 900 miles of river to find
tequileros and whiskey runners.[7]

But instead of meeting these challenges, of acquitting themselves heroically in such critical times, the Rangers fashioned a dismal record of murder and injustice. To every Mexican-American
they became a threat, definitely regarded as killers with legal hunting licenses for brown-skinned people. Nor were such fears unjustified. Throughout the brush country, stories of prisoners tortured or
mysteriously shot ran rampant. Hence, many innocent Mexicans,
when ordered to halt for Ranger inspection, broke and ran, then received a bullet for their mistake. In fact, between 1915 and 1919
this reign of terror, this bloodbath along the Rio Grande, claimed
as many as 5,000 Mexican lives. Or, as historian Webb put it:
"Lead . . . [sank] more men in the Rio Grande in a year than gold
. . . [did] in a decade."[8]

Despite such wanton slaughter, Anglo-Texans along the border understandably condoned these excessive actions. After 1914
they became enveloped in a wartime hysteria which made all Germans and Mexicans suspect. Then the next year they discovered
through the Plan of San Diego that the Mexicans had marked them
for death in a forthcoming invasion of Texas and the Southwest.
Again in 1917 the Zimmerman Note, whereby Germany offered
Texas, New Mexico, and Arizona to Mexico for its support in case
of war with the United States, reaffirmed Anglo-Texan suspicions

Members of Company B camped on the San Saba River in 1896 are from left, Edgar T. Neal, Allen R. Maddox, Tom Johnson (cook), Dudley S. Barker, and John L. Sullivan.

— Courtesy Texas Ranger Hall of Fame Museum

Company B members camped in the Bill Doran pasture on the San Saba River during the Buzzard's Water Hole Mob trouble. From left are Ollie Perry, Jack Harrell, Dr. Donnelly, James Bell, Billie McCauley, Dudley S. Barker, Van Lane, Robert McClure, and Capt. Bill McDonald.

— Courtesy Texas Ranger Hall of Fame Museum

and increased their fears. But, more than anything else, Mexican attacks upon innocent travelers and isolated ranchers, the senseless murdering of Americans simply for being *gringos,* and the constant rumor of an impending bandit raid like that led by Pancho Villa at Columbus, New Mexico, in 1916, drove Texans to approve desperate measures. So during these years of violence, Texans were not too concerned that Governors James E. Ferguson and William P. Hobby began using the Rangers for political patronage. Nor did it seem to bother them that the force was being "packed" with hundreds of incompetent cronies, inexperienced lawmen, and obvious "cutthroats and murderers." The primary concern was that these "Special" Rangers protect them. And no wonder such concern existed. According to a United States Senate committee headed by Albert B. Fall of New Mexico, which investigated "Mexican affairs," Americans "killed, wounded, or outraged" from November 10, 1910, to September 30, 1919, numbered 785, and property damage was estimated at $50,481,133. Possibly E. W. Nevill, a veteran pioneer near Van Horn who lost a son when fifty bandits attacked his ranch on March 25, 1918, best expressed the temper of Texans. Testifying before Fall's committee, he stated that conditions were "worse than when we had to contend with the Comanches every light moon. We knew what we were going up against when we seen a bunch of Comanches; there were two things to do, fight and run. You meet a bunch of Mexicans and you don't know what you are going up against."[9]

Consequently, the war of extermination went on, with no letup in sight. Time and again bandits struck the huge Indio Ranch near Eagle Pass, stealing large numbers of cattle and goats. Farther up the river, in the Big Bend country, the Cano brothers — Chico, José, and Manuel — raided isolated outposts and ranches, then ambushed those who tried to pursue them. And at Brownsville, because of numerous minor incidents in the area, citizens continually feared a large-scale attack from across the border. In turn, Rangers harassed many Germans and Mexican-Americans, accusing them of spying or giving comfort to the enemies of the United States. They also kept the border country in seething turmoil by questioning young Mexican-Americans suspected of evading the draft.

But since their main goals were to prevent or at least to discourage further banditry and rustling, the Rangers oftentimes were extremely cold-blooded and unjustified in their tactics. For instance, on the night of January 28, 1918, Captain J. M. Fox and Company B ran into an ambush outside of El Pourvenir (at the southern tip of the Big Bend). In the ensuing gun battle they did not lose a man; however, all fifteen Mexican prisoners in their custody were killed. Two months later, Captain Will Wright, with a posse of concerned citizens and twelve Rangers, trailed thieves south of the Rio Grande and, in a brief but bloody encounter, killed several Mexican nationals. In September, Sergeant J. J. Edds, one of Wright's men, was "forced" to shoot one handcuffed prisoner in the back during an attempted escape, and then to kill another Mexican for resisting him. In both cases there were no witnesses; therefore, the authorities decided not to prosecute.[10]

Such atrocities, however, could not remain hidden for long. With the end of World War I and the cooling of ardent nationalism, many Texans became disturbed over reports suggesting that the Rangers had murdered "more innocent people . . . on the border than outlaws." Then, in January 1919, Representative J. T. Canales of Brownsville introduced a bill in the state legislature to reorganize the force almost completely — and the whole sordid story was exposed. During the first two weeks in February, a seven-man House committee aired Ranger conduct on the border. And through witnesses willing to relive a number of terrible incidents, the committee learned of Ranger drunkenness and debauchery, of vicious pistol-whippings and brutal intimidations, and — even more appalling — of cold-blooded murders. For instance, Captain H. L. Ransom of Company C, who considered himself "an instrument of justice," herded Mexican prisoners "out in the woods" on several occasions "and shot them." With much the same attitude, Charles F. Stevens of Company G frequently entered private homes, without a warrant, in search of firearms. Upon being asked by the committee on whose authority he had acted, he candidly replied that he "didn't pretend to have any." Yet in spite of such flagrant breaches of public trust, Senior Captain W. H. Hansen had conducted investigations "with the idea of justifying . . . [Ranger] actions," indeed of whitewashing their atrocities.[11]

Fortunately for the Rangers, Canales actually wanted the force personnel "purified" and brought to a high state of "efficiency, not destruction." For that matter, a majority of the committee soon agreed, as did the legislature, that Texas Rangers "properly supported, officered, equipped and managed" would again contribute significantly to state progress and welfare. On March 19, 1919, therefore, they passed an act which temporarily helped restore public confidence in the organization. In a complete overhaul they reduced the force to four regular companies, each with a captain, a sergeant, and fifteen privates, created the position of quartermaster (with captain's rank), established a headquarters company of six men commanded by a senior captain, and allowed the governor to increase Ranger personnel in case of an emergency. In regard to salaries, which, it was hoped, would attract "men of high moral character," wages for captains were set at $150 per month, sergeants at $100, and privates at $90, with minimal expense accounts (although Rangers still had to provide their own horses and much of their equipment). And to curb future misconduct in office, citizens were encouraged to make complaints against Rangers suspected of wrongdoing.

The legislators, however, failed to eliminate a number of serious organizational flaws. No specific qualifications were provided for enlistments; physical condition, formal training and education, or previous law-enforcement experience were not examined. And with all appointments still resting with the governor, the Rangers continued to exist precariously from one state election to the next, their jobs hanging on the current official's whim or favor. Hence, they had no tenure in office, no continuity, no sense of security. For that matter the legislature undermined them even more, oftentimes reducing their size and effectiveness through miserly appropriations.[12]

But despite such limitations, the Canales reforms were still most fortunate and opportune, for during the 1920s law enforcement was incredibly difficult in Texas. With the enactment of prohibition, Rangers were constantly on duty patrolling the Rio Grande for *tequileros* or watching for moonshiners in the forests and out-of-the-way areas of North Central and East Texas. Because of the rapid changes in society partly brought about by the war, they also had to confront Ku Klux Klansmen, those self-appointed protectors and guardians of the "old American way of life," who arbitrarily infringed upon individual liberties. Or they were called upon to prevent property destruction during labor strikes and to quiet transportational and industrial flareups. Of equal importance also was their careful handling of the continuing East Texas "tick war." Frequently they protected federal and state inspectors who forced recalcitrant farmers and ranchers to dip their cattle in order to prevent the spread of disease. But increasingly they were ordered to tame the lawless, frontier-like oil-boom towns which sprang up overnight in such unusual and often isolated places as Desdemona, Mirando City, Mexia, Wink, and Borger.[13]

During these difficult years, three captains particularly upheld Ranger tradition and reputation. In terms of deeds and previous service, Will Wright was by far the best known. A former deputy marshal and sheriff, he had first joined the Rangers in 1898, patrolling the border country with Captain John H. Rogers. Then, in 1917, he also earned the rank of captain; in fact, the Mexicans called him *El Capitán Diablo* (the devil captain) — and rightfully so. No one was more knowledgeable of Southwest Texas or enforced the law more vigorously. Against border bandits and rustlers and *tequileros* he was like a rock, hard and unyielding, a formidable barrier to their lawless activities. And in handling boom towns he set the pattern for later Ranger procedure after successfully taming Wink and the surrounding area in 1927–1928. Although small in stature, he was deadly in combat, thereby commanding the loyalty and respect of his men.[14]

Of somewhat different makeup was Tom Hickman. A tall, lanky cowboy-type, he was the politician-showman of the Rangers. Appearing in parades and as a rodeo judge across the West as well as in Chicago, New York, and London, he publicized and promoted the organization worldwide. Because of his special talent for cultivating the favor of Texas governors, he was the only continuous link in Ranger service from 1921 to 1935. But make no mistake, he was an outstanding peace officer who was responsible for curbing moonshining traffic, for breaking up organized gangs of bank robbers, and for restoring order to oil-boom towns in northern and eastern Texas. Yet perhaps his greatest ability lay in selecting men to serve under him; from his Company B in Fort Worth came such an outstanding officer as Manuel T. "Lone Wolf" Gonzaullas.[15]

Of all the Rangers of this era, Frank Hamer would be the most remembered; the legend of Bonnie and Clyde would see to that. A cowboy and frontiersman who trained himself to be "like an Indian," he was a throwback to the Rangers of the Mexican War and of McNelly's time, yet found himself having to exist in an increasingly urban society — and therein lay both his strength and weakness. Like his primitive Indian heroes, he developed extraordinary sensory powers during his youth. Webb and other admirers claimed that Hamer could hear an airplane thirty seconds before his companions, smell burning flesh to which others were oblivious, and see bullets "before they hit." Consequently, with this Ranger in pursuit, no outlaw was safe. He was a crack shot; he had the patience, the physical equipment (6'3 and 198 pounds), and definitely the know-how to track down any fugitive; and he was, as one old comrade reminisced, one of the few men who was utterly fearless, who "didn't give a damn whether he lived or died." As a law officer he viewed his role rather simply, in much the same terms as a frontier marshal: he was charged with protecting the innocent and punishing the guilty, if need be, personally and without mercy. After all, in that brutal land along the Rio Grande or in the rowdy oil-boom towns or even in the violent young cities of Texas, the law was as unsophisticated as the people in the 1920s. And so was Hamer. In moving through an unruly mob he often used the hard toe of his boot as a means of painful intimidation, while against bank robbers, rustlers, and Mexican desperadoes he despaired of modern technology, commenting on more than one occasion to his Ranger company that "nothing was as effective as a .45 slug in the gut."[16]

In spite of such leadership and a gradual improvement in personnel (partly due to an earlier salary raise), the Rangers were seriously handicapped in 1930. Because of the Great Depression, the state legislature necessarily slashed budgets; therefore the force, which at full complement could number seventy-five men, varied between thirty-five and forty-five. Besides being undermanned, they had also become antiquated by modern science and urbanization. While criminals in high-powered automobiles "shuttled between distant cities like commuters," the Rangers had to rely on free railroad passes or provide their own cars — with a monthly allotment of fifty dollars per company for "repairs and upkeep." And as for weapons, although receiving from the state "one improved carbine [usually a lever-action Winchester .30-.30 or .30-.06 rifle] and a pistol [single-action Colt .45] at cost," they were hard-pressed, historian Steve Schuster noted, to compete with gangsters who used Thompson submachine guns and Browning automatic rifles "acquired at no cost."[17]

Yet briefly during the early 1930s the Rangers performed beyond expectations. With the appointment of William W. "Bill"

Sterling as adjutant general in January 1931, they responded to his encouraging support, especially after he selected outstanding lawmen as captains and increased their transportation allowance substantially. For instance, along the border, Will Wright and several other captains were particularly effective against Mexican rustlers and bootleggers. From their base of operations at Austin, Frank Hamer and Headquarters Company raided gambling halls near San Antonio, broke up a highly organized automobile theft ring in the San Saba-Comanche area, and continually thwarted the widespread efforts of energetic moonshiners. Then, in the vice-ridden Dallas-Fort Worth area, Tom Hickman with Company B constantly interrupted the lawless activities of gamblers, honky-tonk operators, and bank robbers. During 1931–1932 he and his men were even more impressive in handling the new East Texas oil boom centering around Longview and Kilgore. By high-handedly issuing "sundown orders," liberally using both ends of their Colt .45s or Winchesters, and handcuffing hundreds of "bad actors" to Sergeant "Lone Wolf" Gonzaullas's "trotline" (a logging chain which was firmly secured to a pulpit at the First Methodist Church in Kilgore), they ruthlessly "outtoughed" the criminal elements and prevented them from taking over the wildest oil rush ever witnessed in Texas.[18]

But late in July 1932, the Rangers made a grave error in judgment: they openly supported Governor Ross Sterling against Miriam A. "Ma" Ferguson in the Democratic primary — and lost. So in January 1933, upon assuming office, the new governor fired every Ranger for his partisanship — forty-four in all. The results were disastrous. Besides the state legislature reducing Ranger salaries, eliminiating longevity pay, slashing travel budgets, and limiting force personnel to thirty-two men, Mrs. Ferguson appointed new officers, many of whom "by any standard," Schuster candidly asserted, "were a contemptible lot." In less than a year one private was convicted of murder; several others in Company D, after having raided a gambling hall in Duval County, were found to have set up their own establishment with the confiscated equipment; and still another, a captain, was arrested for theft and embezzlement. But even worse, the governor began using Special Ranger commissions, as her husband had done during World War I, as a source of political patronage. Within two years she enlarged this group to 2,344 men, thus prompting the *Austin American* to comment that "about all the requirements a person needed . . . to be a Special Ranger was to be a human being."[19]

Consequently, with Rangers once again becoming a source of patronage, corruption, and ridicule, the effects upon state law enforcement were, of course, catastrophic. During the Ferguson years, crime and violence became widespread, bank holdups and murders commonplace. Soon few states could boast of a more vicious assortment of gangsters or provide a safer sanctuary for the criminal element. For instance, residents in the Dallas-Fort Worth area alone included George "Machine-Gun" Kelly, Raymond Hamilton, and "mad-dog killers" Clyde Barrow and Bonnie Parker. And who besides "Ma" Ferguson was responsible for this breakdown in the public defense? To most Texans the answer was obvious. As one newspaper sarcastically remarked, "a Ranger commission and a nickel can get . . . a cup of coffee anywhere in Texas."[20]

In January 1935, however, Governor James V. Allred obviated the causes of such derision. Having campaigned the previous year to "overhaul" the state law-enforcement machinery, he pushed through the legislature a bill creating the Texas Department of Public Safety (DPS). To supervise administrative policies and procedures he appointed a three-man Public Safety Commission, which in turn selected a director and an assistant director. The new state agency had three basic units: the Texas Rangers, the Highway Patrol, and at Austin a newly created Headquarters Division, which was to be a modern scientific crime laboratory and detection center. Thus, on August 10, 1935, with the official initiation of the DPS, the Rangers became an important part of a much larger law enforcement team. And although Walter Prescott Webb sadly predicted their demise as a separate entity, fearing that they would lose their identity and be absorbed by the more sizable Highway Patrol, such was not the case. Through reorganization came much-needed reform and state support, and the modernization of the force began.[21]

During the summer and fall of 1935, the three Public Safety commissioners appointed by Governor Allred — General Albert Sidney Johnston, George W. Cottingham, and Ernest Goens — met continually in Austin to set departmental policies. At these sessions they effected many significant changes in the Ranger organization. Immediately they allayed individual anxieties by leaving the basic structure of five companies intact, even rehiring all Rangers that Governor Ferguson had dismissed and offering them tenure. Then they established individual standards, which had been wholly lacking in the past. Thereafter, for appointment to the force, examinations and recommendations instead of political patronage would be important, while for promotion, seniority and performance would be the determining factors. As for those aspiring to become Rangers, future applicants would have to be thirty to forty-five years of age, at least 5'8, and "perfectly sound" in mind and body. To qualify fully they would also receive instructions, as the commissioners strongly recommended and later required, in the latest techniques of fingerprinting, communications, ballistics, and records. And they would be crack shots. In regard to education, the commissioner set no stipulations, no penalties, except possibly taking a written exam and submitting an "intelligent" weekly report of all activities. For most Rangers this task proved neither difficult nor time-consuming. For instance, in explaining the laborious tracking and the carefully planned ambush of Bonnie and Clyde, Frank Hamer tersely announced: "We've done the job."[22]

Ever mindful of previous Ranger criticisms and of obvious drawbacks to the force, the commissioners were determined to institute other necessary reforms. Dividing the state into five parts, then six in 1937, they assigned a Ranger captain and his company to a specific area. In turn, privates received duty stations in key towns throughout each district, and under no circumstances could they leave their home territory without orders. If perchance they were seemingly exiled to some small, out-of-the-way Texas community, it would not be forever; transfers were frequent and easy to obtain. Despite lack of funds from the legislature, the commissioners also increased Ranger mobility. Although unable temporarily to purchase state-owned patrol cars, they did increase automobile allowances substantially, while along the border they used airplanes furnished by the United States Coast Guard Air Patrol and provided much-needed horse trailers. At the same time, they increased Ranger armament and fire power, obtaining automatic weapons, including several Thompson .45 submachine guns, through private donations. By such reorganization they thus hoped to bring the force into the twentieth century, to make each Ranger a link between rural and urban Texas. In other words, these modernized state lawmen, trained in the latest scientific methods of crime de-

Sgt. Lee Trimble riding shotgun with Arch Miller at the wheel on July 8, 1924, in Marathon on the way to Glenn Springs in the Chisos Mountains.
— Courtesy Texas Ranger Hall of Fame Museum

One major and five captains: (standing, from left) J. A. Brooks, J. H. Rogers, (unknown) Waite; (sitting) L. P. Sieker, J. B. Armstrong, and Bill McDonald.
— Courtesy Texas Ranger Hall of Fame Museum

Group of Texas Rangers at Headquarters in Austin, 1937: (from left) Col. Horace H. Carmichael, director of the Department of Public Safety; Roscoe D. Holliday, Leo Bishop, Levi Duncan, Dick Oldham, Ernest D. Daniel, former Ranger Capt. Roy W. Aldrich, and Bill Lay.

— Courtesy Texas Ranger Hall of Fame Museum

Texas Rangers Tom Hickman, Lone Wolf Gonzaullas, Bob Crowder, and Clint Peoples.

— Courtesy Texas Ranger Hall of Fame Museum

tection, would have at their fingertips the invaluable resources of the Identification and Records, Intelligence, and Communications bureaus in Austin, even though stationed in remote areas.[23]

Despite these helpful and necessary reforms, the Rangers were still fearful of the future. Surely some agreed with Webb (and later with former Adjutant General Bill Sterling) that they would lose their identity, their freedom of action, their privileged status, and be swallowed up by the much larger Highway Patrol — at times contemptuously called a "bunch of motorcycle jockeys." Others were equally concerned when on August 27, 1935, Governor Allred ordered the Rangers to stop enforcing the state prohibition laws and turn such investigations over to local officers. But they were even more alarmed over the shaky status of their leadership. In November 1935, the likable and respected Senior Captain Tom Hickman was forced to resign because of circumstances surrounding an unsuccessful raid in Fort Worth; several months later (May 1936) Louis G. Phares, the first director of the DPS, was pressured into retiring; then, on September 24, 1938, his replacement, Henry Carmichael, who definitely favored the Rangers, suddenly died of a heart attack.[24]

From such body blows the Rangers were obviously reeling, their morale and spirit at low ebb. But when the commissioners appointed Homer Garrison, Jr., as director, all segments of the DPS became secure and were thereafter in safe hands. For the Rangers especially, this 6'2, square-jawed, bespectacled new leader was an ideal choice. A former deputy sheriff at Lufkin who had joined the Highway Patrol at its inception, he understood these rugged, individualistic men and therefore was able to integrate them into a well-organized structure without blunting their initiative and pride. In fact, they considered the Colonel as one of their own; he was a man of unquestionable integrity who demanded loyalty and discipline and pride, traits of character which they identified as those of a Ranger. More and more over the years, they came to appreciate his tact and diplomacy, his strong support, his ability to "handle legislators." Thus the Garrison legend began to build, growing to gigantic proportions during the next thirty years.[25]

From the beginning, Garrison worked adroitly and patiently to build the force. Whenever a major criminal case occurred in the state, he immediately sent Rangers to investigate, thereby enhancing their prestige as well as giving them the freedom of movement so ingrained in their character and tradition. Against the new governor, W. Lee "Pappy" O'Daniel, and a legislature that was on an "economy jag," he struggled to maintain appropriations. In 1939 the Rangers lost two captains and five investigators because of a cut in funds. But Garrison's "educational approach" eventually began to have the desired effects upon state leaders. In 1939–1940 he repeatedly ignored gubernatorial entreaties to place the Rangers again in the Adjutant General's Department, hence under political domination. Most important during the next few years, he surrounded himself with men who had the ability and courage and dedication to uphold the world-renowned reputation of the force. He encouraged A. Y. Allee, Hardy Purvis, Leo Bishop, Manny Gault, and Zeno Smith to continue their service, while luring into the organization such outstanding lawmen as future Captains Manuel T. "Lone Wolf" Gonzaullas, Bob Crowder, Johnny Klevenhagen, Raymond Waters, Eddie Oliver, J. C. Paulk, and Clint Peoples.[26]

In September 1941, because of Garrison's persuasive counseling, the legislature increased the Rangers to forty-five men — and just in time. After Pearl Harbor on December 7, they had many additional duties thrust upon them. Immediately they, together with the Highway Patrol and the FBI, rounded up enemy aliens and placed them in detention camps near Kenedy, Crystal City, and Seagoville. In turn, they were directed to keep close surveillance over the thousands of German-Americans in Central Texas and the few Japanese-Americans in the Lower Rio Grande Valley, although finding little reason for such orders. Then, with Garrison accepting the chairmanship of Defense Police Mobilization in Texas and soon thereafter other important home-front duties, the Rangers were called upon repeatedly to show films on the training of air-raid wardens, to take statewide inventory of the armament and munitions of all law-enforcement agencies, and to instruct civilians and local police in the latest techniques of defending factories, refineries, generating plants, dams, and vital industries from sabotage. At the same time, because of their experience along the border, they tracked down prisoners-of-war as well as escaped convicts who were trying to reach Mexico.

Despite these diverse responsibilities, the Rangers still carried out their regular police work, which was equally time-consuming and often dangerous. In June of 1943, for instance, Rangers Johnny

Klevenhagen and Eddie Oliver apprehended two criminals in downtown Houston after a running gunfight, while in Beaumont Captain Hardy Purvis and several of his company helped maintain order after a bloody race riot near the shipyards.[27]

Nor did Ranger duties lessen in post-World War II America; with demobilization a serious crime wave enveloped the nation. Under these circumstances Colonel Garrison impressed state legislators with the need for more efficient law enforcement; therefore, the DPS budget rose from $1,549,831 in 1944 to $4,717,400 in 1950. With such encouragement, Garrison strove to improve the DPS, the Rangers specifically reflecting his demand for greater excellence. In 1947 he increased their number from forty-five to fifty-one men, equipped them and the Highway Patrol with seventy-five state-owned automobiles (which were furnished with three-way radios), and required the Bureau of Education to instruct them annually in the latest crime-fighting techniques. By the next year he further aided investigative methods by providing them with additional mobile receivers and transmitters as well as the newest AM and FM power equipment. And in 1949 he broke ground for new buildings in Austin, which by 1953 would house a modern crime-detection center.[28]

The Rangers responded accordingly, making headlines continually during the 1950s by acts of daring and heroism. In 1951, for instance, Max Westerman, who became a Ranger pilot-investigator after the DPS acquired an airplane in 1949, captured an escaping arsonist near Huntsville by landing in front of the fugitive's car. In 1955 Captain Clint Peoples used a U.S. Army half-track to evict a crazed killer who had barricaded himself in an isolated farmhouse near Thornton. In an equal feat of bravery, Captain A. Y. Allee in 1954 added to Ranger invincibility and tradition by scuffling with the powerful "boss" of Duval County, George Parr, and bloodily extracting a promise from him to discontinue openly carrying live-action Winchester rifles in his home domain. Then, in almost unbelievably courageous episodes during 1955–1956, Lewis Rigler, in "plain sight" and unarmed, marched up to a rifle-toting, crazed farmer near Muenster and disarmed him; Captain Johnny Klevenhagen hunted and eventually killed a vicious desperado in the tangled underbrush of the Brazos River bottom near Houston; and Captain Bob Crowder faced rioting and armed patients in the state mental hospital at Rusk and talked them into surrendering without further bloodshed. Yet, of the 8,000 yearly cases that fifty-one Rangers were investigating during the 1950s, these incidents were not too unusual. As Captain Bill Wilson rather graphically commented to the author (and with obvious pride): "Hell, Ben, whenever there's a mean ass, they call on us."[29]

But in spite of such an overall performance — a personnel increase to sixty-two men in 1961, better training, able leadership, and more comprehensive service — the Rangers came under heavy political fire in the 1960s. Charged with being *"pistoleros"* (hired gunmen) of the governor, "strikebreakers" against labor unions, and "the Mexican-Americans' Ku Klux Klan," they found themselves in an impossible situation, having an image nearly as disreputable as in the corrupt Ferguson era of the early 1930s — and to a man they did not like it. Because of the Supreme Court rulings after 1954, they felt "handcuffed" by the judges, their previous methods of police procedure under question, their attempts at law enforcement stymied by legal technicalities. Nor did the Civil Rights Act of 1964 and subsequent amendments improve their public standing or personal temperament, especially with Mexican-Americans charging them with violations at every turn. More than anything else, their involvement in 1966 with *"la huelga"* — a strike involving stoop farm laborers at the well-irrigated, 1,600-acre La Casita Farms near Rio Grande City — proved to be a source of irritation, a bewildering, unpleasant assignment which brought into question their methods of law enforcement, even an excuse for the dissolution of their organization. In trying to keep peace between management and labor, protect property, and uphold the law, they were, in the eyes of a generation facing the riots and violence of a Newark or a Detroit, ineffective. Or as one DPS commissioner observed, they tried "to cope with current problems by using yesterday's tools." They therefore became a political football that Texas liberals could kick at conservatives, a club that United States Senator Ralph Yarborough could swing at his inveterate enemy Governor John Connally, a straw man that organized labor could attack to strengthen the cause of farm unionism in Texas, even a symbol of oppression which Mexican-Americans could use to help stir a social revolution in the Lower Rio Grande Valley. Probably Captain A. Y. Allee, a crusty veteran of thirty-five years on the border, reflected Ranger feelings best in stating to State Senator

Don Kennard of Fort Worth: "Son, this is the goddamdest thing I've ever been in."[30]

During the next few years, such criticisms gained momentum. In January 1968, with Mexican-Americans increasingly vocal, State Senator Joe Bernal of San Antonio threatened a bill to abolish the Rangers by having them "taken over by the DPS." G. I. Forum pointed to the racism within the organization, especially since no blacks or Mexican-Americans were members, and no visible attempts were being made to recruit them. Again in January of that year, with the Sixty-first Legislature in session, some state senators, such as A. R. "Babe" Schwartz of Galveston and Oscar Mauzy of Dallas, suggested cutting DPS appropriations, partly because of what they considered to be the Rangers' embarrassing image. Then, in the spring and summer of 1972, during the hotly contested Democratic primary, gubernatorial candidate Frances "Sissy" Farenthold recommended "disbanding the Rangers," but, after immediate negative public response, relented by suggesting their "withdrawal from South Texas." And as late as May 1974, the Supreme Court added judicial condemnation to the continuing furor; it upheld the actions of a three-judge federal panel that had restrained the Rangers and local lawmen from "intimidating" union organizers in the *"la huelga"* controversy near Rio Grande City in 1968.[31]

Meanwhile, such scurrilous attacks, as well as the untimely death of Colonel Garrison in May 1968, would initiate change within the Department of Public Safety. The DPS commissioners took a "hard look" at the Rangers — and, as in the past, from such investigations and "soul-searching" came new guidelines to meet present and future needs. Under the leadership of Colonel Wilson E. "Pat" Speir, the new director of the DPS who had worked his way up through the ranks since entering the department in 1939, and his assistant Lieutenant Colonel Leo Gossett, the Rangers regrouped and reorganized. By November 1969, after the legislature had enlarged the force to seventy-three men (and eventually to eighty-two by September 1, 1971), Speir and the commissioners established a Criminal Law Enforcement Division (Narcotics, Intelligence, and the Rangers) under Chief James M. "Jim" Ray. In turn, they elevated veteran Ranger Clint Peoples to senior captain and soon thereafter (in 1971) Captain Bill Wilson was named his assistant.[32]

From such reorganization the individual Ranger became a more highly trained law-enforcement officer — and was better equipped. Regarding enlistment requirements, the recruit now had to be between the ages of thirty and fifty, have at least eight years of on-the-job police experience, and have an intermediate certificate which entailed 400 to 600 hours of classroom instruction. He also had to submit a vita for background investigation, take a written examination, then appear before an interview board for further evaluation. Upon acceptance he enrolled in special courses running the gamut of law-enforcement experience: detection and apprehension, gathering of evidence, criminal law, and courtroom presentations. At the same time he became proficient in using his equipment as well as learning how to cultivate good public relations. While on the job he attended monthly company meetings where his captain kept him abreast of the latest procedures in criminal investigation and departmental policy. Unlike those Rangers of the Republic and frontier days, or even of the 1920s and 1930s, he now rode in high-powered, state-furnished automobiles which had new radio equipment with numerous frequencies for receiving and broadcasting, as well as an array of firearms, tear gas, all kinds of transport gear, and a scientific investigative kit. He could use personal firearms (as long as he could qualify with them) or the standardized weapons provided by the department — a Smith & Wesson Model 19 .357 Combat Magnum revolver, a Remington Model 1100 12-gauge semiautomatic shotgun, and a Remington Model 742 .30-.06 semiautomatic rifle, equipped with a telescopic sight. For some emergencies he would be issued body armor (commonly called bullet-proof vests) with attachable groin plates which could even withstand armor-piercing bullets from a .30-.06 rifle. In one instance, on July 30, 1974, such protection saved two Ranger captains and an FBI agent from serious bodily injury at an attempted Huntsville prison break. And for the first time, Rangers wore "adopted clothing" (not an official uniform) consisting of western-style tan gaberdine pants and jacket, black boots, tie and belt, a white shirt, and a silver-colored Stetson. The most distinguishing feature was the Ranger badge, a five-pointed star supported by a wheel forged from a Mexican coin — a fifty-dollar gold piece for captains and a silver peso for all others.[33]

Yet, in 1974, the Rangers were still undergoing changes. With the Sixty-third Legislature increasing personnel to eighty-eight in

Texas Ranger Lee Roy Young, the
first black appointee in Ranger history.
— Courtesy Texas Department
of Public Safety

Capt. A. Y. Alee
— Courtesy Texas Ranger
Hall of Fame Museum

Capt. Jim Riddles and Col. Homer Garrison, Jr., 1967.
— Courtesy Texas Ranger Hall of Fame Museum

Senior Capt. Bill Wilson
— Courtesy Texas Ranger Hall of Fame Museum

Senior Capt. H. R. "Lefty" Block
— Courtesy Texas Department of Public Safety

September 1973, and to ninety-four a year later, the force established even higher entry requirements. Besides previous recruitment demands, a candidate (outside of the DPS) was required to have sixty hours of accredited college work. Upon acceptance, the new Ranger would receive $968 per month, longevity pay ($4 a month per annum), a clothing allowance, a fully equipped car, complete hospitalization, and a paid life-insurance policy. When Captain Peoples retired on April 1, 1974 (he became a federal marshal), Captain Bill Wilson assumed command with Captain J. L. "Skippy" Rundell as his assistant, and soon thereafter several requirements of the previous administration were relaxed. For instance, the "adopted clothing," except for boots, hat, and badge, became "discretionary"; so were the options on weapons, although each Ranger had to keep the .357 Smith & Wesson revolver, the .30-.06 Remington semiautomatic rifle, and the Remington 12-gauge semiautomatic shotgun in his car in case his captain needed to send extra ammunition. In other words, Wilson was emphasizing the Ranger tradition of individuality but at the same time maintaining those requirements, he candidly stated, "of a topnotch law enforcement service."[34]

During the Bill Wilson era (1974–1985) the Rangers realized even more changes, adjusting and responding to an urbanized Texas as well as to a computerized and scientific age. Although many enlistment requirements were still the same for each Ranger applicant — eight years of full-time police work, an intermediate certificate, a vita for background investigation, a written examination followed by a review board for those who scored the highest — some revisions did occur. While age was no longer mentioned specifically, the candidate had to be at least twenty-nine years old (because of certification at age twenty-one plus eight years experience, and the last two years now had to be as a "commissioned officer" and "presently employed" with the DPS). A stringent physical examination also apparently stressed youth for the force, or at least that has been the result. Whereas the mean age of the Rangers was fifty-three in 1967, the average decreased to forty-six in 1989.[35]

But even greater effects occurred regarding equipment and law-enforcement techniques. The state continued to furnish automobiles which had radios with many frequencies for receiving and broadcasting. In August 1985, however, the force already had on order DVP (Digital Voice Privacy) radios, whereby two officers could scramble frequencies so that no one could tune in on their conversation. Each Ranger still was issued such standardized weapons as a Smith & Wesson Model 586 .357 Distinguished Combat Magnum revolver (based on the newer L frame which gives better balance and greater control with full-power service loads), a Remington Model 1100 12-gauge semiautomatic shotgun, body armor, tear gas, and a scientific investigative kit. Instead of the Remington .30-.06 semiautomatic rifle, he now routinely carried a .223 Ruger mini-14, which had twenty-round magazine capacity and was a more effective support weapon.[36]

In turn, the six Ranger companies have been provided with highly sophisticated detection gear that is critical to surveillance and undercover operations as well as on-the-scene investigations. A "body bug" for an informant or undercover agent allows officers to listen to conversations and record them; a "bionic ear" can usually pick up an interchange between two individuals up to 300 feet away or, in the case of a hostage situation, detect the occupants' location in a room or building; and a "following device" (a minute transmitter placed on a suspect's vehicle) sends clear signals to Rangers either in a trailing car or in one of the eight DPS helicopters. In rape cases, an ultraviolet light with a portable dual wavelength is used to find seminal stains, to determine whether indeed an assault occurred. This device also checks for powder residue or metal tracings on a person's hand for evidence of a gun have been fired — and is even more effective than a parrafin test. In extremely critical situations, Rangers continue to use ceramic-plated armor, which will deflect heavy firepower such as a steel-jacketed bullet. And for a "firefight" or a maneuver against dangerous suspects, sniper rifles are equipped with night-vision scopes, thus providing a clear definition of the target.[37]

During the Wilson era, Ranger philosophy necessarily changed somewhat to meet the impending 1980s. Although steeled to lethal situations and geared traditionally to a tough individualistic enforcement of the law, the modern Ranger personified the concept of cooperation more than the stance of "One Riot! One Ranger!" Colonel James B. Adams, the articulate and highly qualified director of the DPS from 1980 to 1987, would argue that their "primary role" has always been "to assist local law enforcement agencies — upon request from them, of course." For that matter, the Ranger leadership has readily agreed. As H. R. "Lefty" Block, who became senior captain upon Wilson's retirement in February 1985, and Assistant Supervisor of the Rangers Maurice Cook both stated: "We have to maintain a low profile." And the reason? If the murder of a prominent citizen should occur in a county where the sheriff had limited personnel and little crime-detection ability or equipment, a call for Ranger help would usually happen. After all, the Rangers have trained investigators, scientific laboratories, and the wherewithal to be successful. But when a felon is apprehended and the Rangers make a "big splash . . . in the press" Block explained, the local sheriff might "not call on us next time" because he "has to live among these people and is elected by them." So, Block said, the Rangers "maintain that type of attitude" of letting "him take the credit . . . It helps him; the job got done; and we're satisfied. That way we don't have any hard feelings from local officers. They know that, if they call, we're not going to run in there and be big glory hunters."[38]

Effective training necessarily had to accompany such philosophy — and it did. While each company assembled monthly (or bimonthly at the discretion of its commander) for briefing on departmental policies and procedures, captains held quarterly meetings. And inevitably they stressed both formal and practical education to improve the force, especially since they began requiring, effective in 1983, a detailed written report for case records. Whereas only one or two Rangers had a university degree in 1974, fourteen had graduated by 1985 and twelve had associate degrees, meaning two years of college work, the overall ninety-four-man force averaging thirty-three college credits. Equally, if not more, important, the Rangers had to attend seminars or in-service training schools (a minimum of forty hours over two years), where they could qualify for advanced and instructor certificates. At times different universities across the state have offered a seminar on some aspect of law enforcement, in which one or two members of the force have been encouraged to participate. Otherwise, Rangers have the opportunity to attend the DPS Academy in Austin, which conducts four or five "schools" each week. In addition, some have attended the FBI National Academy, from which seven have graduated.

And what a wide diversity of courses awaits the modern Rangers. Besides seminars in courtroom procedure, giving testimony, and public relations, the Rangers learn the latest techniques in investigative training: fingerprinting, polygraph, photography, basic interrogation, crime-scene investigation, blood-splattering, hostage negotiations, and forensic hypnosis. Thirteen Rangers were licensed hypnotists in 1989.[39]

As a result, the Rangers have enjoyed as great a degree of success in the 1980s as during any decade in the twentieth century. Although their caseloads have become increasingly heavy, dealing primarily with murder, theft, burglary, fugitive escape, public-service misconduct, kidnapping, and hostage negotiations, Colonel Adams asserted in 1985 that the Rangers were more in demand because their "capabilities . . . were such that in the last few years they have been utilized in some of the more complicated investigations." As evidence, he proudly enumerated a number of cases which the Rangers helped solve, in conjunction with local law-enforcement officials and/or the FBI. After several years of intensive work in the early 1980s, they "cracked" an oil-field theft ring, which was stealing millions of dollars in drilling equipment, and apprehended a gang of extortionists who had been terrorizing a major food chain in the state. In 1983–1984 they also solved the Ultra-lite murders in Grayson County, where four businessmen were brutally slain in an aircraft hangar; the infant deaths at Kerrville in which nurse Genene Jones was convicted; and the "Mom and Pop Case" at Haltom City, where a "modern-day Bonnie and Clyde" had eluded local officers for a decade by robbing only one bank a year. At the same time, Rangers were helping effect the arrest, indictment, and conviction of public officials involved in election fraud in the Rio Grande Valley, working well with local Mexican-American authorities. Then, in 1985, they participated prominently in the successful return of Amy McNeil, the kidnapped daughter of a wealthy Alvarado businessman. And they were called upon to investigate state agencies throughout Texas where indications of criminal wrongdoing by state employees had arisen. Because of their low-profile policy of not attracting attention, the Rangers were able to complete their business without damaging unnecessarily the reputation of innocent public officials.[40]

Yet the Rangers needed to eliminate one last flaw in behalf of their modern-day image — that of racism. As early as June 1987, they began receiving criticism for having no blacks in their organization (although there were six Mexican-Americans). By January 1988, the Austin chapter of the NAACP joined the fray, producing testimony from three black DPS troopers that characterized promotions to the force as being results of the "buddy system." One disappointed black DPS veteran described his failed attempt to be a Ranger this way: "If you're a good old boy, you are going to get promoted. But if you are not in the clique, you can't get anything." The DPS commissioners, therefore, "voted authority" to new DPS director Colonel Leo Gossett to make policy changes in hiring and promotion. As a result, a three-member panel strongly urged hiring "more minorities." On September 1, 1988, forty-one-year-old Lee Roy Young, a fourteen-year veteran who was a DPS investigator in San Antonio, became the first black appointee in Ranger history, and on January 1, 1989, was joined by thirty-five-year-old Earl Ray Pearson, formerly a Highway Patrol sergeant, who proudly pinned on the Ranger badge.[41]

Despite all such changes, the modern Rangers are still regarded as the "elite" in Texas law enforcement. Although their salaries have increased substantially since 1974 (annual base pay for September 1, 1989, was: officers $34,000; sergeants, $37,000; captains, $40,000; assistant commander, $43,000; senior Ranger captain, $46,000, plus hazardous duty and longevity pay of $7.50 a month for each year of service), the reasons for being a Texas Ranger go far beyond monetary considerations. Specifically, those reasons are pride, esprit de corps, and tradition. Colonel Adams succinctly summed up their attitude this way: "The new recruits coming in . . . would pay to be a Ranger."[42]

II.

Bill McDonald
and the Brownsville Affray

Ranger Captain Bill McDonald was an uncomplicated man, unwilling — or unable — to view life in complex form. To him no shades of gray existed. People were either good or evil, right or wrong, scoundrels or honest individuals. In regard to law enforcement he obviously applied this simple principle, regardless of its logic. In a confrontation with him, rustlers had the choice of surrendering or drawing their guns; a mob bent upon lynching a prisoner could either disperse or have him "cut down on anyone who . . . [took] a hand in it"; and strikers, instead of demonstratively protesting for better working conditions, should "go back to work and tell . . . [management their] troubles afterwards." Nor did being outnumbered or threatened with death cause him to hesitate or alter his course of action because, he philosophically stated, "no man in the wrong can stand up against a fellow that's right and keeps on a-comin'."[1]

Direct, straightforward, with a quaint flair for phrasemaking and an unusual ability to seek — and find — the limelight, Bill McDonald chose the right profession for his talents in late nineteenth-century Texas. Since more than half the state was still a raw frontier, or sparsely inhabited, Texas Rangers were essential to the protection of pioneer settlers, and McDonald in particular, because of his extraordinary talents as a manhunter, was in demand. Hence, he was not looked upon as a relic of a bygone age, as an anachronism or throwback to another era, but rather most Texans and contemporaries appreciated and admired him, even to the

24

point of eulogization. Every two years they accepted his role as the sergeant-at-arms at the Democratic state convention, where he sported, as a symbol of ultimate authority, two seemingly oversized pearl-handled Colt .45 revolvers on his wiry, somewhat frail body. They delighted in knowing that, after wolf hunting in Oklahoma with President Theodore Roosevelt in 1905, he hesitated in accepting an invitation to the White House because he did not "know how to put on a plug hat and one of these spike-tailed coats and pigeontoed shoes" and in turn was advised: "Come exactly as you are." They also pridefully told and retold the story, and in no way did McDonald protest, of his preventing Bat Masterson from striking a perturbingly slow Chinese waiter with a "table-castor." When asked by the notorious gunman if "maybe you'd like to take it up," he calmly replied: "I done took it up." Nor did it seem to matter that McDonald, unlike other such famous Ranger captains of the time as John R. Hughes, J. H. Rogers, and J. A. Brooks who "were willing to direct their men and keep themselves out of the public eye" whenever possible, "dominated his men, kept himself in the foreground, and used them for background." After all, he seemed to epitomize Ranger tradition, to be the personification of all the great Ranger captains — especially after he arrived alone in Dallas to prevent an impending prize fight which had all the earmarks of evolving into a riot. When the disappointed mayor asked where the rest of his men were, McDonald coined the most famous phrase in Ranger history by responding: "Hell! Ain't I enough? There's only one prize fight." Then, in August 1906 the Brownsville Affray occurred, and overnight he acquired a national reputation.[2]

Born on September 28, 1852, in Kemper County, Mississippi, William Jesse McDonald enjoyed what biographer Albert Bigelow Paine described as "a semi-barbaric childhood." The eldest son of Enoch and Eunice Durham McDonald, he lived on a large plantation near the Alabama border, where his father ruled like "a feudal baron" over many acres worked by half a hundred slaves. Swimming at a nearby lake, hunting and fishing, and joining in the chase with the hounds for deer and fox or occasionally a bear were often everyday pursuits. He thus obtained very little "book-schooling," yet learned invaluable lessons in preparation for the Texas Rangers, such as riding and shooting or tracking a quarry. He became so adept with a gun that one admirer stated that he "could throw a nickel up in the air and hit it before it touched the ground," while another testified that he "could pick cherries with a rifle." [3]

In 1861, however, this pattern of life gradually changed, and none of it to McDonald's liking. With the eruption of the American Civil War in April, his father, whom he admired and adored, enlisted as an officer in the Confederate army and was encamped nearby at Meridian. How young Bill Jess thrilled at visiting the camp amidst so many uniformed soldiers and the paraphernalia of war; how he took pride that his "hero" was promoted to the rank of major for bravery; then how disconsolate he became with the saddening news that his father had been killed at the Battle of Corinth in October 1862. At age ten he thus became the "man of the house." At age twelve, with Mississippi overrun by Union soldiers, he faced the breakup of the family plantation, with slaves running away and crops unattended. And at fourteen he and his mother lost their land and therefore accepted an invitation from her brother to migrate to Rusk County in East Texas. [4]

In this new environment Bill McDonald did not thrive and prosper; instead, he was a rebellious teenager, bitter at the changes which had taken place in his life and hostile to authority. After working all day on the family farm or cutting and hauling wood to the nearby village of Henderson, the Rusk County seat, he oftentimes went "coon huntin' " alone all night and at times frequented a "stillhouse" which produced whiskey in considerable quantities. When his mother scolded him — without effect — for carousing and then attempted to administer punishment, he seized her whip and defied her authority; that is, until one night while he lay sleeping, she "pinned him securely in a bed sheet" and thrashed a "permanent" taste out of him "both for liquor and disobedience." Yet she would do nothing to curb his hatred of Yankee soldiers, the likes of whom had "shot dead" his beloved father. Together with a companion named Charley Greene, whose brother had been murdered a few months before and whose assailants were still unapprehended, he decided to confront the Union military which had been sent to Henderson to suppress lawlessness late in the 1860s. After a running confrontation with a group of Union soldiers, they chased their adversaries into the courthouse, and Greene, with pistols cocked, attempted to storm it. Within minutes he was seized from behind and subdued. During the confusion, McDonald was able to slip away undetected, but within a few months he too was caught and was imprisoned at the army stockade at nearby Jefferson, charged with the crime of treason. Although he was eventually acquitted by a jury, months of confinement and the conviction of Charley Greene sobered his passions and tempered his bitterness.[5]

Whatever the reasons, McDonald altered his thinking significantly after 1871, never again placing himself opposite the law. Over the next five years he experimented with a number of professions, all of which were remunerative enough but none of which were really gratifying. In 1872, for instance, he studied briefly in New Orleans at Soule's Commercial College and, upon graduation, returned to Henderson to teach a class in penmanship. By the next year he had switched to overseeing a small general store and operating a ferry on the Sabine River between Henderson and Longview. And in 1875, at the growing railroad terminus of Mineola, he opened a grocery which was so successful that he felt financially able to marry Rhonda Isabel Carter in January 1876.[6]

Yet McDonald did not find the "right" profession until, by accident, he was forced into a confrontation with a local bully. In 1876 George Gordon was a large, disagreeable man who owned several equally offensive bulldogs. Living on the outskirts of Mineola along the major road, he seemed to delight in "siccing" his pets upon some unsuspecting stranger or weaker animal. If anyone offered resistance, Gordon was not averse to violence, reputedly having killed several people either with his "constant companion" — a revolver — or a Bowie knife, which was in a scabbard "down his back." Early in 1876, though, he made a serious error in judgment which could easily have proved fatal. While he was visiting one day in Mineola, one of his vicious bulldogs attacked McDonald's prize pointer, maiming it horribly, whereupon McDonald drew his pistol, intent upon eliminating the brutal animal. In a complete reversal of character, Gordon, possibly because of his opponent's impressive reputation with a gun, pled in behalf of his dog, promising never to allow it in Mineola again. The issue was seemingly resolved. But in case more trouble should occur, McDonald persuaded the sheriff to deputize him. Such action could have been called providential because a few days later Gordon returned to town heavily armed and "liquored up," vowing that "nobody could arrest him." Within minutes McDonald had disarmed and jailed him, much to the relief of the townspeople. After this experience he was "hooked for life" as a lawman.[7]

McDonald enjoyed his new job immensely, even though it oftentimes proved difficult and dangerous. As deputy sheriff he gained invaluable on-the-job training in handling individual "toughs" as well as mobs of people who, through numbers, sought anonymity and therefore security for their lawlessness. From a nearby International and Great Northern (I&GN) camp, as many as 300 railroad tiecutters inundated Mineola on Saturday night, drunkenly challenging anyone who might try to curb their license. Patrons at numerous saloons also created a number of problems for law-enforcement officers, while transients and self-willed individuals who felt no obligations to the community repeatedly challenged any symbol of authority. But McDonald applied his talents effectively, because Mineola soon became, somewhat reluctantly, a "moral town."[8]

By 1883 McDonald was thus looking for new challenges, for other ways to utilize his ability. As a result he gradually migrated northward and westward, first into Wichita County, then to Hardeman County, and eventually into the desolate prairies and vast wastelands of the Texas Panhandle and Indian Territory. And with each new challenge he built an enviable reputation. During the 1880s he became known as a relentless pursuer of desperadoes, as a manhunter who enjoyed his work, as a man of nerve who single-handedly, or with a partner, sought out his quarry, no matter what the odds, no matter how great the danger. In Wichita Falls he survived an ambush and then captured his assailants; near Quanah he rounded up the notorious Brooken gang, which was wanted for cattle rustling and robbery and murder; and in No Man's Land (between the Texas Panhandle and Indian Territory) he and a sidekick named Lon Burson, "with plenty of grit and endurance," invaded this outlaw wilderness and performed what was considered to be "the impossible," returning safely with six desperate men who had surrendered rather than face his guns.[9]

McDonald's appearance was somewhat inconsistent with his growing reputation. Slender of build and medium in height, he appeared to be mild-mannered, at times quiet and gentle, with eyes as blue "as the summer sky," which would "turn to [needle] points of gray" when confronting any kind of opposition. Although biographer Paine obliquely observed that McDonald had "the ears of a wild creature, a hunter," actually they were prominent, especially under a wide-brimmed western hat, not because of size or shape but due to their outward extension from his head. As for his nose, which Paine described as "stately Roman architecture which goes with conquest because it signifies courage, resolution and the peerless gift of command," it was narrow and straight, with nothing unusual or outstanding about its construction. Nor did it give prominence to or accentuate the rather full mustache over his upper lip nor disrupt the even features of his tanned, weather-beaten face.[10]

Unmistakably, McDonald could be — and was — a formidable adversary, having the natural instincts and animal cunning which characterized a successful frontier marshal. Despite his lack of education and an inordinate desire for publicity, the man was a superb peace officer. Like other famous Ranger captains, he was apparently, in times of danger, unafraid of death or at least oblivious to it. For instance, after three assailants ambushed him at Quanah in December 1895, wounding him four times, he was still able to kill one and rout the other two. Although exclaiming, "I think I'm a dead rabbit," he directed the doctor — and without anesthetic — not to "fool around" with the slugs in his arm and neck but to "go after the one in the small of . . . [his] back, and let out the blood. There's a bucket of it sloshin' around in there." As for tactics and techniques in enforcing the law, he usually was able to use "a tone of voice" and "needle-pointed eyes," together with his reputation, to petrify and vanquish anyone who considered doing violence. In more critical situations, however, he chose to square off with an opponent at daybreak, charging him head-on. "If you wilt or falter, he will kill you," he candidly explained to his men, "but if you go straight at him and never give him time to get to cover, or to think, he will weaken ninety-nine times in a hundred." And if perchance his adversary turned out to be that rare exception, McDonald had the quickness and agility as well as the lethal ability to dispatch him to Boot Hill.[11]

In January 1891, after learning about the resignation of Ranger Captain S. A. Murray of Company B, McDonald sought to elevate his law-enforcement activities to a more prestigious level. He thereupon obtained an audience with newly elected Governor Jim Hogg, whom he had known for more than twenty years. The interview was unique and in many ways revealing in regard to the character of the two men. Upon being informed as to the purpose of the meeting, Hogg reprovingly responded: "Why didn't you let me know sooner? There are two other applications for the place, both from good men, with long petitions and fine endorsements." When McDonald replied that letters equally supportive of his candidacy would soon be forthcoming, the governor enigmatically and somewhat mischievously announced: "That's all right, Bill, you have already got the best endorsements I ever saw." Then he reached into his desk and pulled out a stack of letters that he had received during the previous four years while serving as Texas' attorney general and which complained that McDonald was "a ruthless and tyrannical official." Among the more serious charges were his use, at times, of boxcars as a temporary jail and the handcuffing of prisoners to long iron chains securely attached to hitching posts. When McDonald readily admitted to the truth of such accusations, Hogg replied: "By gatlins! Those endorsements are good enough for me. They carry the flavor of conviction; I appoint you Ranger Captain on the strength of them."[12]

Over the next fifteen years Hogg would never have cause to regret this judgment. Near the newly created railroad town of Amarillo, McDonald established a Ranger camp where eight men, besides having to furnish their own horses and guns, had the responsibility of controlling a vast frontier grassland. Within a year they had made "unpopular" cattle rustling (which had been, next to cattle raising, "the chief industry" in the area). In fact, the Rangers were so successful that it was rumored that Panhandle desperadoes had vowed "to shoot Bill McDonald on sight." Because of his impressive accomplishments and growing reputation, he was called upon to perform many law-enforcement duties throughout the state, such as quelling riots or strikes in Dallas, Fort Worth, Thurber, Wichita Falls, and on one occasion in the Gulf Coast towns of Orange and Port Arthur. Yet, while achieving widespread fame as a fearless peace officer, McDonald also became known as a man who "never" surrendered a prisoner to a mob, who would not back down no matter what the odds or provocation. Few Texans had not heard of his exploits at Wichita Falls in 1896, when he verbally excoriated an angry mob of armed men who were intent upon lynching two killers in his custody: "Damn your sorry souls!" he growled. "March out of here and get away from this jail, every one of you, or I'll fill this yard with dead men." He was also assigned an equally formidable task, beginning in 1892, of controlling Democratic delegates — or at least of preserving order — at their biennial state convention. Then, in 1906, came his greatest challenge: the Brownsville Affray.[13]

Situated at the southern tip of Texas along the Rio Grande nine miles from the Gulf of Mexico, Brownsville was a sleepy little town of approximately 8,000 inhabitants, steeped in history and tradition. In May 1846, the first battle of the Mexican War had occurred there when American soldiers under the command of General Zachary "Old Rough and Ready" Taylor had withstood heavy shelling and bombardment from Mexican army cannon well ensconced on the bluffs at Matamoros, on the southern side of the river a few hundred yards away. After Major Jacob Brown had been mortally wounded in this attack, Taylor respectfully designated the earthworks and foxholes in the river sands as Fort Brown. Within two years, the small hamlet of Brownsville became the Cameron County seat and two years later was officially incorporated as a city. During the 1850s it developed into a busy trading center, despite its remoteness and the threatened — and real — invasion by Juan Cortina, the "Red Robber of the Rio Grande." With the establishment of the huge King Ranch empire by Richard King and Mifflin Kenedy just to the north, it became the principal outlet for hides and tallow, for sheep and cattle. Then in 1861, after the eruption of the American Civil War, it took on added significance as a port for Confederate cotton and Texas foodstuffs as well as a center for incoming goods. As a result, Brownsville, with more than four-fifths of its populace Hispanic but controlled politically and economically by Anglos, continued to be an important but almost forgotten part of Texas during the latter half of the nineteenth century.[14]

And to the men of the First Battalion, Twenty-fifth Infantry (Colored), Companies B, C, and D, who had served with distinction against the Sioux on the Great Plains, the Spaniards in Cuba, and the Philippine rebels on Luzon, Brownsville should have remained forgotten. Although garrison duty at Fort Niobrara, Nebraska, had been tedious, even debilitating at times over the past four years, their new assignment, briefly at Camp Mabry in Austin and then on to Fort Brown, paled in comparison. Besides being sent to what appeared to be a hellishly out-of-the-way spot, more than 200 miles from civilization and five minutes from the nearest Mexican brothel, they would have to endure not only the ennui of a Texas border town but also Southern tradition. To blacks, that meant just one thing: second-class citizenship under a denigrating system of segregation known throughout the South as Jim Crow laws. Yet even worse was the fact that they were soldiers whom local businessmen often despised personally while welcoming the advantageous economic effects from their trade. Taken at best, this assignment could only be trouble. Just prior to departure, Chaplain Theophilus G. Stewart, the battalion's only black officer, prophetically wrote his superior this memo: "During my whole experience in the service the only time that I have been assaulted by uncivil and ribald speech by a man in the uniform of a soldier was at Fort Riley, Kansas, and the man who did so was a Texas militia man." Then he concluded: "Texas, I fear, means a quasi battle ground for the Twenty-fifth Infantry."[15]

How prophetic this statement was. Upon arrival in Brownsville on July 28, 1906, the 170 men of the Twenty-fifth Infantry (Colored) suffered the ambiance of Southern tradition and the indignities of a segregated race. Instead of receiving applause or cheers while marching through the streets from the train depot to Fort Brown at the lower end of town (as was the customary polite response when soldiers arrived for a new assignment), they passed by unsmiling townspeople, coldly and grimly silent. Soon, however, a verbal reception was forthcoming, the gist of which was "to show Niggers their place." While all Mexican saloon keepers welcomed their business, just two of four Anglo proprietors would accept them, but only in a back room away from the regular customers. One Anglo named H. H. Weller frankly admitted that he "did not want these colored soldiers to come" and braggingly asserted that the townspeople "would get rid of them some way before very long." But others were even more blunt. "We don't want them damn niggers here" became a constant chorus for many of the citizenry because, they reasoned, "niggers will always cause trouble."[16]

Over the next sixteen days the townspeople were increasingly convinced of this statement, regardless of the illogic of their reasoning, regardless of the facts in three separate altercations. On Sunday night, August 5, Privates James W. Newton and Fank J. Lipscomb, both of Company C, were strolling down Elizabeth Street. After walking single-file past a group of white women who were occupying the sidewalk while busily talking, and possibly brushing against one of them, Newton heard some movement behind him before being knocked senseless to the ground. Hovering over him with a drawn Colt .45 revolver was customs inspector Fred Tate, the husband of one of the women, who angrily pistol-whipped him for such "rude" and "insulting" behavior. "In the manner of the South," one witness later testified, the black should have stepped off the sidewalk onto the street. Again the next Sunday night, August 12, two other black privates, somewhat inebriated and noisy, were returning to Fort Brown after visiting Matamoros. When they began arguing and scuffling near a ferry on the Rio Grande, mounted inspector A. Y. Baker either knocked or pushed one of them into knee-deep water in an attempt to restrain them. And the next afternoon at 5:00, August 13, a Mrs. Lon Evans reported that a man, whom she could only identify as a "large Negro soldier," had attempted to rape her by grabbing her by the hair and throwing her to the ground. For some reason he had been scared off, leaving her frightened but "suffering no bodily harm." News of this outrage spread through Brownsville like wildfire, the intensity of which caused Major Charles W. Penrose, the battalion's commanding officer, to restrict Companies B, C, and D to their barracks by 8:00 P.M.[17]

It was a clear, dark night on August 13, the moon having set early with only stars lighting the summer sky. At Fort Brown, despite rumors that the townspeople were greatly excited and demanding satisfaction for a dastardly crime, all was peaceful, the men of Companies B, C, and D seemingly in good spirits and unperturbed by the furor swirling about them. At 11:00 P.M. taps sounded and lights went out; at 11:30 P.M., Officer of the Day Captain E. A. Macklin, the commander of Company C, made his rounds and, finding everything quiet, retired to his room. Then it happened. At approximately ten minutes after midnight, rifle shots rang out near the garrison wall by Company B barracks, shattering the stillness of the night. From the direction of the bullets, some investigators believed that the first volley was fired from twelve to fifteen feet above the ground (which seemed to indicate that the shots came from the gallery of a company barracks). But be that as it may, approximately fifteen to twenty men gathered after that at Cowen's Alley, a narrow passageway running parallel to and halfway between Elizabeth and Washington streets and just across from Garrison Road and the three-foot stone fence that separated Fort Brown from residential Brownsville. Upon moving away from the fort, the group fired indiscriminately at buildings on both sides of the alley, barely missing Mrs. Louis Cowens, her five children, and a Mexican maid in their home. Crossing Thirteenth Street at the rear of the Miller Hotel, they encountered a Brownsville mounted police lieutenant, M. Y. "Joe" Dominguez, whereupon they shot his horse out from under him while shattering his right arm below the elbow, so much so that it was amputated the next day. They also fired at guests peering out the windows of their rooms at the Miller Hotel. From there the rioters split into two groups. One proceeded up Cowen's Alley midway into the next block and fired a volley into the rear of the Ruby Saloon, killing barkeeper Frank Natus and slightly wounding Pauline S. Preciado; the other went half a block to Washington Street, turned left, and riddled the home of Fred E. Starck with bullets. Then there was silence, approximately eight to ten minutes having elapsed since the affray first began. Surprisingly, the rioters vanished, without even one witness being able to testify as to their whereabouts or the path of their retreat. If, perchance, they had been members of the Twenty-fifth Infantry, the escape route became more easily explainable since their barracks were only two short blocks away.[18]

In the aftermath of this foray the reactions throughout Brownsville were intense but very predictable. Running from his home toward the rifle fire, Mayor Fred Combe was warned by a city policeman at Twelfth and Elizabeth to go no further because "the Negroes are shooting up the town." As a result of such rumors, clusters of armed men, outraged and angry, began gathering in increasing numbers, intent upon storming Fort Brown and administering justice to the black perpetrators; that is, until Mayor Combe dispersed them by threatening to "arrest any man who remained on the streets." At the same time, Major Penrose had ordered his command to take up defensive positions along the garrison wall, believing the fort to be under attack. But ten minutes after the last rifle report, he had Companies B, C, and D assembled for roll call, whereupon all were reported "present or accounted for." Unable to find Officer of the Day Captain Macklin, he authorized Captain Samuel P. Lyons, the commander of Company D, to reconnoiter the city with a detail of sixty soldiers and find out who was responsible for the rifle fire. When Captain Lyons encountered Mayor Combe near the Miller Hotel and learned about the civilian interpretations of the foray, the officers at Fort Brown were dumbfounded and completely taken aback. Consequently, Major Penrose ordered another roll call, with the same result, and com-

Bill McDonald, famous captain of the Texas Rangers.
— Courtesy Texas Ranger Hall of Fame Museum

MAP OF BROWNSVILLE

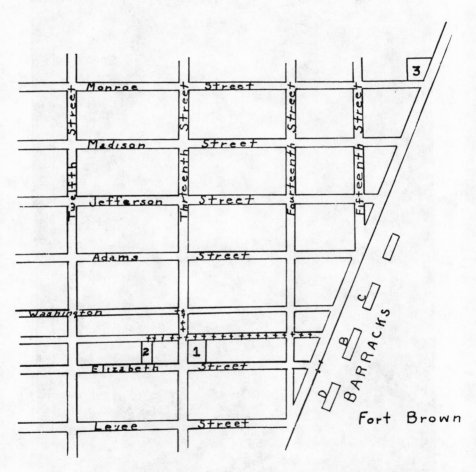

+ + + + Route of Attack
1   Miller Hotel
2   Ruby Saloon
3   Allison's Saloon

manded all personnel to remain at their posts until 3:30 A.M.[19]

By midmorning on August 14, circumstantial evidence against the men of the Twenty-fifth was mounting, and overwhelmingly so, in volume. At 9:00 A.M. Mayor Combe apprised Major Penrose of all testimony and rumors. He displayed fifty to sixty empty shells, one empty rifle clip, and a few unfired cartridges which were found at the Miller Hotel and along the two-block route from Cowen's Alley to Fort Brown. The ammunition was from Springfield 1903 rifles, which only soldiers used. Next, he presented Lieutenant Dominguez's testimony that his assailants wore "the uniform of soldiers" and "were colored"; he also stated that many other witnesses had vowed that the rioters either were blacks or sounded like them. So conclusive did the evidence appear that, even after checking the battalion's weapons and finding nothing incriminating (in other words, the rifles were clean and showed no traces of having been fired), Major Penrose and his officers were convinced that the guilty parties were somehow from Companies B, C, and D.[20]

Yet with no confessions and no witnesses available to identify specifically a single rioter, the investigation, because of its limitations, continued for a week in an unproductive and therefore unsatisfactory manner. Mayor Combe immediately appointed four prominent townspeople to choose a Citizen's Committee of 15, which would then investigate the raid thoroughly as well as cooperate fully with the military at Fort Brown. Within the next two days the members listened to the testimony of twenty-two Brownsville citizens, eight of whom positively identified the rioters as "Negro soldiers" but none of whom could pick out an actual participant. At the same time Major Penrose was even less successful in questioning the 170 soldiers of Companies B, C, and D who, to a man, gave almost an identical statement — that they "neither participated in the riot nor knew of anyone who had." To aid this military inquiry President Theodore Roosevelt instructed Major Augustus P. Blocksom, the assistant inspector-general of the Southwest Division, to proceed at once to Brownsville. After arrival on August 16, he soon became convinced that the raid was "preconcerted," that many of the soldiers knew "something tangible as to the identity of the criminals," but he too was unable to penetrate the Twenty-fifth Infantry's wall of silence. In this unwholesome atmosphere of uncertainty, with local citizens armed and patrolling the streets, and with the Brownsville *Daily Herald* at its yellow jour-

nalistic best declaring that the "people [are] fully prepared to defend themselves" against another "dastard outrage" by black soldiers, Major Blocksom recommended the immediate removal of the
Twenty-fifth Infantry (Colored), because a confrontation might
occur if, in the eyes of the public, justice were not done.[21]

Meanwhile at Dallas, 600 miles to the north, Bill McDonald
was serving as sergeant-at-arms at the Democratic state convention
while at the same time closely following the events at Brownsville
with avid interest. Yet, with each passing day in which neither the
Citizen's Committee of 15 nor the military uncovered any concrete
evidence, he became increasingly perturbed and impatient. Actually he had hoped that Governor S. W. T. Lanham would order
him "to handle" the situation, especially since Brownsville was in
his home district. Then he was given to understand that Texas Adjutant General John A. Hulen and state troops, who were at the
time holding maneuvers in Austin, would promptly respond. But
after several days of inactivity, McDonald hurried to Austin, no
longer able to control his anxieties and suppress his unhappiness.
At Camp Mabry he learned, to his astonishment, that General
Hulen had no intention of interfering at Brownsville because an un-
authorized investigation of Federal troops might "invite a charge
. . . [of] treason." Unconcerned with legal ramifications and distraught over Hulen's attitude, McDonald angrily and somewhat
simplistically retorted: "Treason! Why, them hellions have violated
the laws of the State, shooting into people's houses and committing
murder. I don't care what else they are, they're criminals. It's my
sworn duty to investigate such business as that, and I'm going to
do it."[22]

So, like a frontier marshal who knew no other way to face a
dangerous situation but head-on, McDonald boarded the train for
Brownsville, convinced that his duty was clear. Nor did he vary in
procedure or waver in resolve. At Ranger headquarters in Alice,
Texas, he selected two trusted comrades, Sergeant W. J. McCauley
and C. T. Ryan, to aid his investigation. At Corpus Christi he met
one-armed District Judge Stanley Welch, also en route to Brownsville, who strengthened his determination by encouraging the
Rangers "to take such steps and to use such means as were necessary to identify and punish the offenders." And at 6:00 P.M. on
Tuesday, August 21, he arrived with his men at Brownsville and
immediately sought out Mayor Combe and the Citizen's Commit-

tee chairman to inform them of his intentions. In the course of being brought up-to-date, the Rangers soon learned that no one was any closer than a week before in discovering the identity of the rioters but that Major Penrose was determined to unravel this mystery even "if it took him ten years." McDonald, with characteristic bluntness, exclaimed: "Ten years! What does he need all that time for? He could do it in ten minutes, if he wanted to and tried. He knows his men, and he could find out who was absent during the shooting. And he knows just about who would be likely to get into a gang like that." Thus seemingly caught up in his own rhetoric, and on center stage, he boasted: "I'll find them out, myself, and I won't be ten years about it — nor ten days, neither."[23]

After such statements, McDonald had to produce — especially since Mayor Combe applaudingly added him to the Citizen's Committee of 15. So with his men he literally began working round-the-clock, and the results were extremely gratifying to him. Fortunately for his investigation, two Ranger Company B members stationed at Harlingen, Blaze Delling and Sam McKenzie, had arrived in Brownsville several days earlier to help maintain order and had already gathered some "valuable" information. They had available Mexican witnesses who, during the affray on August 13, had "followed the track of the raiders by the flash of their guns." They also had discovered that the newest saloon for blacks curiously had closed early that night (failing to consider that the soldiers were restricted to their post after 9:00 P.M.). And, most important, they had located two former black soldiers who, they believed, either had participated in the raid or knew the ones involved. Quick to follow up on this lead, McDonald found one of these luckless blacks in the city jail, whereupon he tested the man's bravery and nudged his memory with what his biographer described as "a sort of 'third degree' examination." At the same time he erroneously concluded on the basis of facts from several sources that, when Captain Lyons with a company of sixty soldiers had been ordered to reconnoiter after the affray, his purpose "was to go and finish up the job [begun by the raiders]."[24]

Elated by his progress and armed with what he considered to be sufficient evidence to question the military, McDonald marched on Fort Brown the next morning, August 22, despite warnings that "they [the soldiers] will shoot you down." In the past he had always been successful when attacking early in the morning and charging his opponent head-on, never giving him "time to get to cover, or to think" — and he did not intend to change this formula of success. With only Sergeant McCauley, armed with a Winchester repeating rifle, as his backup, having purposely left behind Rangers Ryan, Delling, and McKenzie to organize the townspeople in the "event of a fight at the entrance," McDonald steadfastly walked toward the front gates of Fort Brown. With two pearl-handled Colt .45 revolvers obviously on display and an automatic shotgun deftly cradled in his arms — "the only pass I want [into Fort Brown]" — he disregarded a command to halt, even with twenty rifles of the Twenty-fifth leveled at him. As he continued forward unwaveringly, he yelled out so that no one could mistake his purpose: "You niggers, hold up there! You've already got into trouble with them old guns of yours. I'm Captain Bill McDonald of the State Rangers, and I'm down here to investigate a foul murder you scoundrels have committed." Then, in his best authoritative tone, he announced: "I'll show you niggers something you've never been use' to. Put up them guns!" And without hesitation they did.[25]

Once inside Fort Brown, McDonald became the authority, the expert with a plan, the man in control. Irritated by military indecision, which looked to him like a coverup, he brusquely questioned Major Penrose about his black troops (with Major Blocksom content to be an observer), his attitude overbearing to the point of being insulting. When challenged by Major Penrose to take over the investigation if he knew a "way of getting it [the information] out of them," McDonald quickly agreed to do so and for the next hour conducted his own unique brand of inquiry. To Corporal Willie H. Miller of Company C, who was outside Fort Brown the night of the foray with a twenty-four-hour pass, he fired questions in staccato fashion, finding the answers at times contradictory. At one point, though, when Miller's reply sounded sullen and morose, McDonald threatened: "You scoundrel, don't you give me any of your back talk! You answer my questions, sir!" With Private C. W. Askew of Company B, however, he took another approach, repeatedly pressing him to produce his military cap. Then, at a propitious moment, he showed him one with the initials "C.W.A." inscribed in the lining, demanding to know if it was his. When Askew said "yes," McDonald revealed that it "was found in the street the morning after the raid." As his interrogation of both officers and enlisted men continued, he found their stories to be "confused, contradictory, and full of guilt."[26]

But to Major Penrose, as well as Captain Macklin (who had been officer of the day at the time of the affray), McDonald was especially contemptuous and scornful. "When I came here," the Ranger lectured, "you told me you couldn't find out anything. I've been here half an hour and I've found out enough, with what I got last night, to warrant me charging a bunch of your men with murder. How do you explain that?" When Major Penrose replied that "you have more experience in such matters and understand better how to go at it than I do," McDonald thundered back, revealing the full depth of his anger and suspicions. "Yes, I have only asked for the facts — that's all. I didn't try to get anybody to tell me a lie. I've found that a whole bunch of these niggers was out that you and your captain said was in. You all are trying to cover up this matter, and it makes you just as sorry and as guilty as those niggers, making you accessories to the crime." In fact, he raged, "You are sorrier than these niggers because you, as officers, and as men of the United States Army, ought to be the first to hunt out the guilty ones, instead of trying to hide them."[27]

After this bitter diatribe, McDonald was as popular as a rattlesnake at Fort Brown. Yet he continued unabashedly to press his investigation, unconcerned that he had alienated the military. After all, he had made his reputation by being a maverick, by being outspoken, regardless of the people involved. On Wednesday morning, August 23, he persuaded Judge Welch, with the assent of the district attorney, to issue warrants for the arrest of thirteen people — one former soldier and twelve men of Companies B, C, and D. Next, he marched into Fort Brown, again brushing aside orders to halt as contemptuously as he had the day before, and presented the warrants to Majors Penrose and Blocksom. With their consent, although Penrose was at first understandably hostile to any of his suggestions, McDonald placed the soldiers in the fort's guardhouse because, he explained, the local sheriff was "no good" and would take too many men away from the continuing investigation to assure their safety. Besides, McDonald was surely aware that arresting United States troops was one thing, but taking them out of federal territory and from their officers would be difficult if not impossible.[28]

For the moment McDonald was a hero, receiving countless congratulatory responses from the people of Brownsville — but not for long. Because of the many legal and technical ramifications which could be precipitated by his actions (not to mention the unfavorable publicity), local businessmen as well as state and national leaders were anxious to smooth over and, if possible, eradicate this embarrassing problem. After all, what power or authority did a state official in the form of a Texas Ranger captain have to arrest United States personnel and on federal property? As a result, the War Department, on the recommendation of Major Blocksom and with the approval of President Roosevelt, ordered the Twenty-fifth Infantry (Colored) to leave Brownsville immediately for Fort Reno, Oklahoma Territory, and instructed Major Penrose to transfer the twelve prisoners under state warrant from the Fort Brown guardhouse to Fort Sam Houston in San Antonio. Upon reflection, Judge Welch was also persuaded to demand of McDonald the return of all warrants issued to him.[29]

Only one obstacle remained: Bill McDonald. Because of his reputation of never bowing to pressure, especially in regard to prisoners, the Brownsville authorities were afraid that he might not be compliant. They were right. Early on August 24, with rumors rampant in Brownsville that the Twenty-fifth Infantry (Colored) was departing — and with all of its men — McDonald sought verification, but was assured by Judge Welch that "no movement looking to the removal of the prisoners was in progress." Still not completely convinced, he voluntarily escorted a company of black troops en route to the train depot, at the same time checking their personnel to make sure that none of his "prisoners" were sandwiched between them. But when a second company, upon seeing him and his men, stopped and retraced its steps to Fort Brown, he became highly suspicious. Once again he located Judge Welch, this time in the company of Major Penrose and Captain Lyons, and fiercely announced: "Judge, those niggers are not going to be moved from here. They are my prisoners and I'm going to hold them. I'm going to wire . . . the Governor for assistance to help me."[30]

By evening, however, McDonald realized that he was fighting a losing battle, that both the local authorities and the military had "conspired" to take his prisoners; yet he remained undaunted. Upon noticing that a number of prominent citizens, including Mayor Combe, Judge Welch, the district attorney, and Congressman John Nance Garner, were collecting at Judge Jim Wells' office, he decided to confront them. Immediately Judge Wells expressed the feelings and fears of the group: "Bill, you won't listen to us. You're going against the law and you're going to start a row here that can't be stopped without terrible sacrifice. Those nigger soldiers won't go away and leave those prisoners behind without breaking out again, and next time it will be a good deal worse. They think those prisoners will be lynched, if they're left here." Then he pleaded: "Don't, for God's sake, get us into another row, Bill." In reply, McDonald asserted that the Rangers had upheld the law by arresting the guilty parties involved in the affray, thus calming the situation, and that under no circumstances was he going to release them without orders from Governor Lanham. "Furthermore," he candidly announced, "I don't believe the people of Brownsville want them taken away from here, and I'll tell you right now that so long as I and my men are here, them niggers are in no danger, nor the people neither." Distraught and obviously angry at such intransigence, Judge Welch impatiently blurted out: "You haven't any sense, McDonald. You're running up against the local authorities as well as the United States. I'll settle this thing, right here," he concluded. "I want those warrants." Yet McDonald still would not yield, stating that, by law, the warrants were "not returnable until the third day of September" and that he was "going to hold that bunch of niggers" unless Governor Lanham instructed him otherwise.[31]

With the two sides irreparably at odds, McDonald departed, since further discussion would be unproductive. More determined than ever, he decided to station his men in the street near the Miller Hotel, where they would have a clear view of the gate at Fort Brown. Then, once again, a confrontation occurred. At twilight he became aware of forty or fifty armed men, appearing at first glance to be soldiers dressed in khaki, moving toward him. As they drew nearer, however, McDonald recognized Judge Welch, the district attorney, and the sheriff in front of local townspeople. After he somewhat sarcastically commented, "What's the trouble now, Judge? Looks like you're going to war, with all those armed men," Welch curtly retorted: "I've come for those warrants. I've got an order for them." Because of the fading daylight McDonald moved into the lobby of the Miller Hotel to examine the piece of paper handed to him, a sea of menacing faces surrounding him and his Ranger force of four men. As a crowd of people also gathered in the mezzanine balcony, McDonald slowly read the document and then said incredulously: "This is your own order, Judge. What is the meaning of this?" Once again Welch loudly reiterated his position for all to hear, fiercely intimating that, one way or another, he was going to retrieve the thirteen warrants.

During this lengthy harangue the air became increasingly electric, fraught with tension and danger. McDonald, against any kind of threat or violence, always seemed to react badly, as far as an adversary was concerned, and responded contrary to usual behavior patterns. Fully aware of his situation, he measured his opposition, while fingering an automatic shotgun, and then contemptuously hissed: "I'll tell you, Judge. You all look like fifteen cents in Mexican money to me." And, he asserted, if the mob wanted action by attempting to overpower the Rangers, he was ready to accommodate them. "So let it fly," he challenged.[32]

Fortunately for all concerned, McDonald did not have to test the mob, for at this critical moment someone rushed in and handed him a telegram from Governor Lanham — and the confrontation quickly dissolved. He was ordered immediately to turn over the warrants for the twelve soldiers and one ex-soldier. Without protest McDonald dutifully carried out his instructions by handing over the warrants to Judge Welch. All during the night he and his men patrolled the streets of Brownsville to make sure that no outbreak occurred either by the soldiers or the townspeople. And at 6:00 A.M. on August 25 they escorted the Twenty-fifth Infantry, without incident, to their train. The Brownsville Affray was over.[33]

Yet in the aftermath of the affray, controversy continued to plague many of the participants as well as those involved in the decision-making. On August 27, 1906, the Twenty-fifth arrived at Fort Reno, Oklahoma Territory. During the next three months the War Department attempted to untangle the mystery which enveloped the foray. And when the black troopers maintained their "conspiracy of silence," President Roosevelt (upon recommendation from Inspector General E. A. Garlington) ordered a "discharge without honor" of every enlisted man of Companies B, C, and D, forever barring them from reenlistment in the army and navy or employment in any civil-service position. In the meantime a grand jury in Cameron County complicated the issue even more by "no billing" the twelve soldiers whom McDonald had arrested. As a result, Senator Joseph Foraker of Ohio, an inveterate enemy of the president, questioned the validity of Roosevelt's decision, especially since the soldiers had received no trial, and demanded an immediate investigation. For more than three years the inquiry continued to linger, with a military tribunal appointed by Roosevelt reexamining the individual case of every trooper. Eventually, in 1910, approximately twenty of those discharged were allowed to reenlist in the army.[34]

No one emerged from the incident more controversial than Bill McDonald. Within two months he retired from active Ranger service and accepted an appointment as the state revenue agent of Texas. Then, in 1912, he acted as bodyguard for Woodrow Wilson who, later as president, named McDonald to the federal marshalship of the Northern District of Texas. In this position he served until his death at Wichita Falls on January 15, 1918. Yet he would always be associated with the Brownsville Affray, the most dramatic incident of his Ranger career. In a letter to Ranger historian Walter Prescott Webb in December 1934, Judge Herbert Davenport of Brownsville reflected: "I have never found a Border man who had the slightest respect for Bill McDonald. He was, to them, a troublemaker, an advertiser, a teller of tales of which he was himself the hero, inclined to act — and act violently — on false or doubtful information, vain, and self important." Major Augustus P. Blocksom, however, remembered McDonald in a different light. Impressed by the unbelievable foolhardiness of a lone Ranger captain who, with only one man as a backup, walked unflinchingly into the rifle sights of twenty black soldiers and ordered "Put up them guns," he admiringly reported: "Bill McDonald would charge hell with a bucket of water."[35]

III.

Red Burton and the Klan

A wave of fear swept across Texas in the summer and fall of 1921. Masked men in white robes paraded triumphantly; flaming crosses illuminated the sky, eerie and ominous in the darkness; and bands of nightriders, vigilante style, tortured or murdered their victims in the name of law and order. At crossroads and in Texas towns, billboards demanding "One Hundred Per Cent Americanism," "Booze Must and Shall Go," "Love Thy Neighbor as Thyself but Leave His Wife Alone," "Keep This a White Man's Country," apprised citizens that a new force, supposedly patriotic, most assuredly moralistic, definitely restrictive, was moving into their community. Preaching racism and religious bigotry, the Invisible Empire of Kleagles and Imperial Wizards and Grand Dragons called for a war against malevolent groups such as radicals, foreigners, and "niggers" to keep them from undermining "pure" American institutions. And how? The Ku Klux Klan had the answer. The best element of society must purge all "alien" forces, no matter how great the cost, no matter what the method.[1]

For $10 "true" Americans could join the Klan; for $10 they could help save the United States. At last they had found an effective vehicle for alleviating the frustrations of a rapidly changing world, for fighting against conditions both disturbing and startling. To them it was shocking how much society was degenerating, how immoral people were becoming. The family, with its spiritual and moral base, was showing signs of fracturing, even of disintegrating. Some women were choosing a career instead of marriage; divorce in preference to self-sacrifice for their children; plunging necklines and rising skirts in defiance of modesty and decency. Yet political leaders on both the national and local levels, although staunch advocates of law and order, were apparently helpless to combat trends toward the disruption of society. Prostitution and gambling were increasing; "racketeer" and "speak-easy" and "booze" were becoming familiar terms in the English language; and that "Noble Experiment," the Eighteenth Amendment, was ineffective — and laughable.[2]

To make matters worse, American institutions seemed to be under heavy attack. Since the Bolshevik Revolution of 1917, "true" Americans believed that Communists and radicals were trying to undermine the American system. United States Attorney General A. Mitchell Palmer had moved in the right direction by ferreting out those "traitors" in the government and bringing them to trial. But this "witch hunt," as the radical press called his actions, had definite limitations; in no way could he noticeably affect local situations. At the same time, the New Immigration, alien and Catholic, spouting strange political philosophies that were often critical of the American way of life, was also weakening this nation by its "mongrelizing taints." Those dark-skinned peoples, who lived in slums and tended toward vice and corruption, usually could not speak English, much less understand how democracy functioned. Equally alarming were attempts to paralyze the economy, to engulf the United States in depression. And who was to blame? Obviously, the "true" Americans agreed, it was the alien element, such as the "Uncle Shylock," the avaricious Jew who kept prices high and wages low.[3]

So in October 1921, Klansmen were marching in Texas almost 100,000 strong, raising the fiery cross and the American flag in unison, denouncing the cancerous evils and corrupting vices in their midst, then enrolling "good solid middle-class citizens" in their ranks: lawyers, doctors, bankers, businessmen, even ministers and policemen. Already they had organized and paraded in Houston, Beaumont, Dallas, Fort Worth, Waco, Austin, and San Antonio. Now they were moving into rural communities. In East Texas and along the Gulf Coast their gospel spread like wildfire; on the Black Prairie in North Texas they were equally successful. The next region to "educate" lay in the center of the state, a land of rolling prairies dotted with small, fairly prosperous farming villages. But here the Invisible Empire hit a snag in the form of two law enforcement officers, Red Burton and Bob Buchanan.[4]

Born on August 10, 1885, near Mart, Texas, Marvin "Red" Burton was the youngest son of John F. and Alice Cubley Burton. Originally from Montrose, Mississippi, his parents had migrated to Texas in the early 1880s and bought a farm between Mart and Waco. In that locale Red Burton grew to manhood, a typical product of his environment and of the era. Like most farm boys in Central Texas, he had specific family chores, helping his father in the fields and his mother around the house. Whenever possible he went to school, but scholastic endeavors did not prevent him from learning to fish, ride, and shoot well. Overall, life was not easy for Red; work hours were long and tasks often tedious. The span from childhood to maturity was brief.[5]

Consequently, when only eighteen, Burton married a local girl and assumed the more difficult responsibilities of making a living. Starting without "a dollar in the world," he worked wherever possible, but essentially his life was without purpose or direction. In 1905 he landed a job on a ranch near Wortham, Texas. Then, in 1913, he returned to the Waco area and, with the savings of the last eight years, purchased a lot and built a house. Once again he was penniless and out of work, lacking even "money enough to buy . . . groceries."[6]

But in 1914, after pouring concrete for stormsewers (and not too regularly), Burton informed his wife one morning: "I'm going to work at somethin'. I don't know what it does; I don't care what it pays. I'm going to work." Determined and almost desperate, he applied for a position with the Cleveland Construction Company. When the foreman sarcastically announced, "Sonny, we have work to do here but you wouldn't do it," Burton bristled, "You don't know me, man; I'll do anything honorable." And looking at the lean-muscled, 6'2 farm boy, almost skinny at 180 pounds, the foreman suddenly changed his mind. Perhaps something in Burton's voice, his clipped, terse comments, his firm, positive tone, carried conviction. Or possibly his appearance — light blue eyes, sandy red hair and ruddy complexion, a mask of defiance and resolution, huge hands, noticeably scarred and calloused, hanging like hamhocks from his shirtsleeves — made the foreman recognize a difference in this applicant. But whatever the reason, he found himself saying: "I'll tell you what, Sonny. You come over here tomorrow morning and . . . we'll run you off." That was one thing no one ever did. Burton stayed three years.[7]

After that day, Red Burton never went hungry again; he was too much in demand. Within three weeks he was elevated to foreman, even though obviously inexperienced. When he expressed feelings of inadequacy, his boss explained the promotion this way: "I know you don't know a whole lot but you will work. I'll help you if you get in trouble." He never had to, however, for Burton learned his trade well. But even more importantly, he won the respect of the men under him. Those who met his standards could count on steady employment, while those who were "toughs" or troublemakers (and there were plenty of that sort in construction work) learned to steer clear of him or quit. He would — and could — back up his decisions.[8]

In August 1917, Burton decided to change jobs, but not because he was unhappy. It was a matter of economics. The United States government, upon entering World War I, contracted the Grace Construction Company to build an airfield at Richfield, a few miles west of Waco. Since thousands of men were enlisting or being drafted into the armed forces, labor was hard to come by and even more difficult to keep. The Grace Company officials therefore offered Burton a job as foreman at double his present salary. They knew his reputation: that he was a tough taskmaster, that he inspired loyalty, that his men were ready to fight for him.

For two and a half weeks at Richfield, Burton measured up to all advance notices. Then, in an unexpected turn of events, the Waco Police Department drafted him into its ranks. Although the city council could in no way enforce such an act, Burton decided to serve for six months. He liked the idea of public service, of doing "things for other people." Besides, he was overworked, almost exhausted, and here was a chance, he reasoned, to "rest up" before returning to his old job.[9]

How wrong he was! At nearby Camp MacArthur thousands of soldiers, mostly from the Midwest, had arrived and were inundating Waco, causing the usual problems between townspeople and the military. For the first few months, therefore, Burton had his hands full directing traffic as well as learning police procedures and gaining an understanding of the problems and techniques of law enforcement. Then he was assigned to night duty, patrolling residential and outlying districts on a motorcycle — and the orientation process began all over again. Gradually, as the months rolled by and as he became more involved, thoughts of returning to construction work faded away; each day he found "policing" more and more fascinating.[10]

But in 1919, with the passage of the Eighteenth Amendment, Burton was caught in a situation which law officers have always dreaded. Besides having to enforce an unpopular law, he watched it corrupt some of his colleagues, thereby placing him in a difficult position. Because he was not "on the take," word went out to "get Red Burton lined up." After all, contraband liquor was bringing high prices and police salaries were low. Yet in spite of all inducements — promises of money, promotion, and favors — he steadfastly refused. So one morning in September his chief informed him that "for the good of the department" he was transferring him to a daytime schedule. Incensed over this roundabout way of curtailing his effectiveness (most of the contraband arrived at night), Burton replied: "Well, sir, if I thought it was better for the department, I wouldn't say a word" — and he quit.[11]

Actually Burton only changed jobs, not professions. Because of his fine record, Bob Buchanan, the sheriff of McLennan County, offered him a deputy's commission. What a lucky break it was for both men. Besides seeing eye-to-eye concerning law enforcement, they became close friends. And on October 1, 1921, at Lorena, Texas, approximately thirteen miles south of Waco, they had need of each other. Together — and alone — they faced the Klan.

Robert "Bob" Buchanan was a rugged law-enforcement officer and a formidable opponent, cut from the same mold as frontier marshals and Texas Rangers. Although fifty years old, he looked much younger, possibly because of his smooth, tanned face and black, wavy hair. Physically he was an impressive man, carrying 225 pounds easily on a sturdy 6′1 build. A huge Colt .38 "thumb-buster" on a .45 frame strapped to his left hip made him even more imposing. Yet his eyes, coal-black, piercing, at times ominous and unfathomable, were his dominant feature. When someone challenged him, they were like gale warnings, prominent and threatening. No one was going to run over Bob Buchanan. He represented the law — and that meant fair, impartial enforcement. Never did he allow political pressure or expediency or friendship to interfere with duty. Of course, this strict adherence to the law, this tough application of justice, was also an Achilles' heel. But he knew no other way; to him any other conduct was unthinkable.[12]

Even with law officers like Burton and Buchanan in Mc-Lennan County, the Klan leaders decided to act on October 1. Having already organized thoroughly in Waco, they planned a Saturday evening rally at Lorena, where they would march with fiery crosses through the black section of town and then convene, ironically enough, at the Baptist Church for an ice cream supper. Throughout Waco and the surrounding areas they tacked up notices, announcing in bold, black type: "The Ku Klux Klan Will Parade Tonight at 8:30."[13]

Surprisingly, neither Buchanan nor Burton was aware of these arrangements. Both were busy investigating a cotton theft in the nearby towns of Leroy and Mart. Yet while on the job they came to an understanding concerning the Klan. Each soon discovered that the other was not a member. In fact, they both voiced grave misgivings as to its purpose and activities, especially since a demonstration in Mart the previous Saturday had caused considerable damage. "If there is ever another parade in McLennan County while I am sheriff, I intend to find out who is responsible," Buchanan asserted emphatically, "and if I am out of the country, I want you to do it." Burton agreed. The matter was closed. Both sensed, however, that a "bad situation" might soon develop.

The two men had no idea that a confrontation was imminent. Upon their return to Waco that afternoon, however, several citizens from Lorena were waiting in Buchanan's office to inform him of a scheduled mass meeting and to appeal for help. Within a few minutes they had their answer. Turning to Burton, the sheriff asked, "Will you go down there with me?" And when Red replied he would, they were on their way.[14]

It was a beautiful autumn afternoon as they rode to Lorena. The air was crisp, the sun bright, the countryside a greenish-brown, not quite ready to succumb to winter. With approximately 350 inhabitants, Lorena resembled many other Central Texas farm communities in the 1920s. Situated on a rolling black prairie, it rose into view easily, the spires from its several churches and the roofs of rambling two-story frame houses surrounded by large shade trees, obvious landmarks. Like so many small towns it had two principal avenues: Main Street, comprising most of the business district, and Highway 81, cutting through the best residential area. Where these two thoroughfares intersected, townspeople had built a funeral parlor, bank, Ford agency, and combination drug and general store, symbols of a permanent and growing community. Except for market day, Saturday mornings, and holidays, the atmosphere was always easygoing, relaxed, often phlegmatic.[15]

But by the time the two lawmen arrived that evening, Lorena had changed dramatically. On the outskirts hundreds of cars, surreys, and wagons were parked haphazardly along the highway or in nearby fields. Along the streets vast throngs, estimated at 15,000 to 20,000 people, were milling about restlessly, though apparently in a festive mood. And as the sun quickly receded and the evening shadows lengthened, they eagerly anticipated the forthcoming events, for less than half a mile to the north hundreds of hooded, white-robed figures were assembling in a cotton field.[16]

In order to maintain some semblance of authority and keep the peace, Buchanan promptly sought out the town leaders. Although known to be "pretty hotheaded" at times, he was extremely calm and "reasonable" that evening. Carefully, he explained his position. He had not come to stop their parade; on the contrary, as far as he was concerned they could march all night. But as sheriff of McLennan County, he announced, "I think I'm entitled to know who's responsible for it, so if anything happens I can know who to look for." For instance, he explained, whenever a circus came to town, the owners always made arrangements with him and the police regarding the parade. Consequently, if the leaders would identify themselves to him by raising their hoods when marching by, he would be satisfied.[17]

Within thirty minutes, after much huddling and conferring, two McLennan County officials who were well-known to both Buchanan and Burton stepped forward to assume responsibility. Jovially the sheriff remarked that they need not lift their hoods because he would "know either of their hides in a tanning yard." So the matter was resolved — but not for long. A majority of the Klan leaders would not accept this agreement. Unhappy with the two officials for violating one of the basic rules of membership — that of secrecy — they rejected Buchanan's proposal, confident that their decision would cause no significant reverberations. After all, what could two law officers, alone and without public support, do? How could they prevent thousands from parading? The answers were obvious, the questions rhetorical. After taking precautionary steps, just in case the lawmen should react foolishly, the Klansmen

Texas Ranger Red Burton
— Courtesy Texas Ranger Hall of Fame Museum

Sheriff Bob Buchanan
— Courtesy Mary Buchanan Dollins

Sheriff Red Burton raiding a gambling house in Waco in the late 1940s.
— Courtesy Texas Ranger Hall of Fame Museum

quickly formed into lines of white-hooded figures, raised several American flags, lit huge crosses (one man, however, had wired one electrically), and began the march.[18]

Meanwhile, Buchanan and Burton were chatting amicably and visiting with friends at the main intersection, unaware that the Klan was not going to cooperate. Then the situation changed dramatically. Out of the crowd the two county officials emerged in front of Burton, told him what had just happened, and rather fearfully asked if the sheriff would "think hard of them" if they did not participate. Rushing across the street, Red was repeating the conversation to Buchanan, who was listening silent and grim-faced, when a resounding roar announced the beginning of the parade. Out onto Highway 81 the Klansmen came, a sea of white-clothed figures outlined against the night. Without a word to anyone Buchanan, with jaw set, and wearing a mask of determination, began walking toward the marchers. Burton, remembering that the sheriff had earlier told him to "stay close" in case of trouble, followed some fifteen to twenty feet behind. Nearer and nearer they moved toward the mass of white, the crowd closing in behind them, both hostility and fear apparent in the expressions of the people.[19]

Now the antagonists were face to face, just a few feet apart; yet Buchanan never hesitated or wavered. Whether unafraid of the consequences or feeling that he had no choice, he reacted bravely, even heroically. Confronting the first two leaders who were carrying a flaming cross, he reached out and slammed it to the ground, then raised up the hood of the nearest figure and resolutely declared: "I don't know you, but if I ever see your face again I will."[20]

As Buchanan moved toward the second man, all hell broke loose. Stealthily, a robed form, later identified as a Waco policeman, crept up behind him and either with a blackjack or billyclub knocked him to the ground. Then, upon seizing the sheriff's pistol, the outraged Klansmen swarmed over him as he lay prostrate in the road, hitting and beating him repeatedly. At the same time Red Burton "was completely covered with men," two or three holding him while others pounded at his face and body. Physically powerful and doubly so because he was fighting for his life, he repeatedly broke away from one group only to be grabbed by another. Suddenly, two pistol shots rang out, startling the melee into silence. Buchanan, hurt and bleeding, yelled out: "Red, they've shot me."[21]

Now the action became deadlier. Flicking out a pocketknife

with a four-inch blade, the sheriff, even though badly wounded, slashed and stabbed two of his antagonists. Then Burton, like a man possessed, wild and uncontrollable after seeing his comrade fall, reacted almost unbelievably in the next few minutes. Never losing sight of the man who had shot Buchanan, he managed to pull a small .38 Colt automatic from his left pants pocket and fired two shots. The would-be killer dropped. Oblivious to the punishing blows from men who were still pommeling him, Burton fired the remaining seven bullets at Klansmen near the sheriff, definitely hitting one and possibly several others. For some reason the mob had failed to take his holstered single-action .41 Colt; but in his highly excited state of mind he had no time to ponder such an oversight, for he needed the weapon. Wrenching his pinned right arm free, he unsheathed the .41 Colt and stuck the barrel into the stomach of a prominent Lorena businessman, T. C. Westbrook, who was still trying to hold him. In a cold, deadly voice he said: "Mr. Westbrook, I love you like a daddy, but if I am not released I'm going to kill you." And for the first time since the fight began he was free of fists and arms and bodies.

Bruised and blood-smeared, Burton quickly assessed the situation as he stood in the highway exposed and unprotected — and it was not to his liking. In front of him, some ten yards away, the sheriff was staggering but on his feet, bleeding profusely from wounds in his right chest and leg. Approximately fifty feet to his left a robed Klansman was leveling a pistol at Buchanan, while at about the same distance on his right someone was also shooting at the sheriff.

Instinctively, Burton swung into action. With two shots he ended the threat to Buchanan, the man crumpling to the ground in a heap. Then he whirled to face his own assailant. In haste he fired several times, missing on each attempt but causing the man to flee. In fact, upon realizing that Burton could not be stopped and with bullets hitting indiscriminately in their midst, the crowd had dispersed, men and women scattering frantically in all directions.[22]

Burton then turned to help Buchanan, but during the last exchange of gunfire someone had carried him to the drugstore at the intersection. So Red Burton hobbled and stumbled down the highway, unaware that he had been wounded in the right thigh. All about him was confusion. In a few short minutes Lorena had become a hate-filled disaster area. The town was a shambles, white robes and debris strewn everywhere, the streets spattered with blood, Klansmen confused and disorganized, their leaders striving to regroup. In the middle of the intersection a former Waco judge was damning and cursing the two lawmen at the top of his lungs, encouraging the apprehensive to more violence. For a fleeting moment Burton had "an evil thought," but with only one bullet left in his .41 Colt he decided not "to waste it on the old son-of-a-bitch."[23]

After considerable physical exertion, Burton finally reached the front door of the drugstore, fearful that his comrade was mortally wounded because boastful Klansmen were shouting that they had killed Buchanan. Once inside he took command, threatening and cursing those who seemed to be more afraid of the Klan than of him. To Wiley Stem, a Waco policeman, he gave specific instructions to bolt the door and let no one in "unless someone had been injured." At the same instant he flipped back Stem's coat, grabbed his .45 Colt automatic, and grimly said, "Wiley, I need this and you have no use for it, so I'm taking it." Then he hurried over to Buchanan, who was sitting upright in a chair, obviously in pain and having difficulty breathing, blood flowing profusely from his chest. "Burton, they've killed me," the sheriff weakly exclaimed, to which Red replied: "No, Bob, those sons-of-bitches can't kill you; you just can't die."[24]

But for the moment Burton could not be sure that anyone would not die. Outside the building Klansmen were milling about, venting their hate and frustration by angrily shouting: "Get a rope! Get a rope! Let's hang 'em." Inside, the foul stench of sweat and blood grew stronger, the moans of suffering men reverberating through the room as more and more wounded were brought in. Among them were Louis Crow, a prominent Waco businessman and ironically a close friend of the sheriff, with a deep stab wound in the chest; Ed Howard, a Waco policeman, knifed in the stomach; Carl West of Lorena, shot in the neck; and at least five others suffering from bullet or knife wounds. Already medical assistance was on the way, for Burton had summoned ambulances from Waco. But with the mob threatening to break in at any moment, and with an enraged Red Burton fingering a fully loaded gun and ready to kill anyone who threatened the wounded Buchanan, the chances of another bloodbath seemed definite.

Buchanan, however, realizing that trouble would continue as long as he and Burton were in town, repeatedly pleaded with his "friend" not to wait for the ambulance. Unsuccessful at first, he used the one argument which Burton could not resist. "I have always thought you were the best friend I had in the world," the sheriff declared, "and if you are, you will take me to the hospital." To that plea there could be only one answer. So Burton instructed Wiley Stem to "get a car" and bring it to the side entrance on Highway 81. Then he asked for someone to help him with the sheriff, but everyone shied away, fearful of what the Klan might do. He therefore draped Buchanan across his shoulder and back, holding him with his right hand, and dragged him across the room and out the side door through the crowd to the waiting car. Just in case the Klansmen intended to carry out their threats, he had Stem's .45 Colt automatic in his left hand, cocked and ready for action. But they had had enough of Burton for one night; they wanted no more. In silence they let the lawmen depart.[25]

At breakneck speed Burton drove along the narrow winding highway to Waco, his thoughts a mass of mixed emotions. Worried and increasingly concerned, he kept checking on Buchanan, who was coughing spasmodically and sometimes gagging, watching him push a forefinger into the chest wound to stop the flow of blood. As ambulances passed by, clanging and screaming in the night, he bitterly reflected upon the events of the evening, the threats and violence, the unreasoning hatred of the mob, the feeling of loneliness when no one would help him. Suddenly, robed figures appeared on his right, running across a cotton field, and instinctively he reached for his .45 Colt automatic, feelings of vengeance and retribution welling up inside him. As if reading his mind, Buchanan spoke out almost pleadingly: "No, Burton, I think they whipped us; let's not have any more trouble."[26]

So onward they raced toward Waco, Burton blaring the car horn to clear the way after reaching the city limits. Upon arrival at the Colgin Hospital, just across from the county jail (which was also the sheriff's home), they proceeded with the help of an attendant to the second-floor emergency room. Then events quite similar to the drugstore scene at Lorena happened all over again. With the Buchanan family and Burton standing guard at the door, doctors worked feverishly on the wounded and suffering men who streamed into the operating room. In the corridors, newspaper reporters and law officers, as well as county and district officials, were trying to piece together from the participants exactly what had happened, while outside in the street, thousands of people began gathering, surly and hostile, threatening to storm the hospital and lynch the two lawmen.[27]

In all this frenzied commotion Burton remained calm and seemingly unmoved. Now painfully aware of both the multiple bruises on his body and the gunshot wound in his leg, he slumped into a chair to rest while listening without comment as I. Mac Wood, Buchanan's office deputy (and a Klansman), told what the mob was plotting. To pleas that he sneak out the back way and barricade himself in the county jail, Burton replied: "No, Mac, I have never had to be locked in jail yet." If, however, the Klansmen wanted trouble, he would accommodate them, Burton informed Wood, because he intended to come out soon.

At 4:00 Sunday morning Burton left the hospital. Although limping badly, he opened the front door, hobbled down the steps, and moved defiantly through the crowd, never speaking to or noticing anyone, yet expecting a confrontation each step of the way. After a few hushed, extremely tense minutes he had run the gauntlet and was safe within the county jail. For the moment he had faced the mob and had backed them down.

But the issue was by no means resolved, for the Klansmen were determined to win out. With Buchanan incapacitated, Burton was now in charge and therefore the key to the situation. Yet every attempt to outwit, pressure, or scare him failed miserably. When a fellow deputy, with whom he had worked closely, told him "to line up with the Klan" or "be a damn fool," Burton grabbed him by the back of the neck and the seat of the pants, unceremoniously dragged him into the county clerk's office, and ordered one of the secretaries to stamp "Canceled" across his commission as a deputy sheriff. Later the same day, two county commissioners tried still another approach, offering him a thirty-day paid vacation (to begin immediately) because they were afraid for his safety. Thanking them for their concern, he resolutely announced that he had "no intention of leaving." And if Klansmen wanted him, they would find him "in the sheriff's office," he asserted, "eighteen or twenty hours each day."[28]

For over a week the pressure continued to mount, but Burton remained adamant. No matter that friends and prominent citizens asked him to submit to the Klan, no matter that public opinion was overwhelmingly against him and the sheriff, he would not back down, even after Crow died on October 4 and most of Waco turned out to mourn a "fallen hero." Scornful of hundreds of posters offering a "$5,000 Reward for Red Burton, Dead or Alive," he purposely appeared more prominently in public, challenging the Klan by his presence. Against a barrage of threats on his life, he countered with equally violent actions and statements. Whenever drivers happened to pull up beside him in a car, they found an automatic shotgun pointing out the window. During one difficult day after visiting Buchanan, who was still on the critical list, he bitterly and unwisely declared: "My greatest desire is that I may live to see . . . the streets of Lorena grow up in weeds."[29]

Consequently, the Klansmen realized that only one course of action was left: Kill Red Burton! Throughout McLennan County and Central Texas word went out for Klansmen to assemble in Waco, whereupon they would march on the county jail and lynch Red Burton. On Wednesday afternoon, October 10, men began gathering on the city street corners, whispering their thoughts and plans. But as their numbers increased into the hundreds and then thousands, they boldly announced their intentions. Under the cover of darkness, with fiery crosses illuminating the sky, they were going to demonstrate what would happen to those who opposed the Klan.

By late afternoon Red Burton recognized the full extent of the danger. Yet he could do nothing. The Klansmen had the offensive; it was their move. That was the worst part — the feeling of helplessness, the loneliness, the waiting. To say the least, Burton was "considerably worried"; he knew that his opponents were deadly serious.[30]

Darkness came quickly that October night in Waco. A light, cold mist was falling, the dampness bringing shivers to those in the streets. At approximately 8:00 P.M. three prominent citizens entered the county jail to see Burton, and to his surprise they wanted to help. "If you knew what all we know, you couldn't be in Waco, let alone sitting here in the sheriff's office alone," one of them began, because "[the Klan is] coming over here . . . to kill you." Under no circumstances could they condone such behavior; therefore, they were offering their services. They had already decided to hide him in one of their homes, to protect his family, and if necessary to stand with him against the mob; for, as one of them put it, "We need you, but we need you alive."[31]

To accept their aid was definitely the sane choice, the human one; to reject it seemingly foolhardy. But Red Burton, even though deeply moved by their concern, would not run. After all, if the Klansmen really wanted to kill him, they would "finally do it," he explained, "so they had just as well get through with it tonight." He was not certain, however, that when actually facing him — and also the possibility of his retaliation — they could do murder. "But I am going to give them a chance," he told his startled friends. Presently he intended to make his usual nightly check around town.[32]

As Burton recalled later, the next thirty minutes were a nightmare. Almost instinctively he reached for a sawed-off shotgun and placed it under his raincoat. Then over "strong protests" he opened the door and stepped out onto the street. With the sidewalks jammed with people, he had to push through the crowds, his ruddy face reflecting his grim determination. Up Austin Avenue to the Raleigh Hotel, then back to city hall and the police station he walked, catcalls and threats of violence all about him, a mob of people following and closing fast behind him. Crossing over to Sixth Street, he stopped at the Riddle Cafe for a cup of coffee. Sitting at a table near the back, he readied his shotgun as the angry crowd pressed against the large glass window panels. At that moment Mrs. Riddle hesitantly approached him, tears running down her cheeks, and whispered: "Mr. Burton, when you get ready to leave, my car is at the back door and . . . I am going to drive you away from here, because if you don't, those people are going to kill you." Burton again refused help. "Those men think they want to kill me but they don't," he replied, "because they realize that . . . some of them will be killed." Besides, he announced, while rising to pay his check, "I didn't come in your back door. I am going out . . . just as I came in." And he did, with no one challenging him or even attempting to slow him down en route to the sheriff's office.

Later, Burton readily admitted that he "really had no hopes of returning to the office alive." But now he felt safe. Perhaps his three friends, jubilantly returning to the jail, most accurately assessed what had just happened. As one of them put it: "Burton, you have done the smartest thing that a man ever did . . . we thought you were crazy but . . . if you had run as we advised you, this thing would have never ended; but now they have gone home with their tails tucked like a bunch of whipped puppies."[33]

The violence was over; however, the evil effects, the cancerous suspicions, the hatreds and animosities, lingered. When Texas

Governor Pat Neff ordered an immediate investigation, the Klansmen in Lorena and Waco withheld information and obstructed justice, threatening anyone who might think of testifying against them. Consequently, the McLennan County grand jury returned no indictments but issued "a sweeping rebuke" to Bob Buchanan for his actions. The citizens of Lorena acted in the same spirit; approximately 300 of them signed a petition, vindicating the Klan of its part in "the trouble" and damning the lawmen "for the blood that was spilled." So the bitterness would continue in the county, with people blaming one another for what had happened. And even though the Klan would continue to thrive in Central Texas for several years, the Lorena affair alarmed many thoughtful citizens and thereby aroused staunch opposition against the organization.[34]

No one was a more outstanding opponent of the Klan than Bob Buchanan. A constant reminder of that terrible night, he continued to live for seven years, somewhat crippled by the bullet still in his right leg and physically unable to run for sheriff again. But he never apologized for his actions; instead he battled the Klan, whenever possible showing people what it really stood for. During the next few years he also fought several civil suits brought against him by those wounded at Lorena — and each time he won. In fact, so great was his reputation, so dominant his presence, that the Klan did not parade in Waco until after he retired from office on January 1, 1923.[35]

As for Red Burton, Lorena was just the beginning of a long career in law enforcement. Because of Burton's dedication and valor as a chief deputy in McLennan County, Governor Neff appointed him a Texas Ranger in 1922; he was never disappointed. During the next eleven years Burton became almost a legend in the Ranger service, especially in cases concerning bootleggers, oil boomers, and Klansmen. Then, in 1933, he returned to Waco to serve as chief of detectives and later as chief of police. Upon retirement in 1951, despite all his many contributions to law enforcement over a thirty-five-year span, he would best be remembered for that night in Lorena — for the example that he and Bob Buchanan had set, where two peace officers, disregarding personal safety, faced the Klan and fought it to a standstill.[36]

IV.

Leo Bishop and the
San Augustine Crime Wave

Leo Bishop hated Mexicans — and he had a reason. Near Sonora in Sutton County, Texas, when he was only six years old, a Mexican sheepherder tried to kill his father, Buck Bishop, with a "big bolukie — a butcher knife." In the ensuing fight the Mexican was killed with one shot, a .22 bullet in the heart. Two years later at Rock Springs another Mexican, armed with a .30-.30 rifle, surprised his grandmother, who was washing clothes under a tree at her ranch. When she ran for the house, he shot her five times; the last bullet, Bishop bitterly recollected, "blew her head practically off." The next year at Carta Valley, some forty-five miles north of Del Rio, a Mexican man broke into the Bishop ranch house late one night while Leo's father was away on business. During the next few minutes young Leo, together with his five-year-old brother, fought the intruder, who was trying to rape their mother. Although thrown against a wall and almost knocked unconscious, he afforded his mother time to grab a .30-.30 rifle and kill her assailant. Approximately twenty years later, upon becoming a Texas Ranger, he constantly fought rustlers and smugglers on the border, learning the art of survival because of his Mexican adversaries.[1]

Leo Henderson Bishop was born at Junction, Texas, on January 15, 1903. The eldest son of Aileen Henderson and John Cyphus "Buck" Bishop, he understood, early in life, the hardship — but enjoyment — of frontier ranching. Because his father "hired out" to local cattlemen, the family was often on the move, like camp followers, living a nomadic, uprooted existence. When only four years old, young Leo received a small saddle which rested on a very gentle horse. Consequently, after chores for mother were done — milking cows and carrying wood to the stove — he rode the range, devotedly following after his father.

In 1911, Buck Bishop had accumulated enough money to buy a small ranch near Carta Valley. By modern business standards he made a bad deal; but a "scrub ranch" was all he could afford. In this land of mesquite and scrub brush and cactus, which was grimly desert-like in appearance, the soil was at best hard and gravelly, at worst difficult either for people or livestock to subsist upon. Few American frontiers were more desolate and lonely and inhospitable than the South Plains of Texas. The closest neighbor to the Bishops was five miles distant, the nearest town for supplies forty-five miles. Roads were more like trails, rock-strewn and rutted, winding over scorched hills and through dismal valleys. Water was therefore a most precious commodity, coming from one lone well. The ranch house was an old, weather-beaten frame building which lacked modern conveniences (Buck built another one within a year). As a consequence young Leo carried water to the house for drinking, washing, and cooking; cut brush and sotol for firewood; used a coal oil lantern for light; and frequented a small structure several hundred feet downwind from the living area.[2]

Yet Leo Bishop thrived in this frontier environment; both he and the land were unfenced and unfettered. As he put it, "I grew up kinda natural." Consequently, he never had much "schooling." Although his father hired a young governess one year as a part-time teacher before sending him to a military academy in San Marcos for three semesters, Leo did not finish high school. During most of his waking hours he practically lived on a horse, learning the trade of a cowboy. He was "one helluva bronc buster," whenever possible volunteering his services, hoping for compensation but not demanding it. He was also a successful hunter, good with a revolver but uncanny with a rifle. He could never really explain this talent. But it was there. Instead of taking a bead on a quarry, he fired his rifle from the hip, as if using a forefinger to kill an imaginary foe. And he was more than good. During the 1930s he would be recognized as the best rifleman in the Texas Rangers.[3]

In 1921 Bishop married Ruby Nation, and to a certain extent his carefree life changed. "I had to go to making that woman a living," he announced with a smile. At first, therefore, he worked for other people, "busting" broncs, digging post holes, tending cattle, and herding them to a railhead or to market. Then he bought a small ranch near Carta Valley (Buck Bishop loaned him the money) and settled down to raising a small herd of cattle and a large crop of children. After several years he sold his "spread" and acquired another one in Terrell County, west of the Pecos River.

But Bishop could not do well in this new area, especially after the Great Depression of 1929. Within three years, he recollected, "the people I owed money took that ranch and all my livestock and pitched me out on the road with a sick wife and four little kids." Like the Joads in John Steinbeck's *Grapes of Wrath*, he desperately tried to find work, even part time, but without success. No one had any money, especially on the Southwest Texas frontier.[4]

Early in 1932, however, Bishop found a way to provide for his family. Upon learning that a Texas Ranger had died, thus creating a vacancy, he applied to Governor Ross Sterling for the job and got it. With the state paying $180 a month, he at last had some security — though not much for a family of six. Assigned to a Ranger company at Uvalde, he was sent immediately to the huge Indio Ranch, approximately eighteen miles below Eagle Pass. Although he did receive free railroad passes throughout the state, expenses were high. For instance, he had to supply practically all of his equipment — clothes, bedding, horses and saddle, and oftentimes ammunition for a Colt .45 single-action revolver and a .300 Savage rifle. When en route to a destination he received the fabulous sum of $3 a day for room and board. Therefore, he tried to stay with friends along the way or to sleep in a railroad chaircar.[5]

Once on the job, Bishop was in something of a quandary. He had been given only one specific instruction: "Uphold the law." Yet he had received no formal training as to how to go about it. Not knowing "what to do and which way to jump," he candidly stated, "I just kept my mouth shut." One-armed Ranger Sergeant Arch Miller, a veteran of border warfare and "the meanest one-armed son-of-a-bitch that . . . [Bishop] ever saw," provided him rather meager consolation. "Watch what the other men do," Miller counseled, "and you'll learn pretty quick. You won't have to have a teacher."

And Bishop did learn; he had to in order to stay alive. Already an outstanding shot and an excellent rider who "could talk Mexkin," he had a definite advantage over some of the men. Yet he still

had to acquaint himself with the forty-five-mile frontage of the
Indio Ranch, which touched the Rio Grande and faced Mexico.
Soon he discovered the best river crossings where he could wait undetected and "poison them," on occasion, with "hot lead." He also
learned that in this prickly pear and scrub-brush country, in which
no one could usually "see a hundred yards in any direction," a rifle
or shotgun was a necessary weapon, while a pistol was practically
useless. But most important, he realized that, on the border, life
was cheap, that Mexican cattle rustlers and tequila smugglers, although "poor shots," were deadly adversaries, and that they would
fight rather than suffer capture.[6]

For almost a year Bishop patrolled the border below Eagle
Pass, protecting livestock on several ranches and "poisoning crossings" against all illegal intruders from Mexico. At times he followed tracks for four or five days and never made contact, while on
other occasions he unexpectedly ran into an ambush and "was covered up with sand," as bullets hit close enough to spatter sand on
him. He sometimes participated in two or three gun battles a week,
then had a slack period for ten to fifteen days. But the longer his
Ranger company stayed in the area, the less action occurred, especially after Bishop and Arch Miller illegally crossed the Rio
Grande, captured two thieves who had sought refuge in Mexico,
and turned them over to Mexican authorities. Consequently, in the
fall of 1932 the general manager of the Indio Ranch, Bob Martin,
slaughtered a steer and honored Bishop's Ranger company with a
barbecue. He gratefully acknowledged their effectiveness, stating
that this "was the first time in sixteen years [over a three-month
period] that there hadn't been a robbing or a stealing or killing of
some kind on the Indio Ranch."[7]

Yet in January 1933, despite such excellent service, Bishop lost
his job; in fact, all the Ranger force did — forty-four men in all. And
the reason for this turnover in personnel, this disruption and inef-
ficiency in state law enforcement, was that the Rangers inadvert-
ently became involved in Texas politics. Early in August, Governor
Ross Sterling had received information that "a steady influx of
transients" and a "hoard of floaters" were moving into East Texas
towns to "steal the forthcoming election" for their gubernatorial
candidate, Miriam A. "Ma" Ferguson. Hence he sent three Ranger
companies (including Bishop) from the Valley to prevent any bal-
lot stuffing or intimidation of voters, especially those who favored

him. Because of their high regard for Sterling the Rangers were impolitic in their comments and partisan in their activities. Not until after "Ma" Ferguson won the election did they realize the error of their actions. Three days after assuming office, the governor had her revenge.[8]

So once again, during difficult Depression days, Leo Bishop was in need of work. But with the fabulous East Texas oil boom attracting practically every con man and get-rich-quick drifter in the nation, and with state law enforcement under the Ferguson administration suffering a disastrous setback, his services were soon in demand. After working a month on a ranch between Del Rio and Eagle Pass (for only $25), he received an urgent call from former Ranger Sergeant Manuel T. "Lone Wolf" Gonzaullas, whom the Atlas Pipeline Company had hired to protect its property in the Kilgore-Longview-Gladewater area. The telephone conversation was specific and direct. If Bishop was willing to become a night guard from 7:00 P.M. to 7:00 A.M., Governor Ferguson would appoint him a Special Ranger (to legalize the bearing of arms). The pay would be $5 a night. But he had to come immediately and bring certain necessary equipment: two .45 revolvers and a sawed-off 12-gauge shotgun.[9]

Without hesitation Bishop accepted. Within a week he loaded his wife and five children (he now had "three queens and two jacks") into an "ole jalopy" and set out for Longview. Upon arrival "Lone Wolf" Gonzaullas, who was adept at applying psychology as well as force to maintain order, used Bishop effectively. Since it was rumored, and in some cases proven, that unscrupulous operators in large companies had initiated slant oil drillings under a competitor's property, thereby siphoning off thousands of barrels of "hot oil," gangs of rowdies had been dynamiting pumping stations and pipelines almost nightly. So Gonzaullas assigned Bishop to the Atlas Company's largest pumping station, which was in Kilgore. In taking Bishop to work the first afternoon, he "stopped off" at roadside cafes and beer joints along the way, where rugged oil-field roustabouts and grisly-faced toughs were known to congregate. To the amazed group of spectators Gonzaullas announced that, standing before them, was the newest guard for the Atlas Company, "an ole valley river rat" who was "the best rifle shot in the Ranger service." As Bishop rather proudly but sarcastically put it, "I was scared I was gonna get killed before I ever got the job" because "he would introduce me to the crowds at large and tell 'em what a tough son-of-a-bitch I had been." In fact, Bishop was so thoroughly disgusted after six successive stops that he demanded several more boxes of shotgun shells to defend himself.[10]

This rather unique introduction to the Kilgore community paid off, however, and Bishop would memorize this unusual technique of curbing lawlessness. For four months he guarded the largest company pumping station, twelve hours a night, seven days a week, without incident. During all that time he never used his shotgun in line of duty, although once in awhile to break the monotony "there'd be a stray dog . . . or sumpin' . . . [to] practice on." The word was out: Gonzaullas had "got all the killers in Texas working for him."[11]

Not too surprisingly, Bishop soon tired of the inactivity in his job. He also began longing for the scrub-brush country of South Texas in lieu of heavily forested East Texas. Hence, as he was seeking an opportunity to return to more familiar surroundings, officers of the Federal Intermediate Credit Bank in Houston provided him the means. In the summer of 1933 they hired him to oversee their extensive ranch properties in South and East Texas. For the record, he was an inspector of their livestock, but actually he was a hired gun, what some might euphemistically call "an insurance policy" against rustlers and wrongdoers.[12]

Bishop enjoyed this work, no question about it; yet after eighteen months he accepted another job, one which proved much more challenging as well as extremely dangerous. The reason for such a decision again had to do with politics. In January 1935, James V. "Jimmie" Allred succeeded "Ma" Ferguson to the governorship after having defeated six opponents in the 1934 Democratic primary and a Republican candidate in the November general election. As a result he immediately began implementing his most important campaign pledge to Texans: a war against crime through better law enforcement. Of course, such action meant drastically overhauling the Texas Rangers, and more specifically dismissal of the Ferguson appointees. So on January 18, the day after inauguration, the governor commissioned eight men into the Ranger service, one of whom was Private Leo Bishop.[13]

For his first assignment Bishop was sent to San Augustine. Nestled amidst thick growths of pine interspersed with oak and other hardwood, this historic Texas community was in many ways a replica of the Old South. The ruling gentry was white, Anglo-Saxon, and Protestant; their outlook was rural and small-town, their attitude toward outside interference hostile and at times belligerent. Since most of the prominent families pridefully claimed ancestors who had resided in the area prior to the Civil War, the community was remarkably homogeneous. Families tended to have large numbers of children who intermarried and remained on the ancestral homestead or on nearby property. They therefore appeared to be extremely clannish, Leo Bishop recollected. But one prominent citizen disagreed with this evaluation. "We were kinfolks," he candidly asserted. As might be expected they thus viewed any action by a kinsman as a family matter regardless of its public nature or legal seriousness. Hence, feuds had at times erupted, and local law-enforcement officials had been specifically informed not to meddle. In turn, the blacks in the community and county, comprising approximately one-third of the population, were thought of not necessarily as property but as being associated with or belonging to a family. In other words, Old Mose was "their nigger." Nor was there "any particular problem between the two races," one San Augustinian stated. "Our school system was segregated, but apparently everyone was satisfied because there were no complaints."[14]

Thirty-two miles east of Nacogdoches and "only a stone's throw" from Louisiana, San Augustine was somewhat isolated. While the United States was becoming increasingly urbanized in the 1930s, the town remained immune to rapid change, its 1,247 citizens seemingly content to resist modernization. Besides the Santa Fe Railroad, only two narrow highways provided contact with the outside world. Cotton, corn, and timber continued to be the prime products of the area, with local industries and businesses depending heavily on such staples. Although the county seat of San Augustine County, the town still maintained its sleepy, leisurely paced atmosphere. Most of the downtown area revolved around the central square, thereby facing the most dominant structures of the community — a three-story stone courthouse and a two-story brick jail. Blacksmith shops, a feed store, and a livery stable were important businesses on Main Street; therefore, horses and mules were much in evidence — and a necessary means of transportation — on the red-clay streets which sometimes turned into reddish quagmires during the rainy winter and spring months and a dust bowl in the summer.[15]

In this small East Texas town a situation had arisen over which Governor Allred had become deeply concerned. Just prior to Christmas of 1934, a gun battle had taken place in a local hardware store in which four men were killed. But no grand jury indictments ensued. For that matter the number of assaults, robberies, rapes, and murders in the county had increased significantly over the past two years, again with few indictments and no convictions. Obviously the newly elected sheriff (a local man who had no professional training) and three Ferguson Rangers stationed there could not, or would not, cope with the situation.[16]

During the last week in January, Bishop, together with Captain J. W. McCormick, Sergeant Sid Kelso, and Private Dan Hines, arrived in San Augustine. Quickly they sent the three Ferguson Rangers "packing" and displayed a document which canceled twenty-eight Special Ranger commissions before assessing the circumstances affecting their jobs. If anything, however, they discovered that reports had understated the gravity of the situation. Local citizens lived in fear of their lives. Some merchants kept double-barreled shotguns in their stores, loaded with buckshot and within reach. No one would talk except to very intimate friends, because they never knew whom to trust. After all, any number of people had some blood or marriage ties with the Burlesons and McClanahans, the two families whose several members were responsible for innumerable abuses and illegal acts. For instance, "when someone got killed or got beat up," one citizen recollected, "you would ask, who was it? They'd say I think it was so and so, but I don't know. I wasn't there. And that would end it." As a consequence, even if an incident occurred on the courthouse square at a peak business hour, witnesses were hard to find. And, as a result, the wrongdoers, with help from the Ferguson Rangers, who along with the sheriff recommended twenty-eight of their men to the governor as Special Rangers, became more blatant in their comments, more brazen in their actions. On any number of occasions sheriff's deputies and Special Rangers accosted on the street farmers who had just sold their cotton or produce and forced them to settle their debts or contribute to a "favorite charity." Beatings in the downtown area therefore became more frequent, but no one objected because "they [the McClanahans and their deputies] would arm up, three abreast," one citizen recollected, "and march around the square, daring anyone to step forward." In the surrounding countryside conditions were equally as bad. Sharecroppers, both black and white, were robbed of their hogs and cattle or were ordered to liquefy their corn into "moonshine." Wherever resistance occurred, maiming or murder resulted. As such violence and outrage continued with impunity, the culprits became increasingly contemptuous of public opinion and confident of their immunity. When one citizen was appointed as a mailman, a position one of them coveted, they killed him. Then, upon learning that a United States Secret Service agent was investigating their illegal counterfeiting operation, seven of them, including the sheriff, pistol-whipped and beat him into unconsciousness at the San Augustine Fair Grounds.[17]

Because Captain McCormick had responsibilities as far north as Wichita Falls and Sergeant Kelso was stationed at Longview almost eighty miles away, Leo Bishop and Dan Hines were assigned "to clean up this mess." The two men, much like newly appointed marshals in a lawless frontier town, responded to the challenge. Their first order of business was that of establishing rapport with the community, of opening up channels of communication with the people. And that meant gaining their confidence by providing them security against the local "outlaws." In other words, they had to demonstrate to the citizens their capabilities — that they were tougher than the opposition, that they could handle any situation.

At Kilgore two years earlier, Bishop had learned from "Lone Wolf" Gonzaullas the importance of image and reputation. He therefore looked and played the part of a Texas Ranger. Slender and wiry, weighing only 155 pounds, Bishop appeared to be much taller than a mere six feet. He had regular, pleasant features. His hair was dark brown; his eyes were blue; his skin was tanned and weather-beaten from endless hours on the range. Dressed in cowboy garb, always wearing boots and a large Stetson, he was obviously not an East Texan. Yet with two Colt .45 revolvers strapped to his hips and a .300 Savage rifle in hand as a constant companion, he was much in evidence. Somehow, though, he was unobtrusive, confident but "not strutting," friendly but formidably aloof. Within a few hours everyone knew that he was "the best rifle shot in the Texas Rangers"; and within a week he let it be known that if any "tough" tried "to pick a fight" he would "carry the battle to him in his own manner" — which meant using a rifle or pistol in-

stead of "going to fist city." In this manner Bishop awed the San
Augustinians. Two of them later admiringly reflected: "If you were
to describe a Texas Ranger, you would describe Leo Bishop."[18]

Despite their reputation as rugged law officers, Bishop and
Hines were quite concerned that the opposition would try to shoot
them in the back or have them ambushed. Bishop later acknowledged that San Augustine, not the Valley or Kilgore, "was the
toughest place I ever got into in my life." Consequently, the two
Rangers employed another tactic which had worked successfully in
the border country as well as in the East Texas boom towns. To
gain the advantage over adversaries, they had learned to browbeat
them with words, to run a verbal bluff. "I've called a man an ugly
name and cussed him to paralyze his thoughts for a minute,"
Bishop admitted, because that way "you take charge of him before
he realizes what's happened." Hence, when one of the Burlesons
first met the two Rangers on the town square, sticking out his hand
and introducing himself, Ranger Dan Hines rejected such an over-
ture of friendship and scowlingly hissed: "Yeah, you son-of-a-bitch,
I knew who you wuz before I got here." To some others who were
considered the "roughest toughs," the Rangers calmly proposed
this ominous threat: "We're not trying to make a show, but we're
going . . . to kill you if you make a bobble." So if "you want to live,
be sitting on the jailhouse steps without your guns at five o'clock."
To Charlie McClanahan, who was believed to be the man most responsible for the lawlessness, Bishop was especially threatening
and insulting, berating him on the street with words intended "to
take the hide off." Menacingly he said: "This damn county isn't big
enough for me and you both." Then, in frontier-marshal style, he
announced: "If I catch you on the street again, you'd better be
armed because I'm gonna come a shootin'."[19]

This type of psychological warfare rapidly produced the desired results. Charlie McClanahan immediately fled San Augustine
to nearby Louisiana, while the rest of the gang "made themselves
scarce." Within a week, therefore, with no one around to harass or
intimidate the citizens, Bishop and Hines collected tremendous
amounts of data for the grand jury, especially testimony from eye-
witnesses, who now came forward to corroborate the lawless activities of the past few years. By the second week in March, nineteen
indictments had been returned, including seven against the men
who had beaten up the United States Secret Service agent. Arrests

Ranger Leo Bishop at San Augustine in 1935.
— Courtesy Mrs. D. J. Robbins

Leo Bishop and Dan Hines in 1935.
— Courtesy Mrs. D. J. Robbins

Leo Bishop at his ranch near Carta Valley in the 1960s.

— Courtesy Mrs. D. J. Robbins

quickly followed, and the presiding judge set trial dates. Then the *San Augustine Tribune* reported that Charlie McClanahan had surrendered after authorities guaranteed "safe conduct" from those Rangers who "had chased him from the state."[20]

Seemingly the crime wave in San Augustine was over; yet Bishop had several "loose ends" which still needed "tying up." One especially bothered him. From the voluminous testimony he had learned that the McClanahans and Burlesons had engaged extensively in "moonshining." Besides making illegal whiskey themselves, they had "persuaded" others to do their bidding. So on specific nights they made their rounds in the back country, collecting ten gallons from one farmhouse, twenty from another, still ten from another. Most of the time they also brought with them "a damn mean nigger," Bishop recollected, who "did anything and everything." On one particular night in 1934, after an old black sharecropper had repeatedly failed to meet his gallon quota, this enforcer coldbloodedly pulled out a pistol and murdered the defenseless man in the doorway of his shack.[21]

Leo Bishop wanted "that mean nigger" in the worst way — and as soon as possible. But because the area was heavily forested, almost primeval in nature, with winding trails that disappeared into thickly matted vegetation, he had as much difficulty in locating as in apprehending him. He therefore sought — and found — a reliable informant. For several weeks Bishop had been watching a young black named Ben Sublette, a car-wash attendant at the local Chevrolet dealership. Since his partner Dan Hines had just bought a new Chevrolet coupe, Bishop occasionally stopped by with him to have it washed. Within a very brief time he discovered that Sublette was "gun shy." So in a teasing yet impressive ploy he invariably sneaked up on the black and quickly drew one of his .45 Colt revolvers. "He'd just tear things up, just scared to death . . . his eyes as big as saucers," Bishop chuckled. Then Sublette would plead: "My Gawd, Mr. Leo, don't do that to me." After several weeks Bishop finally agreed to end such menacing horseplay, that is, in return for a favor. He wanted information as to the whereabouts of the black killer. In turn, he promised to keep his source "absolutely confidential."[22]

Bishop did not have to wait long, for he soon received word that the man was hiding in a deserted farmhouse some twenty miles south of the county. After receiving detailed directions, he hastily,

and therefore somewhat recklessly, set out alone on "the hunt."
When unable to locate Hines, he borrowed his Chevrolet coupe and
traveled winding red-clay roads into the forested and at times eerily
silent back country. In less than an hour he arrived at his destination, an old log shack full of chinks and cracks, a foreboding hidea-
way less than thirty feet from the wooded area which was so thickly
matted, Bishop noted, "that you couldn't stick a butcher knife in."

Cutting the motor, Bishop let the coupe roll silently in front of
the cabin. Then, as he jumped from the still-moving vehicle and
ran toward the back of the house, anticipating a possible retreat,
"all hell broke loose." Crashing out the back door, flushed from
cover like a startled quail, a well-built black man (5'9, 175
pounds), with rifle in hand, ran toward the protective trees. Bishop
immediately yelled out "halt" to which the fleeing black reacted by
spinning around and firing an ancient relic of a weapon. At that
range "I thought he was gonna kill me," Bishop solemnly recollected. "He just turned and brought that ole gun up and I was
lookin' right in the mouth of it. I guarantee you . . . [that hole in the
rifle barrel] looked as big as a dinner plate." Instinctively, Bishop
dived sideways to the left while at the same time drawing his Colt
.45 single-action revolver — and it was none too soon. After the
roar of the rifle blast, a slug ripped through his empty holster and
dug into his right hip and buttocks. In desperation he frantically returned the fire and heard his adversary yell out in obvious pain,
then drop "that ole gun." By chance, his .45 slug had hit the rifle
hand of the man, ripping off the trigger and middle fingers at the
knuckles.

As the wounded man stood helplessly before him, begging for
his life, Bishop admitted that he had an almost irresistible urge to
"save the state the expense of tryin' that nigger right there, cause
he needed killin'." But he repressed this impulse because, he
stated, "I never did do that." He thus took charge of his prisoner.
Painfully, Bishop arose from the ground, marched the fearful man
to the Chevrolet, and forced him to lean spread-eagled against it.
Next, he searched the man thoroughly, finding "three or four more
old cartridges . . . none of the same caliber," then handcuffed both
hands in back, and locked him in the turtleback trunk of the coupe.

Stiff and hobbling, Bishop decided to take stock of his own
condition. At first he hesitated examining himself, especially upon
realizing that his "boot was about full . . . with blood." Upon closer

inspection, however, he discovered that the rifle slug — "an ole lead bullet big as the end of my finger" — had nicked him in the hip before hitting his billfold and being deflected through both cheeks of his buttocks. With quite "a trench" across his backside "through all that outside flesh" he had been painfully and, for a Ranger, embarrassingly wounded.

On the return ride to San Augustine, Bishop began reflecting upon what had happened; and once again the teachings of "Lone Wolf" Gonzaullas on the importance of image and reputation affected him. Under no circumstances, therefore, must he let anyone know his condition. After all, "if a damn nigger had come that close to killin' him," he reasoned, then someone else might try to "get it done." So upon arrival in San Augustine he strained mightily to keep from limping, to hide his badly crippled condition. Then, upon locking his prisoner in a cell, he menacingly announced: "If you decide you want to break jail, you just break out cause I'm gonna kill ya when you hit the ground."[23]

With this problem resolved, Bishop had only one other "loose end to tie up." It was in the person of the San Augustine sheriff, who had proven to be both an obstacle and an embarrassment to the Rangers. Besides being incompetent (he was inexperienced, having been in office only since January) as well as an obstructionist to Bishop and Hines, he was engaged in illegal activities. "Two or three blocks from the jail," Bishop vehemently recalled, "that no good s.o.b." was "bootlegging." Complicating the situation even more was the sheriff's son. Late in February he had been arrested at one of his father's bootlegging establishments and, while awaiting arraignment, had broken out of jail through "inside" help.

Bishop thus decided that the sheriff must go, and he was not too particular as to the method. He then contrived to "set up" the local lawman and thus bring about a forced resignation. The plan worked. At his request a good friend who was a Beaumont law officer sent an attractive blonde to San Augustine as "bait" and within a week the sheriff "fell — hook, line, and sinker." A few days later Bishop surprised the couple in a motel room "at the proper time" and obtained a quick confession. Immediately the San Augustine commissioners accepted the sheriff's resignation and then appointed an honest lawman named N. S. Sharp as his replacement.[24]

These efforts would have gone for naught if convictions had

not followed. But Governor Allred, who was determined to "clean up San Augustine," had already anticipated such problems and had set the judicial wheels in motion. As early as the summer of 1934 he had called to Austin newly elected District Attorney Wardlow Lane of Center, who was the chief prosecutor in neighboring Shelby and Panola counties. A young and ambitious East Texan who was a direct descendant of the famous Texas pioneer James W. Truitt, the thirty-year-old Lane "swallowed" the entire "Allred treatment" and, for the moment, believed the flattering assessment of his legal abilities. He thus agreed to prosecute vigorously all cases which any San Augustine judge would transfer to his district.[25]

So in March 1935, Lane (who by his own later admission "didn't have sense enough to be afraid") concluded this scenario in frontier justice. With Bishop and Hines and Captain McCormick as bodyguards and constant companions, he prepared two cases which would test the power and dominance of the Burlesons and the McClanahans. Then in the small East Texas courtroom at Carthage, which was packed to overflowing, he verbally excoriated the tough San Augustine defendants, thereby carrying out Bishop's advice "to peel their butts" so that other witnesses would find courage and come forward to testify. At times Captain McCormick, openly abusive and "vicious talking," intimidated hostile witnesses with threats of bodily harm, while Bishop quietly, although much more ominously, supported Lane by his presence. As a consequence, both trials quickly ended in convictions.[26]

By the end of March a deluge of judicial power and newly found civic responsibility overwhelmed those who had once ruled and terrified the San Augustine area. Indictments, trials, and convictions became the normal pattern, so much so that the Rangers could no longer justify retention in the area, at least not in such numbers. Yet before being assigned to new posts in the state, Bishop and his compadres received the grateful thanks of the San Augustine inhabitants. On Friday night, March 22, 1935, more than 4,000 people gathered at the town square in their honor. To open the festivities Mayor J. R. Bogard introduced Captain McCormick and Bishop, to whom the crowd responded with a thundering ovation. Then W. F. Hays, editor of the *San Augustine Tribune*, read a telegram from Governor Allred commending the citizens for supporting the Rangers and for no longer tolerating "vicious, violent lawlessness." And after several laudatory speeches the Stephen F. Austin College orchestra struck a tune, and Captain McCormick with Mrs. Herman Clark and Bishop with Mrs. J. H. Ellington led hundreds of couples in a street dance which lasted far into the night. Yet what the two Rangers treasured even more was a gift from the city of San Augustine "in appreciation of . . . [their] splendid work" — for each a handsome, short-barreled .38 Colt with an appropriate inscription.[27]

Within a few weeks Bishop left San Augustine. Nothing in his lifetime would ever equal in danger or effect those memorable few months of 1935. For the next year and a half he was stationed at Del Rio and Hebbronville in South Texas before returning to San Augustine for a pleasant, largely uneventful three-year hitch. Soon thereafter, however, he ran afoul of his captain, who was taking "payoffs from gamblers," he asserted, "all the way to Wichita Falls." Upon reporting these irregularities and after seeing no immediate action taken, he quickly became disenchanted with the Ranger service and resigned in 1941, never to return.[28]

But people who came in contact with Leo Bishop would never forget him. Thirty years later, veteran Rangers, when reflecting upon the honest and dedicated men with whom they had served, would still mention his name with respect and admiration. And even today, to the citizens of San Augustine he remains a legendary figure — a steely-eyed cowboy who rode into their midst early in 1935 and almost single-handedly returned the community to them.

V.

Clint Peoples and the Crazed Man

Most boys, while growing up, have aspired to romantic professions, imagining themselves as courageous men of action involved in all kinds of dangerous and exciting situations. Upon reaching manhood, however, they have usually dismissed such youthful dreams and fantasies in favor of more realistic occupations. But not Clint Peoples. From his earliest days he wanted to be a law officer, a man with a badge, a defender of rights and property. His hero was Will Browder, a lawyer who became district attorney and then district judge in Montgomery County, Texas; his idol was Ben Hicks, the mild-mannered, fearless sheriff of Conroe who impressed him by always being well-dressed, who intrigued him by keeping his pistol covered, and who so thrilled his youthful mind — by allowing him to "tag along" — that he "just couldn't see anything else." Whenever possible, Peoples would borrow his dad's old revolver and practice in the woods; just as often he hunted with a rifle or a shotgun. And for what purpose? Obviously, these activities were forms of recreation and pleasure, but they also represented preparation toward being the best in his chosen profession — a captain in the Texas Rangers.

Born at Bridgeport, Texas, on August 25, 1910, Clinton Thomas Peoples was the oldest child of William Thomas and Susie Baugh Peoples. Nothing concerning his ancestors was either exceptional or outstanding. For the most part they were farmers and laborers, law-abiding people who followed the migratory trails to Texas from Tennessee early in the nineteenth century. As long as any family members could recollect, they had claimed the state as their home; and even though their lineage was vague, being Texan seemed to satisfy any lingering curiosity.[1]

But this heritage did not keep them from being poor or from traveling across the state in search of work. Consequently, the Peoples family moved a number of times, apparently willing to go where the job dictated. In turn, they became very close-knit, each hardship holding them more tightly together. At Childress, Texas, Clint's father operated a cafe, but without too much success. Then, in 1915, he worked on the King Ranch as one of its foremen, the small South Texas whistlestop called Ricardo, being their new home. Within two years, however, with armed bands of Mexicans raiding north of the Rio Grande, pillaging and killing en route, he decided to find a safer locale, especially after twenty-five to thirty *banditos* terrorized his house. So, on a hot October day in 1917, he loaded his family aboard an open-windowed, museum-piece of a passenger train, while herding his horses and cattle into several boxcars. After almost a day and a half of such hellish transportation, they arrived late one night at the small East Texas town of Willis. And what a sight they were, standing there on the depot platform, two weary adults with three small, sleepy children, their faces blackened and their clothes soot-covered from the train's coal and wood-burning engine. By morning they found their way to an abandoned farm two miles east of town — their home for the next nine years.[2]

Approximately fifty miles north of Houston and eight from Conroe, Willis was a typical "Piney Woods" community. In 1920 the population was, even by the most optimistic figuring, around 900. The surrounding countryside of red, gravelly soil, heavily forested with pine and oak and sweet gum, did not lend itself to the principal Texas staples of cotton and corn. Overall, the inhabitants were poor and provincial, uninformed about the outside world, but hospitable to those who were willing to settle in their area. For instance, when Bill Peoples began building a home for his family, neighbors from miles around surprised him with an old-fashioned house-raising party.[3]

In East Texas the Peoples family finally found roots. Yet life was not easy, especially for young Clint. As the oldest son, he had additional responsibilities to the family. There were "always chores," he recalled. Up at 4:00 in the morning, he had to milk the cows, feed the stock, and prime the pump (no matter how cold it was) before eating breakfast and walking two miles to school. For five days each week he received the general education and hickory-rod discipline of a rural, two-teacher educational system. On Saturdays he worked all day with his father, either cultivating their truck farm or delivering milk and butter from their dairy. By Sundays he was ready for relaxation, which meant Sunday school, morning service, and evening prayer meeting at the nearby Baptist church or, at times, a religious festival of "all day singing and dinner on the ground."[4]

In 1926 the family moved to a farm six miles south of Conroe. Although quite prosperous and relatively happy at Willis, they felt compelled to leave; it was a matter of principle. For several years Clint's father had become increasingly dissatisfied with the actions of Hi Little, the local constable. Too often it seemed to him that the law was not being enforced impartially, that certain interest groups were openly favored. Despite loud protests by his family, he ran for constable. During the heat of the campaign he proclaimed confidently that "whenever he couldn't beat Hi Little, he'd leave." Soon after the election he kept his word, at the same time vowing never to participate in politics again.[5]

Actually, the move to Conroe proved to be advantageous. Even if daily chores did not change perceptibly, Clint did realize greater opportunities. At the local high school he received a broad education as well as a chance to play on the baseball team. After graduation in 1928 he worked for his father, who had a number of business enterprises. Besides managing a farm and dairy, Bill Peoples operated a service station, hardware store, grocery, cafe, and small hotel; at times, he even served as the town undertaker. More than ever before, he called upon all members of his family to help. As a result, Clint became a jack-of-all-trades — mechanic, salesman, waiter, cashier, desk clerk, mortician — "filling in wherever needed, doing what had to be done."[6]

By 1930, however, Clint Peoples could no longer continue this job of musical chairs. His desire to break away from this monotonous, uninspiring routine, to follow his own ambitions, was too strong. Of course, familial obligations were important to him, but being a peace officer dominated his thoughts and actions. Admiringly, he watched Sheriff Ben Hicks make his daily rounds, and every day he idolized him more and dreamed of working with him.

Finally, he asked his dad to use "his influence" — and it worked. Although only twenty (and therefore legally too young to be a deputy), Clint was nevertheless appointed. Given "an old tin badge" and told to "find" a gun, he naively asked Ben Hicks: "What am I supposed to do?" To which the sheriff replied simply and succinctly: "Enforce the law."

But how? The answer was not an easy one, especially for someone who wanted to excel. Of course, knowledge of the law was most important. Whenever possible, Peoples studied the Texas statutes, familiarized himself with courtroom procedures, and examined the different methods of presenting evidence. Like a man starving, he devoured information pertaining to his profession, questioning judges as to the finer points of law, forever asking lawyers to explain certain legal terminology. In fact, he later reminisced: "At one time I could tell you the penalty for every crime on the books."[7]

Equally essential in his preparation was "the school of hard knocks," for an error as a deputy might prove fatal. Since Conroe was a sleepy, out-of-the-way East Texas town of approximately 2,400 people, geared economically to sawmilling, young Clint received a leisurely education in law enforcement for two years. Almost daily he tapped the vast reservoir of experience known as Ben Hicks; often at mealtime or in the evening he "talked shop" with other officers, exchanging ideas and comparing notes. Gradually, then, he became aware of the "constant process of training" that was so essential to peace officers.[8]

But in June 1932, Peoples had his life rearranged, his world radically changing as the tempo of existence quickened. Six miles from town, George Strake's No. 2 blew in, and overnight Conroe became an oil-boom town. Where once a quiet Main Street existed, a muddy quagmire of a road now teemed with trucks and wagons carrying heavy oil equipment. Small, reputable business establishments gave way to rowdy dancehalls, while tent villages and "cot houses," large, unadorned buildings lined with beds, became commonplace. Causing this transformation, this confusion and turmoil, were the "boomers" — rugged wildcatters and foul-mouthed roughnecks, small businessmen down on their luck, East Texas "dirt" farmers, Arkansas hillbillies, Louisiana Cajuns and "swamp rats," larcenous saloonkeepers and "their girls." These characters poured into the area, more than doubling the population within a few weeks. Although some were carrion-like in nature, waiting to feast on the less fortunate, many were out of work, desperate, at times starving, because of the Great Depression. Consequently, they "would do anything," Peoples recollected, "to get a dollar." And anyone who blocked them from this goal, who limited their actions or restricted their freedom, was looked upon as an enemy.[9]

Into this unpopular and oftentimes unhealthful role, Clint Peoples as a deputy sheriff was obligated to place himself. How easy it had been to take an oath of office; how difficult he found it now to uphold! Conroe was wide open, dancehalls going "full blast" twenty-four hours a day. Almost hourly, craggy-faced, tough-minded men, hungry and at times destitute, roamed the streets, "looking for action," welcoming a fight with anyone. Outside of town, law-enforcement officers were equally hard-pressed, with bootleggers brewing an unwholesome "rot gut" whiskey in almost every large grove of pine trees or with hijackers awaiting an opportunity to steal expensive oil rig equipment.

Peoples therefore learned quickly how to survive in this oil-crazed jungle: it meant being tougher and, if need be, more ruthless than his opponents. During nightly rounds of the town he was forced into as many as three or four fights. Sometimes men would get into trouble, he lamented, because bootleg whiskey, vile to the point of being poisonous, would "drive them out of their minds." A few enjoyed challenging the law, but most of the combatants were simply looking for someone who would give them a physical workout, who would be a worthy adversary. And Peoples, a strapping 6'2, 185-pound young deputy, with more zeal than caution, was happy to accommodate them or, as he liked to put it, "have a little business with them."

Although not consciously wanting to hurt anyone, this rugged lawman fought to win. Like a legendary frontier marshal, he "couldn't afford to get whipped." And if the situation called for "cheating a little bit," using a blackjack or pistol barrel when a fist would not suffice, he would do so; for "losing face" at the hands of a "boomer" would have been disastrous to his reputation.[10]

The Conroe boom continued unabated for five years, and Peoples enjoyed almost every minute of it despite long hours and constant dangers. He also profited quite handsomely since his salary was based upon a percentage of court fines and costs. Yet ever so gradually he grew more and more dissatisfied. With increasing frequency, confrontations became rather "old hat" and law enforcement routine, even though on several occasions a group of toughs, he admitted, "darn near got me." Until 1941 he continued as chief deputy to Ben Hicks; then he resigned and applied for a position in the Texas Highway Patrol, the underlying reasons being pride and ambition. To his father, who had argued vigorously in 1930 against law enforcement as a career, he had promised that one day he would rise to the top of his profession. "I will be," he had candidly asserted, "a captain in the Texas Rangers." He therefore took a $100-a-month salary cut, sold his home, and moved to Austin because the Patrol was a step in that direction.[11]

Peoples never regretted this decision. Already an experienced officer, he was the type of man that the Texas Department of Public Safety (DPS) needed and wanted; as a result, his advancement, though not meteoric, was certainly rapid. After two months of intensive training in modern police procedures and in the most scientific methods of criminal detection, he graduated in January 1941 from the DPS Academy at Austin and proceeded to Kingsville for his first assignment. During the next six years he was stationed in various parts of the state, performing his duties with efficiency and dispatch, always hoping that his record would merit promotion. On December 1, 1946, his faith was justified. An opening occurred in the sixty-two-man Ranger force, whereupon he was appointed a private. Then, on March 4, 1953, two weeks after his father died, he fulfilled a promise of twenty-three years: he was commissioned one of six captains in the Texas Rangers.[12]

As the new commander of Company F, Clint Peoples assumed many responsibilities. With a sergeant and ten privates he had jurisdiction over the vast Central Texas area. In an emergency, however, the governor could — and frequently did — order him to other locales in the state, while Colonel Homer Garrison, Jr., his boss and close personal friend, placed him on special assignment occasionally as an undercover agent. Of course, numerous civic functions were also time-consuming but equally vital to law enforcement. Yet, no matter how favorable the publicity, performance in the field was still the best "PR." In fact, the Rangers had always considered dealing with desperate men, with enemies of the state, as their special prerogative, their reason for existence, a matter of pride and tradition. A case in point was the episode near Thornton, Texas.[13]

N. J. Tynes was a troubled, disturbed man. Although rather

slight, with blond hair, blue eyes, and fair complexion, he was physically strong, his 6'1, 180-pound frame hardened by long, arduous hours of farming. But somewhere in his makeup there was a flaw, a neurotic pattern, a maniacal bent. At the age of thirty-eight he had been in and out of mental hospitals several times, with no permanent relief in sight. Periodically, something or someone would "set him off"; then this "friendly, nice feller," as neighbor John Alston picturesquely put it, became extremely dangerous, for "with a .22 rifle he could shoot a jackrabbit and him a runnin'."[14]

On Saturday, May 14, 1955, at about 9:00 P.M., N. J. Tynes had one of his "spells." No one knew exactly what triggered it. Possibly the knowledge that within a week Sheriff Harry Dunlap of Limestone County would be escorting him to the state hospital at Mexia affected his mental condition. Or perhaps slaughtering hogs that morning, the sight of blood, the gory ordeal of cleaning them, may have been a contributing factor. Whatever the reason, just after dark that night he moved stealthily into a cornfield where eighteen-year-old Johnny Ray Bentley, a fishing buddy and good friend, was plowing. As the tractor, with headlights flashing, made the turn at the end of a row, he raised up suddenly from about fifty feet away and fired a .22 rifle, hitting Bentley just below the left shoulder blade and knocking him to the ground. John Alston, who was nearby, had thought at first that Tynes, even though having "a strange, reddish look about him," was stalking rabbits. Later, Tynes explained simply that "the tractor noise was bothering him."

As soon as Alston recovered from the shock of what he had just witnessed, he ran three miles to the nearest telephone. Sheriff Dunlap now took action. Meeting Alston at nearby Thornton, he followed him to the scene of the shooting. After young Bentley was loaded into an ambulance, Dunlap proceeded with two deputies to the assailant's home, where Tynes, firing several rifle shots dangerously near, "made it plain that he didn't want to discuss the matter with them that night." They withdrew until morning.

Before 8:00 A.M. on Sunday, Sheriff Dunlap, together with his two deputies, met Ranger J. H. Rogers and two highway patrolmen, J. H. Neese and Bob Wright, at Thornton. After a brief conference they agreed upon a plan of attack, one which was quite simple, yet seemingly sound and foolproof. Under no circumstances did they want anyone hurt, especially Tynes, who was apparently insane. They would therefore surround the house, fire in several canisters of tear gas, then persuade him to come out.

By 8:30 A.M., after traveling two and three-quarter miles east of Thornton on a narrow, caliche-type farm road, the officers reached their destination. But the terrain, typical of this Central Texas area where a deteriorating, gravelly red soil was suitable mainly for grazing, did not favor their plan. Out in the open before them and facing west, a two-story frame house, badly in need of repairs and several coats of white paint, rested almost naked on a gentle rise. Except for two scrawny hackberry trees just to the north and three small outbuildings or sheds fifty feet in back of the house to the east, nothing impaired the view for at least 150 yards in any direction. So if Tynes intended to resist, he was at a decided advantage. On higher ground, especially from a second-story window, he could observe their actions as well as prevent them from closing in.[15]

On May 15, a quiet Sunday morning, the air was crisp and clean, the temperature pleasant but already beginning to rise rapidly, as the lawmen moved into position. While Sheriff Dunlap and his two deputies made a wide swing to reach the sheds behind the house, the highway patrolmen, using rifles with telescopic sights, crouched behind their car approximately 200 yards to the north. Then, according to plan, Ranger J. L. Rogers dashed for a shallow ditch twenty yards in front of the house and waited several minutes so that everyone could get in place before raising up and firing a canister of tear gas through a front window.

For the next few minutes there was silence, the officers watching intently but detecting no sign of life within the gas-saturated structure. Then, in the shadows of the screened back porch, Sheriff Dunlap noticed a slight movement. Gradually he made out the figure of Tynes, reeling from the tear gas, and at that moment the sheriff committed a grievous mistake for a lawman. Although unable to see his man clearly, he stepped out from the protection of the shed into the open and shouted: "Come on out, N. J." At first, it appeared that the trouble was over. But suddenly Tynes threw open the screen door, at the same time grabbing his .22 rifle which was leaning against the wall, and fired. With a sickening thud the bullet smashed into the startled Dunlap, hitting him squarely between the eyes. Falling between two large gasoline drums as "if poleaxed," he lay still, his face and upper torso hidden from view, his body seemingly lifeless.

Their plans shattered by one rifle bullet, the officers reacted emotionally without organization or design. After a momentary, stunned lapse they tried "to get" Tynes, leveling a heavy barrage at the house; however, he was "like a cat squirrel," one officer recalled, "running from one window to another, shooting at everybody he could." As their rage slowly subsided, they once more thought about the sheriff, hoping that by some remote possibility he might still be alive. At that moment he moaned and gave an ominous death gurgle and they realized the futility of their situation. With their leader slain and a deadly crazy man preventing them from securing his lifeless body, they were forced to wait forlornly on this scorched Central Texas prairie for reinforcements.[16]

Clint Peoples was en route to Oklahoma City for a police seminar when the tragic news flashed over his shortwave radio. Although over a hundred miles away, he turned his car around and sped toward Thornton; after all, a fellow peace officer had been murdered in his district. In little more than an hour, shortly before noon, he reached the besieged farmhouse, having "slung the rubber off" two tires in his haste. And immediately he took charge. Since J. L. Rogers had already radioed fellow Ranger Trenton Horton of Belton to obtain an armored vehicle from nearby Fort Hood, Peoples decided to await its arrival. Meanwhile he contacted Tynes' sister and brother, hoping that they might persuade him to surrender. Their answer was "positively 'no' under any conditions," Peoples recalled. They "knew how dangerous he was." He therefore followed standard police procedure, first cordoning off the area so that hundreds of curious spectators would be out of rifle range, then calling for an ambulance and fire truck. In turn, he announced that, if possible, Tynes would be taken alive; he reinforced this statement by ordering a highway patrolman, who radioed that the madman was squarely in his telescopic sights, not to shoot him. And when it was suggested that another lawman might be killed, he shrugged his shoulders and replied, "Well, that's an occupational hazard. We can't shoot this fellow. Our primary interest is to take him alive."[17]

So the afternoon of waiting wore on with only an occasional rifle shot from the house breaking the stillness. Yet a side drama was developing: two patrolmen were determined to recover the body of Sheriff Dunlap which was lying exposed and swollen in the blistering sun. Having found a discarded metal table top, thick enough to repel a .22 slug, they rigged it up as a shield. Then they

Senior Capt. Clint Peoples.
— Courtesy Texas Ranger Hall of Fame Museum

Ranger Clint Peoples and Homer Garrison, Jr., DPS director, inspect the armored car used at Thornton.

— Courtesy Texas Ranger Hall of Fame Museum

The N. J. Tynes home, front view.
— Courtesy Dallas Public Library

Back view of N. J. Tynes' home near Thornton.
— Courtesy Dallas Public Library

Officers retrieving the body of Sheriff Harry Dunlap.
— Courtesy Dallas Public Library

Subduing N. J. Tynes.
— Courtesy Dallas Public Library

inched cautiously forward from the sheds until they reached the body and dragged it to safety. To their surprise and relief, Tynes was either oblivious to their actions or unimpressed by their heroism; he did not challenge them.[18]

At approximately 2:30 that afternoon the armored vehicle from Fort Hood finally came rumbling down the road; the short vigil was over. Immediately, Peoples assembled the various peace officers and laid out a new plan of action. While Ranger Captain Bob Crowder of Dallas, Ranger J. L. Rogers, and several highway patrolmen would station themselves behind the sheds, he would advance in the halftrack or "tank" from the front. With an army sergeant as driver and Sheriff Grady Pamplin of Marlin, a friend and former Ranger, as his "cover man," he would assault the house with tear gas. With luck, they would take Tynes alive.

Within thirty minutes everyone was in position and the attack began. Slowly, the tank thundered toward the house, Peoples shoving a .45 automatic in his belt while loading a gas gun. While Sheriff Pamplin covered him with a .30-.06 rifle, he raised up (when within fifteen feet) and crashed a tear-gas canister through the nearest window, then ordered the driver to withdraw a few yards. For at least half an hour he continued this tactic, advancing and firing, retreating and reloading, systematically proceeding counterclockwise around the building. Still no sign of Tynes.

Peoples next moved his crew toward the screened back porch, reasoning that Tynes must be hiding where the fumes were less effective. But as they closed in, the tank almost became their coffin, "about as useful," Peoples recalled, "as a log wagon." In his haste to blanket this last area with gas, the Ranger accidentally exploded a canister in their midst. Coughing and gasping for air, he and Pamplin rose from the protective armor of the tank, trying to escape the fumes. At that moment, however, they suddenly realized a greater danger. From the shadows of the porch Tynes sprang forward, raised his rifle, and yelled: "Goddammit! I ain't a'goin'." *Whang!* A bullet ricocheted off the top edge of the tank, barely missing both men. Reaching for his .45 automatic, Peoples instinctively fired the gas gun in his hand, the projectile crashing through the porch screen, hitting Tynes in the left arm between his wrist and elbow, almost severing his hand.

Now all previous strategy "went out the window." It became a matter of self-preservation — and that meant an immediate neutralization of the madman. After leveling a heavy barrage at the porch area, which missed Tynes but forced him to drop his rifle while fleeing into the inner confines of the house, the lawmen moved in for the final assault. Peoples and Pamplin rushed through a screen door on the left, noticed a trail of blood, and followed it into the living room toward the front of the house. At the same time J. L. Rogers and Bob Crowder crashed through an entrance on the right into a large, old-fashioned kitchen. Sprawled on the floor, face down and motionless, but partially hidden because of the heavy concentration of tear gas, was Tynes. As they approached, he suddenly lunged at them, and Rogers, unable to discern whether he was armed, fired automatically, hitting him in the right shoulder. The impact of the bullet failed to stop him. Like a wild bull, he butted Rogers in the stomach, flailing him with two mangled and bloody arms. Now all four officers, coughing and half-blind, obviously affected by so much gas, grabbed Tynes, then with difficulty dragged him from the house.

What a gruesome, pathetic sight Tynes was in his madness and agony. Although shot in the left leg and right shoulder, with his left hand and wrist hanging grotesquely, almost completely severed at the elbow, he still struggled mightily, slinging blood in all directions, despite the efforts of four powerful lawmen to subdue him. Wild-eyed and uncontrollable, he screamed over and over again: "Get Harry Dunlap. He won't let you do this to me." When informed that he had killed the sheriff, he denied it. "I never do anything wrong," he announced while being strapped into the waiting ambulance. "You fellows come out here . . . to put me in that old place."[19]

As the ambulance streaked toward the hospital, the crowd quickly dispersed, returning to their homes after a tension-packed day. In the aftermath, Clint Peoples, standing in the farm yard, suddenly felt tired and drained; yet his day was far from over. After discussing the case with a number of newsmen, he proceeded to the hospital at Groesbeck where, to his sorrow, he learned that Tynes was not expected to live. He died the next morning.

Peoples drove to Bob Crowder's home in Dallas, where finally he was able to wash away the dirt and blood and tear gas. By midnight he was on his way once again, speeding toward Oklahoma City; and at 9:00 the next morning he was standing before a class, teaching a seminar on law enforcement. In a twenty-four-hour span he had again fulfilled a promise made to his father years before — to be the best in his profession.[20]

VI.

Bob Crowder and the Rusk Hospital Riot

Bob Crowder would have liked historian John D. Hicks, if for no other reason than that they both undeniably rejected the concepts concerning the "Agrarian Myth." Existence in rural East Texas during the late nineteenth and early twentieth centuries was not a life of joyful perfection, of happy contentment by working with nature, of all good things coming from the soil. The idyllic image of an indissoluble link between the family farm and American democracy was well hidden, if in fact it did exist. And the picture of a yeoman farmer, in the spirit of independence and equality, wringing a bountiful harvest from God's soil, was inconsistent with that of a young sharecropper who at best eked a tenuous living from the stubborn earth.[1]

Born near Minden, Texas (Rusk County), on January 29, 1901, Richard R. "Bob" Crowder often knew poverty and toil and hardship during his early life. When only fifteen months old, he lost his mother as a result of lead poisoning after a family shotgun accidentally discharged, hitting her in the ankle and leg. Then his father became incapacitated with recurring fever and coughing which was eventually diagnosed as pneumonia. As a consequence, Crowder, the youngest of three brothers, was parceled out to an aunt for several years. Large for his age, and with the family in dire financial straits, he began doing "man's work" when only nine. On a nearby farm he hired out for $8 a month ($7 of which he sent to his father) plus room and board. Many a morning after that, he recollected, "I . . . [was] on the end of a hoe waiting for daylight to come."[2]

Life, even with age and experience, did not become any easier for Crowder. Although working three years on another farm for $13 a month, he had little respite from a routine which was laborious and seemingly inescapable. Whether in winter or summer he herded cows to the milking barn before sunrise and split kindling each evening for the smoking stove. In the morning for a number of years he attended school in a one-room structure with children from the surrounding area, but he seldom enjoyed it. While arithmetic was his "best" subject, all the others — reading, spelling, grammar, history, and geography — continually plagued him, especially since he had little time to study. Then after school until sundown he toiled in the fields, plowing or planting, hoeing corn or picking cotton.

In 1914, although only thirteen years old, Crowder considered himself "practically grown." At 5'10 and 150 pounds, sinewy and rawboned, his face tanned and windburned from constant exposure in the fields, his hands already calloused and scarred by heavy toil, he carried on a full-time job that would have discouraged lesser men. Besides cultivating fifty acres of cotton, corn, sweet potatoes, and peanuts on the "halves" basis of a sharecropper, he successfully grew five acres of sugar cane which was, he candidly admitted, "the hardest thing in the world." Yet, because of his industry and perseverance, the landlord became greedy, "picked a fuss," and forced him to settle for a mere $30 (Crowder claimed that his half was easily worth $500).

As a result, the disillusioned Crowder forsook farming for less speculative but equally strenuous jobs. For over a year he worked on a country road gang for $30 a month, building bridges and improving dirt paths and country lanes into something resembling crude highways. In 1916 he moved to nearby Henderson, a town of 1,500 people, where he hauled freight from the railroad depot to area businesses and farms in a horse-drawn wagon. After several years, however, he and one of his brothers decided to follow the wheat harvest northward from Texas. After all, $4 a day, despite rustic accommodations and a work schedule "from sun to sun," was good pay for unskilled young men. During the off-season they also found jobs on cattle and hay ranches in eastern Colorado, thereby providing them shelter and a little spending money for Saturday nights.[3]

In 1920, however, Crowder drastically changed the direction of his life, although by accident. Upon hearing about a flood disaster in the Colorado mountains, he and his brother thought that they might find work readily available. They were wrong. So one day in Denver, as the two were walking aimlessly down Market Street, hungry and dirty and penniless, his brother saw a uniformed soldier on the street corner and impulsively blurted out: "Let's join the Marines!" Although preferring the U.S. Navy, Crowder agreed to talk with Marine recruiters, take a physical examination, and decide about enlistment within a week. After several days he "signed up," although his brother, much to his surprise, refused to do so at the last moment.

With orders in one hand and a paid ticket in the other, Crowder boarded a train at Denver, his destination being Marine boot camp in San Francisco. And for the first time in his life he felt utterly and completely alone. Nor did the situation improve over the next four months. Confused and hesitant, he had difficulty finding and reporting to the Marine sentinel at Camp Mabry in San Francisco Bay. "Hell! I didn't even know what a sentinel was," he later confessed. Next, he could not be sworn in and proceed with training because some of his papers were lost for three weeks. And then there was Drill Sergeant Rostosky, a tough, mean-mouthed "little Napoleon" who seemed to delight in berating the lean 6'3, 168-pound country boy from Texas. Crowder "had never been talked to like that" in his life — the verbal abuse, the cursing, the denigrating references and demeaning comments — and he did not appreciate it. As a consequence, he responded negatively. After Rostosky was extremely vile one day and asked any recruit who did not like his methods to step forward, Crowder "pushed his rifle to the boy" next to him and "started out." Immediately he was double timing to a barrel half a mile distant with Sergeant Rostosky's curses ringing in his ears. In fact, he became so rebellious that the path to the barrel could easily have been named "Crowder Alley" simply because the young Texan stubbornly maintained that Rostosky "was not right."

But at some point during those months the training, the esprit de corps, the discipline and rules took hold, and Crowder, along with his fellow sufferers, began to fit into that tough-Marine mold of elite soldier. Other than achieving recognition as an "expert marksman" with a rifle and becoming a disciplined fighting man, he learned how to cope with people — but more specifically with himself. Upon graduation from boot camp he "hunted for" his hated tormentor Sergeant Rostosky and, upon finding him, gloweringly and menacingly said, "Hello, you little son-of-a-bitch." Rostosky immediately defused such provocation by making Crowder "feel about two inches tall" as he replied: "Hi, Bob, sure glad to see you. I know how you feel and I don't blame you. But one day you'll be training recruits and you'll know what I had to go through." The sergeant was right. Two and a half years later Crowder was a drillmaster of recruits at San Diego.[4]

Yet, in dealing with men, Crowder developed a different philosophy, one which he would apply the rest of his life. "People should be led and not driven," he earnestly stated. And when placed in charge of a group of individuals, he intended first to understand them and whenever possible "to work with them — and not over them." For that matter, he tried to disassociate himself from any ego problem. In other words he was willing to subordinate himself, to keep a low profile, to allow one of his men who was "on top of a situation" to take the leadership role temporarily and thereby effect the desired results. The man in charge always had the responsibility, Crowder asserted, of creating a favorable working atmosphere in which the group could "pull together."

For the next thirty-one months Crowder grew into manhood; responsibility and experience were invaluable teachers, especially when dealing with regular Marines and navy men. What a tough lot Crowder found them to be. Assigned to the battleship *Oklahoma*, he became recognized as an expert with all weaponry, specifically of small-arms fire (pistol, automatic rifle, and rifle) and was soon promoted to the rank of corporal. As a Marine he was also responsible for standing guard duty as well as enforcing rules and regulations aboard ship. Yet he seldom had need to exert physical force, even though at times having to confront surly, belligerent men. Because of regular meals and extensive exercise he had filled out his 6'3 frame with 225 pounds of sinew and muscle; he had become a formidable, intimidating figure who warranted discretion if not immediate fear.

By the end of 1923, after three years in the Marines, Crowder decided to return to civilian life; he could not live on a corporal's pay of $44 a month either comfortably or well. Yet in Texas his economic status did not measurably improve during the next year and a half. After a few weeks of "fiddlin' around" in Henderson, where work was difficult to obtain, he moved to Dallas. His first job, that of driving a truck and hauling freight, was with American Express. But he soon "hired on" as a city streetcar conductor because of a better salary scale, then realized what a horrible mistake he had made. "It was the hardest job I ever had in my life," he lamented. The traffic was "nerve wracking," the average passenger "disagreeable," the company supervisor somewhat officious and definitely adamant in maintaining a prompt time schedule. Nor did Crowder ever adjust to this situation. For instance, during one especially difficult day, when riders were constantly dilatory in leaving from the rear exit of the streetcar, he became irritated and angry at being delayed on his scheduled run; therefore, after only a brief interval at the next stop, he exasperatedly slammed the rear door shut. One block later he learned that he had been dragging a man whose arm had been caught.[5]

By the summer of 1925, Crowder was so in need of relief, so desperate for a change, that he applied for a position in the Dallas Police Department and, two days later, the last Friday in June, was accepted. What a strange setup he walked into! Chaos and disorganization best described his first month as a city peace officer. Other than the information on his application form, Crowder was an unknown quantity to the department and totally unprepared to perform his duties. He received no formal — or, for that matter, informal — interrogation, no indoctrination concerning rules and procedures, no explanation about city and state laws, and little or no equipment (he had to buy both uniform and gun). And how did rookies obtain knowledge and understanding about their job? From an "old hand," Crowder retorted. The difficulty with this training method, he lamented, was that the veteran officers were "jealous" of their "experience" and "shunned you."

So Crowder suffered considerably along with his fellow rookies. When asked if he could ride a motorcycle, he stammered: "Yeah! A little bit." To which a police lieutenant replied: "That's good. You'll be a motorcycle officer." Crowder then had only a few hours to learn how to operate his new vehicle before going on duty. He went immediately to the nearest Harley-Davidson shop, explained his predicament to the manager, and for ten minutes, amidst a recurring comment of "God help the people," learned how "to kick it off," shift gears, and "sit" without falling off. Nor was his partner, who was assigned to ride in the sidecar, any help. He too had never driven a motorcycle. And when Crowder asked what their patrol duties were, he replied that, having been on the job "only four days, I guess we're supposed to check doors [of business establishments] to see if anything is open."

In spite of "a lot of spills" and ruining several pairs of shoes (he dragged his feet to help stop the motorcycle), Crowder escaped serious injury until a car haphazardly crashed into his idling vehicle and broke his foot. After a brief recuperative period he was assigned to "walk a beat." And for the first time in a long while Crowder had a change of luck. His name was Louis Buzan, a Spanish-speaking veteran policeman who became a staunch friend. "He taught me how to get along as an officer and what to do," Crowder fondly recalled, specifically standard methods of procedure, safety, and self-preservation. Under Buzan's tutelage Crowder studied the legal and technical problems for an officer concerning those laws which were most often violated. He also learned how to talk to suspects or informers ("that's a real art") and how to demonstrate toughness without necessarily being physical, although at times he was. But, most important, he came to realize that he was "serving the people" and that fairness and honesty were prime requisites for a peace officer.[6]

During the next five years, Crowder served Dallas citizens, routinely performing his duties without furor or fanfare. A fierce competitor and self-achiever, he was determined to master the two-wheeled piece of machinery that had caused him so much grief during his first month in the department; therefore he returned to being "a motorcycle cop" and a good one. Then, by chance, he again changed jobs. In the fall of 1929 he became aware of the newly formed Texas Highway Patrol, because almost daily his partner had been expounding upon the honor of being selected as one of the "first fifty" trainees and "insisted" that they both take the qualifying examination. Although quite hesitant about applying because of his poor educational background, Crowder reluctantly consented. To his complete surprise, he received notification to report for duty in Austin on January 10, 1930 (his partner was not accepted).

Upon arriving at Camp Mabry, which was at that time on the

northwestern edge of Austin, Crowder had a distinct advantage over most of the other forty-nine rookies. He was one of only five or six men who knew how to ride a motorcycle; he was an expert with both a rifle and pistol; and he had been a Marine for three years. His military experience definitely helped him, the routines being quite similar: up at 5:00 each morning for calisthenics, breakfast at 6:00, classroom work from 8:00 to 10:00, then motorcycle training until noon; after lunch, two more hours of class instruction, followed by more motorcycle riding and target practice with a Colt .45 automatic.

Yet even with all his experience Crowder was "scared to death, afraid [that he] was going to bust out." And at times his fears seemed justified, for he now had to deal with academics. From instructors Chief L. G. Phares and second-in-command Lieutenant Homer Garrison, Jr., he received heavy doses of state history and geography. "I didn't know there were 254 counties in Texas," he exclaimed. "I thought there were about 100, if that many." He was also examined thoroughly in regard to vehicle registration, the weighing of trucks to determine license fees, and the state civil and criminal codes which affected highway enforcement. To complete this already overcrowded schedule, Phares and Garrison added to the agenda "motorcycle rallies," whereby the men were hauled out of bed at 2:00 or 3:00 in the morning for a round-trip "motorcyclecade" to Waco or San Antonio. Because Texas roads were only partially paved, but more often of dirt or gravel, spills were frequent and accidents, especially from spewed up debris, common occurrences. And since the winter of 1930 was, as Crowder put it, "colder than hell . . .[with] icicles hanging off the [barrack] showers," these early morning excursions were unpleasant and exhausting and dangerous.[7]

After three months of such intensive training, Crowder received a state highway patrolman's commission and was assigned to Texarkana on April 1, 1930. What a unique experience his first year was! With no tradition to follow, with no directives as a guide except "work and enforce the law," he and his partner E. H. Bruce, who was shorter but also about 225 pounds, must have looked like strange, mammoth creatures from outer space (two huge men stuffed into tight-fitting uniforms and boots) to the isolated farmers of far Northeast Texas. At first no one knew who they were or their *raison d'être;* therefore, they spent most of their time in educational and public relations programs. Whenever possible, they spoke to private organizations and civic groups, explaining the role and function of the Highway Patrol. Instead of arresting people for traffic violations (no driver's license, faulty equipment on a car, no license plates or outdated ones), they informed each citizen about the state statutes and issued "warning tickets," that is, unless someone had flagrantly broken the law.

Because their district was so extensive (larger than Rhode Island or Delaware) and because the roads were so pathetically poor, mainly of dirt and gravel, they often left their home base at Texarkana on Monday morning and did not complete their territorial circuit until Saturday night. Other than having to work seven days a week, they had no time schedule. In other words, they could begin each day's patrol in the morning or the afternoon. But either way they more than earned their state salary of $150 a month (which was cut to $125 in 1933 due to state deficits caused by the Great Depression).

Despite long hours and minimal pay, Crowder truly enjoyed his work — and it showed. Thus, in November 1931, he was promoted to the rank of sergeant and assigned to Camp Mabry in Austin as an instructor for the second training school of highway patrolmen. The appointment was an honor, yet Crowder was a logical choice. He excelled on a motorcycle, was an expert with a .45 automatic, and from his past year's experience could point out in the classroom the many problems connected with being a patrolman. He would also teach Texas history and geography with renewed fervor because such information was not only helpful but indispensable to a state police officer.[8]

Somewhere during 1931–1932, however, Crowder ran afoul of office politics. He always believed that Chief Phares' wife, for some reason, developed a strong dislike for him and influenced her husband negatively. Regardless of the cause, the results were the same; he was neither encouraged nor rewarded during the next five years. Instead of being promoted to lieutenant at the end of the three-month instructional school (as had been hinted), he was shifted out of Austin from one station to another: first to Fort Worth, then to Mineral Wells, and in 1935 to Wichita Falls. Through legislative enactment he even lost his sergeant's stripes in 1933 because the rank was eliminated. Then, in 1937, in spite of his exemplary record, in spite of being highly regarded by his fellow officers, it was rumored throughout the Highway Patrol that Phares was trying to "fire him."[9]

Greatly disturbed, Crowder visited his partner one evening to discuss his deteriorating situation. When he returned home, what appeared to be an ominous note said: "Call operator 13 in Austin." Expecting the worst, he dialed the number. Then came the surprise. On the other end of the line was Manuel T. "Lone Wolf" Gonzaullas, chief of the newly formed Bureau of Intelligence.* Stating that he had heard rumors about Crowder's difficulties with Phares, he tersely asked: "Would you be willing to switch over from the Highway Patrol and work for me?" The response was an immediate and enthusiastic "Hell yes." And the next morning Crowder was sworn in and stationed at Tyler, Texas.[10]

For the next eighteen months Crowder tried to demonstrate his appreciation, to prove that Gonzaullas was not mistaken in his judgment of men. Consequently, he exhausted himself in his job. "We were working day and night, honest to God, that year I lived in Tyler," he exclaimed. "I don't believe I slept two nights all through the night. I was always called out for some reason." But more important were the results of such labors. Besides tending to routine matters which in themselves were full-time work, he toiled extensively on two cases which had baffled local lawmen for several years. After months of "running down" leads, of interrogating suspects, of piecing together disconnected parts of a crime puzzle, he and three other officers "cracked" an interstate ring of thieves who had stolen millions of dollars in oil-field equipment. Again the next year he helped uncover a huge car-theft organization which operated out of Dallas but which extended from Houston to East Texas to the Panhandle.[11]

Crowder thus began building a reputation which would one day make him a Ranger legend. Although a relatively quiet man, he was a demon behind the wheel of a car. Whether such behavior stemmed from his becoming inured to traveling at dangerously high speeds on a motorcycle over gravel and dirt roads or from

---

* In 1935 the Texas legislature, at the insistence of Governor James V. Allred, established the Department of Public Safety (DPS). Under the leadership of a director and with the advice and consent of a state commission appointed by the governor, the DPS was divided into three departments: Highway Patrol, Texas Rangers, and Headquarters Division, which included a modern scientific crime laboratory and detection center.

wanting to be first at the scene of trouble, he never verified. But one fact was certain: he could be counted on to be an early arrival and participant. Equally important, Crowder would work on a case unceasingly until it was completed. Regular hours never concerned him. "This business of going to work at 8:00 and getting off at 5:00, you can't do it," he asserted. "If you get on the trail, you've got to keep going til you come to the end of it." And in that time period, prior to the Miranda decision and civil rights legislation, Crowder was known for his ability to obtain confessions. At times he would "ride around" a suspect — keeping him in automobile custody and away from a lawyer — while doggedly probing each aspect of an alibi. He instinctively knew when someone was lying. "You just know it," he explained. "Then you go to work on him — talk, talk, talk. Hell, I've sat up three days and nights talking [until] I'd get the best of him." But, above all, this large, unassuming man was known for his honesty in dealing with men and his calm fearlessness to threats of violence, thereby maintaining the Ranger tradition of "you can't stop a man who just keeps on a comin' on." [12]

In January 1939, Crowder transferred out of the Bureau of Intelligence to the Texas Rangers. For the next two years he moved about considerably — Wichita Falls, Lubbock, Dallas — not because of any personal difficulties but because of Ranger manpower needs. In 1940, however, he went "home" to Dallas as a sergeant in Company B under Captain "Lone Wolf" Gonzaullas. The two made quite a team. One seemed to offset the other's weaknesses and complement the other's strengths. Gonzaullas, flashy yet dapper in western-style garb, catlike in his movements at 5'10 1/2, 170 pounds, and sporting two pearl-handled .45 automatics, brought a wealth of experience to his captaincy, dating as far back as the early 1920s when on the border with Captain Frank Hamer. A master psychologist, he tried to intimidate men with his appearance and reputation, allowing the press to print that he had killed more than eighty men in performance of his duties. Crowder, on the other hand, was the steady, quiet enforcer, an omnipresent, giant shadow of Gonzaullas, who took vicarious pleasure in his captain's growing fame and fanfare, much like a deputy in the Old West who protected his sheriff from "backshooters." Yet such respect was mutual, because Gonzaullas always consulted Crowder before determining a course of action. Consequently, together they fashioned an enviable record. [13]

In 1947, therefore, when a Ranger captain vacancy occurred in Lubbock, Crowder was an obvious replacement. Then, in 1951, when Gonzaullas retired from the force, he returned once again to Dallas as the captain of Company B. But he had no time to celebrate. Besides the heavy demands of the daily routine, he had to deal with a highly explosive problem involving integration. For the past several months blacks had been moving into certain areas of the city by buying homes through realtors. Upon learning about the activities of these so-called "blockbusters," the white citizens of the area, who feared an immediate devaluation of their property, protested vehemently through mass neighborhood meetings and petitions. After their efforts proved fruitless, remonstrations turned to violence; a group of men began tossing dynamite into these black homes and literally blowing them "to pieces." Through his usual schedule of working day and night (and in close conjunction with the Dallas police), Crowder helped apprehend these "mad bombers" — and his captaincy in Dallas was off to a propitious beginning.[14]

Yet no matter how outstanding his achievements, no matter how impressive his excellent record as a peace officer, Texas lawmen would remember one incident in Crowder's career that set him apart from all others — the riot at the Rusk State Hospital.

Actually, the underlying causes for such an outbreak of violence were not uncommon to that decade immediately following World War II. Texas, like many other states, had woefully neglected the mentally ill. Time and again the state legislature had failed to provide necessary funding for adequate facilities and special care; therefore, the Rusk State Hospital was a product of such oversights. Although first used as a state penitentiary late in the nineteenth century, it was converted into a hospital for the mentally ill in 1919 and then, after a building program in the 1930s, had a Maximum Security Unit (MSU) added in 1954. In all, the institution housed 2,500 inmates, including approximately 600 criminally insane, in twenty relatively well-constructed buildings of wood or brick. For those unfortunates or "prisoners," Rusk was the end of the world, a veritable "Hell Hole"; the public had deposited them in this out-of-the-way place and had thrown away the key.[15]

And why were the patients without hope? Even a cursory examination of conditions revealed a number of disturbing answers. In the MSU compound, for example, where three brick buildings were surrounded by two fences (one of which was electrically charged), 600 men lived in senseless degradation. At best, their living quarters could be called Spartan. While most were assigned flimsy spring beds with thin mattresses, some had to use the floor as a pallet. Other than a few tables and chairs, the most notable pieces of furniture were long wooden benches in the hallways where the inmates "would just sit," one investigator put it, "like cigar-store Indians." And again, why? The patients had nothing to do — no entertainment, no organized sports activities, no adequate counseling and instruction, no therapy programs (except electroshock treatment and lobotomies). Nor were the Rusk Hospital administrators necessarily to blame. After all, with limited funds, they were terribly understaffed, employing only one supervisor for every thirty to fifty patients. They therefore created a work pool of attendants or "floor bouncers" who were trusties with a license to "discipline" fellow inmates. As a result, brutality became a way of life at Rusk because, one observer noted, while some "bouncers" were "as crazy as bedbugs," others "were just plain mean."[16]

So at 9:30 on Saturday morning, April 16, 1955, eighty-one black inmates in the Maximum Security Unit of Rusk State Hospital rebelled against a system which had allowed such intolerable conditions. Led by twenty-two-year-old Ben Riley and his lieutenant, Joe Murphy, a wounded veteran of World War II, the men of upstairs Ward 7 "went after" and severely injured one of their antagonists, a "floor bouncer" named Robert Williams. When two attendants, Joe Taylor and Bill Curtis, attempted to break up the fight, they too were overpowered and beaten. Then, with keys to Ward 6 in their possession, the rioters rushed downstairs and brutalized two "bouncers" with icepicks, baseball bats, mop handles, and broken parts of chairs and benches. At that moment Unit Physician L. D. Hancock and Assistant Supervisor (of Wards 6 and 7) Clyde White arrived at the building to make their morning rounds, unaware of what had just occurred. To his credit Riley quickwittedly duped the two by yelling out: "Hurry, doctor, there's been a fight and somebody's been hurt." And upon rushing into the building, they also were beaten and subdued. In fact, the inmates unsuccessfully tried to administer to Dr. Hancock, whom many considered to be "arrogant" and "highhanded," some of his own prescribed medicine — "a dose of ole Sparky," the electroshock machine.

To finalize this takeover, Riley knew that he must deal with one other individual. He therefore forced Hancock to telephone Dr. Charles Castner, the hospital superintendent, and ask him to come immediately to Ward 6. Within five minutes the sixty-six-year-old Castner arrived at the MSU compound and was lured inside the building by Riley, who employed the same ruse once again: "Doctor, there's been a big gang fight upstairs and Doctor Hancock's been hurt." A veteran of thirty-nine years experience with the mentally ill, Castner quickly surveyed the situation and, realizing that Hancock "was in pretty bad shape" (suffering from a concussion and multiple stab wounds), authoritatively insisted that the injured men be treated immediately at the base hospital. After a brief hesitation Riley agreed, then stipulated that one doctor must remain as a hostage. "It's either you or Hancock," he announced. So Castner volunteered to remain.[17]

As Hancock and several others were allowed to leave the MSU compound, the second phase of this little drama began to unfold. Emmett Whitehead, the fair-complexioned, sandy-haired, twenty-nine-year-old editor and publisher of the *Rusk Cherokeean,* was "no hero." But when good friend Cecil Parrish, the Rusk Hospital business manager, telephoned him, asking for his help because "the patients were creating a problem," he responded at once, driving the short distance to the hospital in a few minutes. Nor did he hesitate to enter the MSU compound when informed that a black named Ben Riley wanted to see a newspaper reporter. After all, covering the news was his job; but more important, Charles Castner was "like a second father to him." So Whitehead found himself walking up the compound road past several structures to the farthest building and knocking on the door of Ward 6.[18]

And then, out onto the steps, emerged one terrifying individual, who was obviously, by his bearing and actions, the leader of the rioters. At 6', 220 pounds, wearing only a pair of light-colored pants, Ben Riley was an impressive physical specimen, his well-muscled torso almost dwarfed by huge, log-like arms. Rather nimble for a big man, he bounded within four feet of Whitehead and, under the glare of an April sun, his completely shaven pate perspiring profusely, he began spouting forth the rioters' complaints. He was seemingly unconcerned that lying unconscious between them was the black "bouncer" Robert Williams, bleeding from the ears and mouth, with a sizable indentation (the width of a baseball bat)

in his forehead. Besides wanting better counseling, organized exercise periods, and an end to inmate "beatings," the men of Wards 6
and 7, he asserted, were seeking the same rights that "the white patients" enjoyed, specifically in regard to meals and bathing and
freedom of movement. Because of all this furor and suffering, they
were expecting, indeed demanding, that the news media give extensive coverage to their grievances and that a "hearing" with state officials be arranged. As if to emphasize each of his points, Ben Riley
jabbed an icepick toward the young newspaperman, obviously intent on intimidating him, although Whitehead later pointed out
that "at no time did he threaten me." And then, to demonstrate
further the determination of the rioters, Riley announced that they
would "slaughter" Dr. Castner, White, and Curtis if police officers
entered the compound or disregarded their protest demands;
"there's nothing these sons-a-bitches can do to us," he malevo-
lently told Whitehead, "'cause we're already crazy."[19]

In an attempt to placate Riley and ease the situation, Whitehead was most agreeable, especially with an icepick being continually thrust at him. Meticulously he listed each one of the inmates'
complaints; next, he obtained permission for the *Rusk Cherokeean*
photographer Riley Shattuck to take pictures of those inmates who
Riley claimed had been abused physically; further, he vowed that
within a few hours an "Extra" edition would be printed which
would explain the causes of the riot. He even promised that by late
afternoon James M. Windham, a close friend who was a member of
the State Hospital Board, would be in Rusk for a hearing. He then
went to his office and, after working furiously for two hours, produced 100 "Extras" of the *Rusk Cherokeean,* specifically for Riley
and the men of Wards 6 and 7.[20]

In the meantime, at Dallas, the third and final phase of this
drama was beginning. Returning from lunch around 1:00 P.M., Bob
Crowder received a phone call from the director of the Department
of Public Safety (DPS), his old friend and "boss" Colonel Homer
Garrison, Jr. Although Rusk was outside the territorial jurisdiction
of Company B, it was suggested that he "ought to get down there."
Nothing more needed to be said. After ordering one Ranger to meet
him at the State Hospital and two others to bring tear gas, nauseat-
ing gas, and "all other riot equipment," he "burned up the road"
in a new 1955 Oldsmobile, covering the 120 miles to Rusk in the almost unbelievable time of ninety minutes.

Senior Capt. Bob Crowder
— Courtesy Texas Ranger Hall of Fame Museum

Psychiatrist Charles Castner (left) and Ranger Crowder are interviewed just after the riot at Rusk State Hospital.

— Courtesy Emmett Whitehead

Ben Riley, riot leader (right), points to another patient to show marks allegedly made from beating by attendants. Later it was proven that burn scars were present before admission to the Rusk State Hospital.

— Courtesy Emmett Whitehead

Publisher Emmett H. Whitehead printed the Cherokeean's *extra almost single-handedly during a riot at Rusk State Hospital's maximum security unit on April 16, 1955.*

— Courtesy Emmett Whitehead

Crowder clocked such high speeds because, besides being a "wild man" in a car, he was familiar with the road. Although seventeen years had elapsed since his being stationed at Tyler, the area had remained relatively unchanged. In the forty-mile stretch on Highway 69 south of Tyler, the countryside was rustic, picturesque, in many ways almost primeval — except for the small town of Jacksonville and an occasional farm or fruit stand along the way. No question about it, Crowder was traveling through the heartland of the Piney Woods, through the rolling hills and red-dirt countryside of East Texas where pine tree forests rose eighty to a hundred feet in height and dense vegetation and undergrowth covered the ground. At the Rusk city limits he came over a rise, the highest point in the region, and to his right on the downward slope of a hill was the State Hospital, its buildings somewhat hidden by the heavy foliage.[21]

Upon arriving in front of the Maximum Security Unit at 2:45 P.M., Crowder easily photographed the scene in his mind. On the south side by the double row of fences hundreds of uniformed lawmen were milling about, with most clustered in front of an electronically operated gate. Inside the compound to the north on slightly elevated ground were two dormitory-style buildings, while behind them on the continued incline was the two-story structure occupied by the men of Wards 6 and 7. It was easily recognizable because several "lookouts" were on the roof; thus, no surprise foray to free the hostages could possibly go undetected.[22]

But Crowder had no time to investigate further, much less to receive detailed reports of the day's events; for, to his surprise, he would be immediately "on stage." Just prior to the Ranger's arrival Ben Riley had been demanding to speak to an official of the state or, as one observer quaintly phrased it, "The head Nigger said he'd talk to a Ranger captain if he represented the government." And since Crowder was the only Ranger captain at Rusk, his duty was clear. "O.K.," he agreed, "I'll go in and talk to him if he wants to talk." He was therefore led to a phone at the corner of the compound, a number was dialed, and a voice answered. Into the receiver Crowder identified himself and asked directly, "Do you want to speak to me?" Ben Riley answered with a simple "Yes." In that case, Crowder asserted, "I'm ready to come in there, but I don't want no foolishness." After Riley replied, "Me neither," Crowder laid out the rules for this critical, possibly fatal confrontation in terse, clipped statements, the intent of which could not be misunderstood. "I want to tell you one thing," he announced. "I'm not comin' in unarmed because you've already got three people over there as hostages and I don't want to be the fourth one — and I'm not going to be." Then Crowder grimly said to Riley: "I just want to tell you this. If somethin' goes amiss, I know who's going to fall first."[23]

With time now precious, Crowder needed to know specifically what he "was walking into." Calling aside Emmett Whitehead, he asked what the conditions were inside Wards 6 and 7, what Riley was like, and who had influence with him. For almost ten minutes he listened carefully to the young newspaperman detail his experiences earlier in the day and calmly probed him for information which would provide a "key" to the situation. He also talked briefly with several State Hospital employees before moving toward the electronically operated gate.[24]

At 3:10 P.M. Crowder walked resolutely northward past the first two buildings in the compound toward Wards 6 and 7. Within five minutes he had reached the designated doorstep, whereupon Ben Riley emerged to face him. Calmly, but firmly, Crowder began to speak, measuring his adversary, ever alert to the effect of his words, soothingly applying just enough pressure "to get Riley to back down." During the exchange between the two, which lasted approximately twenty minutes, Crowder emphasized that the inmates were doing "something that's wrong," that their actions "can't help," that if the hostages were mistreated "it's just going to be worse for you." In response, Riley listed, as he had earlier to Whitehead, the grievances of the eighty-one rioters and asked for a hearing in front of "whoever's in charge of the hospital." At that critical moment Crowder used the necessary lever. "O.K.," he replied, "I'll see that you get a hearing." Then, authoritatively, he ordered, "You just call all your people down here, tell them to bring their weapons . . . and pitch them down in front of me." After an effective pause, he said, "I want the superintendent and the two attendants down here unharmed." With Crowder now in control Riley reacted accordingly. Dramatically slamming his ice-pick and scissors to the ground, he signaled the others to do the same. Slowly, each inmate filed past Crowder and Riley, discarding a varied assortment of weapons into one large pile. And, at length, Dr. Castner, White, and Curtis emerged from Ward 6, shaken but safe.

Operations now became routine. Crowder first had the inmates "shaken down," just in case some had second thoughts about retaining a weapon. Then, within an hour, James M. Windham of the State Hospital Board arrived and patiently listened to different grievances, thus complying with Crowder's promise to Riley. And along with Castner and several other officials Crowder viewed the damage done to Wards 6 and 7. The riot was over.[25]

In 1970, after having retired as the senior captain of the Texas Rangers, Crowder modestly reflected upon that day at Rusk by saying: "Well, I think I got there just probably at the right time." But others knew better than that, especially his Ranger colleagues and specifically Ben Riley. Unknowingly, Crowder gave the most perceptive insight concerning his effectiveness that day when asked if he had any alternative plan of action. "Now if, when I got down there, it hadn't worked that way, I don't know what the story would have been," he candidly admitted. "But I know one thing. I had two .45s with eight shots in each of them, and that's about as far as I know."[26]

VII.

Fred Gomez Carrasco
vs. Texas Law Enforcement

On Wednesday, July 24, 1974, routine and sameness were expected as necessary patterns inside "The Walls" of the Huntsville State Penitentiary. Both the inmates and prison personnel needed to know what to anticipate each day, what programs to acknowledge, what procedures to follow. For example, in the three-story, brick, classroom-library building opposite the prison hospital and catty-cornered on the left to the chapel, regularity was definitely the norm. While the first floor/basement area was used for storage and freezer vaults as well as a small officers' mess, the middle floor incorporated the inmates' dining hall, where prisoners ate throughout the day in designated and carefully structured shifts. The third level, which had recently been remodeled, was "an open-concept educational center," well-lit, air-conditioned, and immaculately clean, complete with reading tables and bounded on all sides with bookshelves. Its thick concrete floor was covered with acoustical tile and a thin carpet; its brick walls plastered over and solid, with no windows.

For access to the third floor, architects had designed a rather unique outside structure which was the only entrance — a zigzag, three-tiered ramp which began on an upward rise from a spacious inmate yard, then split to both left and right angles and, after two more ninety-degree turns, came together again when nearing the top, in some ways resembling an oriental or pagoda-like design. Inmates then had to pass through heavy double-glass doors into a small reception area (10' by 20') enclosed by a three-foot high railing called the "picket fence." With no hindrances except for one desk where a guard was stationed, they could enter two large spacial bays (90' by 60') with an unenclosed classroom area on the left and a reading room on the right. In the center, directly behind the reception area and separating the two bays, were offices and restrooms, divided and offset either by thin wooden walls or Plexiglas windows. Here especially a timetable was in evidence, with regularly scheduled classes such as typing and English beginning at fifteen minutes before the hour.[1]

But at a little before 1:00 P.M. on that July day, this picture of disciplined serenity, of ordered direction, quickly dissolved. Just as classes were about to settle in for the next time period, an inmate in traditional white cotton prison garb, obviously of Spanish descent, stood in the middle of the large library complex and began gaining recognition by brandishing a "blue" revolver (actually a .357 Magnum) over his head. For those who were concentrating on other matters and still unaware of his presence, he startled them by firing several shots — and a different type of order began. Upon hearing gunfire, Sergeant Bruce Noviskie hurriedly ran up to the steep, three-tiered ramp from the inmate yard, only to receive a "slight" wound in the foot from several rounds of bullets which passed through the double-glass doors of the library. At the same time, Lieutenant Wayne Scott was cut by fragments of flying glass and spewed chips of concrete. Since regulations forebade prison personnel from carrying weapons within "The Walls," they wisely retreated.[2]

As threats from the outside momentarily subsided, the lone gunman now began securing his position. Together with two companions who also had "blue" revolvers, he herded seventy fellow inmates into a far corner of the library complex; next he separated five civilian teachers into a special grouping; and then, after ordering heavy metal file cabinets to be placed in front of the glass doors and stationing a lookout there to prevent a surprise attack, he began searching for people still unaccounted for.[3]

During those same frantic minutes after 1:00 P.M., others within the third-floor complex had experienced a number of emotions and had reacted accordingly. Bobby Heard, a dark-haired, clean-cut, twenty-seven-year-old guard, was unable to reach the safety of the ramp. He therefore used an obscure closet stairway to the attic inside one of the center offices, trying first to hide and then hopefully later to escape. Linda Woodman, an assistant librarian, was cataloging books in the center offices along with three other colleagues when Assistant Principal Novella Pollard rushed in and yelled: "Hit the floor. There's a man out there with a gun." Laboring under the debilitating combination of myopia and a woman's vanity (she refused to wear glasses at work), Woodman strained to find the disruptive inmate, naively unafraid of what she could not see. But when several shots reverberated throughout the complex, her attitude quickly changed. She and Novella Pollard ducked beneath a desk and then, in an incredible exhibition of strength, using mainly their legs, the two frantically pushed a large wooden filing cabinet (which later took four men to move) to block the office entrance. Within minutes, however, Ron Robinson, one of the five teachers already held captive, knocked on the door and persuaded them to leave their meager "fortress." Otherwise, Woodman recalled him saying, "they will kill some hostages." So out came Pollard, Woodman, and three women librarians.

Now the search for Bobby Heard intensified. Positive that he was in the attic but unable to find the stairway, the gunmen tried to tear a hole in the ceiling; they also, in frustration and anger, fired several shots into the attic; then they applied a terrifying logic. "If you come down now, we'll spare your life," they yelled. "If we come up and find you, we'll kill you." Soon thereafter Heard emerged from hiding, his clothes "wringing wet" from the stifling heat of the unairconditioned loft. He was then gagged, bound tightly, and placed on a table while ten civilian hostages — seven women and three men — were led to some chairs and seated in a row. Fred Gomez Carrasco was making his bid for freedom and immortality.[4]

Having turned thirty-four just after arriving at the Huntsville unit in February 1974, Carrasco had a notorious reputation with both inmates and prison officials. Whether affectionately called "El Viejo" (the old man) by his followers, or more reverently "El Señor," he was intelligent and cunning, a man to be reckoned with, deadly to the point that murder left no conscionable imprint on him. For instance, he once frankly admitted to prison chaplain Joseph O'Brien: "Padre, I have killed many men. I killed six men in one night in Nuevo Laredo. Killing is nothing to me." And obviously his life was a testimony to those statements. Along with three older brothers he had grown up in one of the toughest areas of

Library and prison yard at the Huntsville Unit showing the library and education unit and the maximum security ramp.

— Courtesy Bob Wiatt

A closeup of the three-tiered ramp at Huntsville Prison where the escape was attempted.

— Courtesy Bob Wiatt

Principals of the attempted escape from "The Walls."

FRED GOMEZ CARRASCO

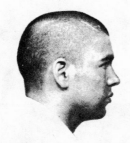 

RUDY S. DOMINGUEZ

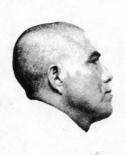 

IGNACIO CUEVAS

San Antonio, a district the police called the "hell hole." At age fifteen he was arrested for shoplifting, at sixteen for brawling and drunken driving, at eighteen for murder and auto theft. Upon serving twenty months at Huntsville after pleading guilty to the lesser charge, Carrasco was paroled — and ready for an advanced degree in the school of crime.

From 1960 to 1973 he became heavily involved in drug trafficking, building an extensive criminal network which stretched from northern Mexico to San Antonio (and possibly as far as Chicago). Known by local police as the "Mexican Connection," he maintained his "heroin empire" despite serving short sentences in both American and Mexican prisons; for he persuaded his followers with fear and his enemies with brutality, reputedly having murdered fifty men. In fact, while he became the subject of an intensive police manhunt in July 1973, a popular song called "The Ballad of Fred Carrasco" began winding its way through the cafes and bars of South Texas and northern Mexico, praising his machismo and marveling at his exploits. Although vowing never to be taken alive, he was captured by San Antonio detectives after miraculously surviving four bullet wounds — and his legend continued to grow.[5]

In appearance Carrasco belied the stereotype of a Mexican *jefe,* of a rugged, virile *bandito* like Emilio Zapata. At 5'7, 207 pounds, he was stocky and overweight, fleshy rather than muscular. His face was oval and heavy-jowled, his hair black and wavy, his skin olive, denoting more Spanish than Indian blood. Surprisingly, at least as far as most of the women hostages were concerned, the look in his eyes was "soft" and his voice tone very gentle, thereby giving the impression that he "was kind" and "would protect us" — that is, Linda Woodman recalled, "when he wasn't threatening to kill us." As for personal appearance he was "rooster proud," Father O'Brien asserted, clean shaven and neat, constantly "primping," combing and recombing his hair, seemingly ever-conscious that his devoted wife Rosa, "the perfect female," should be proud of her macho man.

But make no mistake: Carrasco was a formidable and dangerous adversary. A man with high leadership qualities, he had an unusual instinct for survival. He wanted no opposition to his authority and would brook none. With grudging admiration, Texas law-enforcement officers at Huntsville marveled at his highly developed paranoia, at his almost unbelievable animal cunning, at his ability to anticipate their moves and countermoves. Thus, on the third floor of the Huntsville Prison library complex, Carrasco would apply his years of experience, his knowledge of the street, and often, one observer noted, "would display emotions of anger and frustration, but never lose control."[6]

With the prison officials still in a state of confusion and shock, Carrasco moved swiftly to consolidate previous gains and carry out his plans. After tying the hands of the four male hostages behind their backs and taping their mouths — and sometimes their eyes — with four-inch bookbinding tape, he and his two confederates placed Bobby Heard in a chair atop metal file cabinets with his back next to the double-glass doors. As further protection against a surprise attack, they rigged mirrors at such an angle near the entrance so that a lookout could see down the ramp without exposing himself to a possible attempt by a police sharpshooter with a telescopic sight. In a less dramatic but equally essential action, they recovered canned goods — peaches, chili, and tuna — as well as crackers, which had been "stashed" earlier in the library. And after they untaped ammunition from around their legs, Carrasco made a bandolier of bullets and draped it around his shoulder and chest.

When Father O'Brien voluntarily walked into the library a little after 2:00 P.M., acting as a go-between but hoping somehow to end such madness, Carrasco was in full command. In the image of a bandit chieftain, his orders "sharp, curt, and forceful," he at first demanded from Warden Hal Husbands fifteen sets of handcuffs and a television set. Then later in the day he sent a typewritten note, via the priest, with an additional list of requirements: six M-16 rifles, five magazines and 100 rounds of loose ammunition, three bullet-proof vests and combat helmets, and three walkie-talkie radios on the same frequency; otherwise, he was willing "to shoot his way out" and, he intimated, the hostages would die.[7]

Jim Estelle, at that time director of the Texas Department of Corrections (TDC), was an experienced law-enforcement official. Since his father had been an employee in the California penal system, Estelle was, so to speak, "a prison brat," receiving his first diploma from the San Quentin grammar school. Although vowing never to follow in his father's footsteps, he became a correctional officer at Folsom Prison in California after marriage determined, between his freshman and sophomore years in college, that "someone needed to pay the light bill." Soon thereafter he decided to qualify himself for promotion, to acquire more academic sex appeal; therefore, he graduated from Sacramento State College with a B.A. degree in police science and correctional administration. And over the next eighteen years, while attaining the position of assistant warden in the large California system, he continued to take courses toward a graduate degree. In 1970 Estelle was selected to be the warden of the Montana prison at Deer Lodge, where he served for two years until moving to Texas as the assistant director of the TDC, being the "hand-picked successor" to long-time Director George Beto, who was retiring in August.

At 6', 200 pounds, with even features, ruddy complexion, and dark, wavy hair, Estelle looked the part of a successful Texas business executive, neat and well-dressed, but not overly so. Only his cowboy boots and a wad of Copenhagen tobacco in his left cheek possibly belied that image. Soft-spoken and deliberate in his statements, except when overly provoked, his hazel eyes, which could "chill you," were the real signals of "gale warnings ahead." He moved with an air of confidence, his every action testifying to the fact that, at age forty-three, he knew his business — and knew it well.[8]

But Estelle soon realized that "there never was, or ever will be, a cookbook written to cover a hostage situation," especially with so many variables involved. After interrupting a luncheon speech in San Antonio upon being informed of the library takeover, he arrived at Huntsville by 3:00 P.M. and was "briefed" concerning the state of affairs. Then he began writing his own cookbook. With the "hostiles," as Estelle called them, "in complete command and control of the situation," he had to play a waiting game, buying time by delay and subterfuge. Since prison policy concerning hostages inexorably stated — and all inmates knew the rules — that no illegal freedom, no amnesty, no immunity from prosecution was possible. Estelle had "to say and do things that seemed to belie those basic principles." In fact, he candidly admitted, "I lied more during those . . . days than in the rest of the total of my life." Such machinations, however, were necessary "tactics of combat." He therefore began a deadly game with the wily Carrasco, his main objectives being to save the lives of the hostages and to end the siege.[9]

As a consequence, Estelle rejected most of the "hostiles' " demands, but not all. While publicly stating that "we are considering your requests," he was not about to allow them rifles and ammunition and bullet-proof vests. Everything else was negotiable. Using the sound principle in hostage discussions of "you concede something and we will concede something," he agreed to send fifteen pairs of handcuffs (which would be more humane for the hostages than possible electrical wiring or sash cords) provided that the "hostiles" would release the inmates who had been trapped by the takeover. Using Father O'Brien as an intermediary, he opened negotiations. And Carrasco accepted.

In groups of four and five the seventy inmates were allowed to leave — that is, all but ten who volunteered to remain as helpers, with Carrasco supervising the intervals of departure. As a further gesture of cooperation, Estelle agreed to send up the requested television set, knowing full well that no cable attachment was in the library. Thus, when Carrasco telephoned, obviously upset, Estelle "played dumb" by saying, "Geez! We didn't even think of that. What can we say?" Then to Carrasco's demand that a cable be installed, Estelle frankly replied, "I don't think I can get an electrician or TV technician up there under these circumstances. I just don't have those kinds of volunteers."[10]

Besides the primary concern for those in the library, Estelle had behind-the-scenes responsibilities which were extremely important but in the main escaped public notice. Despite the crisis situation, of lives endangered, he had to be ever cognizant that the three "hostiles" would face prosecution. Preserving a chain of evidence was therefore of utmost importance. Consequently, he established a monitoring system for outgoing and incoming telephone calls, ordered all personnel to keep personal journals and logs concerning daily events, and had TDC lawyers, as well as those at the attorney general's office, instruct his staff on how to follow legal protocol regarding evidence. One especially critical area had to do with Spanish translation; and in this regard Estelle received vital support from an unexpected source. Soon after the first negotiations on Wednesday, Ruben Montemayor, Carrasco's attorney in San Antonio, called Estelle, volunteering his services at his own expense. Although being unknown to TDC officials and somewhat suspect at first, he proved to be of inestimable value. Facile in both English and Spanish, he was extremely able, quick-witted, and bright, translating accurately (along with two TDC interpreters) all calls with the "hostiles." When at times Estelle and Carrasco would be at loggerheads, he was asked to conduct negotiations, to be the spokesman, but never the decision-maker, walking a "fine line" in relationship to his client while serving both the public and the state.[11]

Within the library complex, however, the grim drama continued without much letup. Carrasco handcuffed the women singly at times but more often, usually at night, together in pairs. He also used the library telephone repeatedly, conferring with Estelle or Husbands. He and his compatriots were especially "upset" over the noise from without, claiming that the TDC was trying to tunnel into the library. Estelle's explanation did not completely satisfy them: that the clanging of trays and the clatter of dishes in the inmates' second-floor mess hall were normal kitchen noises, and that the attic was inaccessible except to pigeons, which constantly found their way through the louvers under the tile roof.[12]

But at 6:00 P.M. this mood of confrontation, of continued threats, changed somewhat, momentarily taking a new direction. One of the hostages, fifty-one-year-old Glennon Johnson, became desperately ill, evincing all the symptoms of a heart attack. Hyperventilating and gasping for breath, his skin clammy and an ashen pallor, he appeared to be dying. Carrasco thus decided to release him and allow fellow inmates to take him on a stretcher to the prison hospital — and now the number of civilian hostages was reduced to ten.[13]

For the rest of that long day and evening, despite the prevailing possibility of mass murder, both the "hostiles" and the hostages seemingly tried to achieve some kind of normalcy, to build a new order out of the previous havoc. Carrasco especially eased tension by announcing: "Everyone take it easy, do as we say, and no one will be hurt. We are committed to a plan to leave prison." In much the same spirit he proposed swapping six more inmates for one of his friends, David Robles, who was in the prison hospital. Estelle, hoping to establish firmly a pattern of mutual concessions by both sides, readily agreed to the exchange, thereby leaving only four "volunteers" in the complex — Martin Quiroz, Florencio Vera, Henry Escamilla, and Stephen Ray Robertson — to perform the general "flunkie" tasks. And although Robles, after looking over the situation, wanted "no part of it" and departed, Carrasco seemed to be pleased overall with his position. For instance, he selected Linda Woodman as his unofficial secretary, one of her jobs being to telephone TDC officials, the relatives and friends of the "hostiles," and, at one point, Governor Dolph Briscoe's office. At his direction she also asked for, and obtained from the TDC, pillows, sheets, blankets, and towels, as well as cigarettes, cold drinks, and ice. Then, at 10:00 P.M., she ordered for everyone separate meals, which turned out to be three rather unappetizing sandwiches; no one was particularly hungry anyway.

The greatest psychological boost was that Carrasco allowed the hostages to call their families, even into the wee hours of the morning. Nor did it matter that the complex lights were left on continuously; that Carrasco, ever suspicious and paranoid, moved everyone to a different part of the complex every time Father O'Brien left with a message for Estelle; that Bobby Heard, bound and gagged atop the barricade with his back next to the glass doors, was a stark reminder of their desperate plight. A semblance of order and structure was returning to their lives; they were beginning to know what to expect. In fact, at 3:30 A.M., when Carrasco announced to Father O'Brien, who had acted as a mediator and go-between for the past thirteen hours, that he was "free to leave" but could not "come back" and the Father unhesitatingly volunteered to become a hostage, that act within itself was a stabilizing force. Although unimpressive in size and stature (5'8, 180 pounds), O'Brien was "the bravest man I had seen," Linda Woodman acknowledged. After all, "he didn't have to stay." A veteran of eleven years with the TDC, bald except for a fringe of white hair which seemed to accentuate his reddish complexion and make him appear older than age forty-six, he was a constant source of strength to his fellow hostages. His knowledge of Spanish kept everyone informed about what was being said (except when he protectively told the women "it's best you don't know"), while his Irish wit and unswerving faith alternately relieved tensions or engendered a kind of quiet courage.[14]

At 8:00 A.M. on Thursday, July 25, Carrasco awakened the hostages and, except for Bobby Heard, who was still bound and gagged atop the barricades at the door, seated them in a semicircle of chairs which had been arranged in the reception or "picket fence" area by the desk. At that moment they all became aware, although some had sensed it earlier, that in daily interpersonal relationships Carrasco, despite his sudden fits of rage, was not really a danger to them; however, they could not transfer that same assumption to his two companions. For instance, twenty-seven-year-old Rudy Dominguez, who was serving a fifteen-year sentence for assault to murder, was an obvious psychopath — a vicious, cold-blooded killer who liked to inflict pain and then watch his victims suffer. Slender and willowy at 5'8, 136 pounds, dark-haired and sharp-featured, his eyes continually hidden by smoke-tinted sunglasses, he was a "real loner," surly and unpredictable. No one could control him, not even Carrasco, whom he obviously accepted as leader. The head librarian, Aline House, asserted that Dominguez was like a "rattlesnake," "always coiled in a tight knot and ready to slash his fangs into any threat." His means to transmit venom was a .38-caliber pistol, "his security blanket," which seemed to give him almost unbelievable reassurance as well as added importance. He was never without it, constantly fondling it, using the muzzle to scratch his head or to keep his place while reading a line in the newspaper. It was, Linda Woodman observed, "an extension of his hand," a malevolent companion, with which he terrified the hostages, thrusting it against their temples or point-blank into their faces. Nor did anyone attempt to cultivate him, to fathom the inner recesses of his mind, hoping possibly to elicit sympathy or understanding. He was far too dangerous, especially after not sleeping at all during the first two days, or so it seemed. His accented speech was frighteningly guttural and difficult to decipher; his face a calloused mask of hatred and hidden fury.[15]

Yet in some ways Ignacio Cuevas, slightly darker complected than his two companions, was equally threatening. At 5'4, 140 pounds, he was stocky but still solid at age forty-two, capable of doing numerous pushups on the fingertips of one hand. A Mexican national serving forty-five years for murder, he had difficulty speaking English but could make himself understood. Unlike Dominguez, he was amiable and conversant with several hostages, especially Elizabeth "Von" Beseda and Bertha "Bert" Davis, who had taught him in English and art classes. To the others, however, he was a "real nut," a "mad dog . . . unable to think in a human way." The hostages "felt very unsettled" with Cuevas, Novella Pollard candidly recollected: "You knew that Rudy would kill you, but you didn't know what Cuevas would do." During the second night of the siege he told several of the women that Jesus was condoning everything he did, that he was "saved" even if he killed them. On another occasion he thrust a .357 Magnum point-blank into the face of Father O'Brien, then proceeded to tell him of his "desire to become a minister and save souls." On still another occasion he became extremely upset and paranoid, accusing Linda Woodman of being an "SBI [FBI] agent" who was gathering evidence against them; he vowed to murder her "when we get to Mexico." But possibly Father O'Brien assessed Cuevas best in stating that he was a "stupid" man of "low intelligence" who spoke "with the sincerity of a madman" and who, along with Carrasco and Dominguez, was "capable of killing us quickly, perhaps on whim, without a qualm, without compunction."[16]

At that moment the hostages, in their semicircle of chairs (known as the "fear area"), with Carrasco to their right at a desk (with a telephone), Dominguez pacing back and forth behind them, and Cuevas with his Magnum pressed against the temple of the unlucky hostage who had to sit in the end seat on the far left, began experiencing the real meaning of the word "terror." From a broom closet approximately eight feet in front of them, unmistakable metallic sounds and tapping noises were excruciatingly obvious. Paranoically believing that the TDC was trying to tunnel into the library, Cuevas became highly excited and agitated, pressing his ear to the floor where an open pipe protruded; however, because of all the clanging and commotion emanating from the inmates' dining hall on the second floor, he was unable to distinguish between the different sounds. The "hostiles" thus reacted accordingly. While Dominguez forced teacher Ron Robinson, at gunpoint, to sit upon the open pipe in the broom closet, Carrasco ordered Novella Pollard to telephone Estelle and demand that all noise in the second-floor mess hall cease immediately; otherwise, "Robinson would be shot." But just as she was delivering this ultimatum, Dominguez startled everyone by firing his gun point-blank at Robinson, who slumped lifelessly backward. "Oh, my God! They've killed Mr. Robinson. Oh, this is a nightmare! Warden, do something," Novella Pollard screamed uncontrollably over the phone. For the next few minutes the hostages sat in a complete state of shock, fearful that one, or all, might be shot; that is, until they heard Dominguez gruffly say, "Get up, get up, Robinson. You're not hurt." And although later believing that Carrasco had staged this scene for the benefit of Estelle and the TDC, specifically to demonstrate that he was the controlling factor in this "poker game," they also realized,

Aline House correctly noted, that their "lives meant nothing to these men."[17]

Yet this episode was only the opening round in a long, terror-filled day. For the rest of Thursday morning and into the afternoon the hostages were continually reassembled in their "fear area," as Carrasco set deadlines for his demands over the phone — first at noon, then at 1:00 P.M., and finally at 3:30 P.M. — each time with the threat that the hostages would be shot. Some of the women began carrying a pillow with them each time, although realizing that it was no protection. In some ways, however, it served as "a security blanket," Linda Woodman asserted, because as each deadline neared "you began getting frightened again." Cuevas also added to their trauma, to their fear and uncertainty by deciding to be a "cheerleader." While Carrasco was talking to Estelle and on one occasion to Texas Governor Dolph Briscoe, he forced the hostages to plead for their lives, to "please do something for us." Menacingly he waved his .357 Magnum at them, then thrust the muzzle against the temple of Father O'Brien, who was sitting at the end of the semicircle, and demanded: "Louder! Louder! Make them hear you! Scream for help!"

In between these unrealistic scenes, Cuevas and Dominguez almost went berserk from the outside noises. Although Estelle had ordered the immediate evacuation of the second-story dining hall that morning after the "Robinson shooting," even leaving half-eaten trays of food as they were, the two were convinced that the TDC was still going to attempt a break-in. Pigeons nesting in the attic louvers thus became the hostages' worst enemies, driving the two "hostiles" into "frenzied activity." Besides constantly inspecting the loft area, or sending an inmate hostage to do so, they seemed on the verge, with each new sound, of firing into the library ceiling. Under such circumstances anything could happen; they might shoot someone who moved wrongly or who was unfortunate to be near an outside noise. Equally dangerous, however, was the fact that no one had eaten that morning; the participants were operating only on nervous energy and already badly frayed nerves. Even when the TDC sent in huge trays of appetizing hot steak sandwiches, Carrasco would not let anyone really enjoy the meal. Using Father O'Brien as the "court taster," in case Estelle had poisoned or drugged the food, he announced: "We will wait thirty or forty minutes; then, if the Father is O.K., we will all eat."[18]

Nor was the third day, Friday, July 26, any better; in fact, in some ways, it proved to be even worse. Early that morning Cuevas and Dominguez roused the hostages by saying, "All get up and get ready — maybe today we go." But after having assembled them in the "fear area," the two decided to conduct a personal investigation as to who had lost a ring in "trying to get handcuffs off." When their search proved futile and Linda Woodman offered a reasonable alternative explanation which should have satisfied their paranoia, they concluded with, "Maybe . . . but no one try anything or we kill you." Once again the terrifying specter of death stirred them.[19]

Soon thereafter Carrasco (who usually slept longer in the morning) appeared, thereby calming the situation for the moment; after all, to the women, he was their "protector" from the two "killers," and on every occasion they tried to reinforce their position with him, playing on his vanity and machismo. When he informed them that "when I leave here, I'll need three women and one man," Father O'Brien immediately volunteered, while they all flatteringly responded: "We'll go with you anywhere, Fred." Then, after Novella Pollard, Linda Woodman, and Von Beseda agreed to be the three hostages, Carrasco seemed pleased, especially since they talked to him most frequently and "puffed" him by seemingly being interested in his comments and by their constant "nagging" about and criticism of his two companions.[20]

Yet intermittently throughout the day the tension continued to build, with each new incident compounding their terror. Early in the afternoon, while Carrasco was negotiating endlessly over the phone with the TDC, Dominguez had become increasingly paranoid because of the unexplained outside noises. Suddenly, a book dropped to the floor from a rear shelf in the library, whereupon Dominguez, believing that the TDC was trying to tunnel through, swept other books from their shelves, listened intently with his ear pressed to the wall, and determined that his suspicions were correct. After Carrasco ordered the women to the "fear area" and Ron Robinson and Father O'Brien to lie flat next to the back wall, "Rudy ran back to within about ten or twelve feet from the wall," Aline House recollected, "and fired six rapid shots, spraying the wall where he had removed the books. He put another bullet into his gun and fired it after a few seconds' delay." Even though neither man was hurt, the sound effects and reverberations in such close quarters were so deafening and terrifying, Novella Pollard vividly recalled, that "we jumped with every shot." Later in the afternoon Carrasco also became upset because of movement in the inmate yard three stories below. He therefore ordered Linda Woodman to phone Warden Hal Husbands and demand that all such activities cease immediately; otherwise, "tell . . . [him] to watch the chapel window and I'll show him I can hit what I'm aiming at." Within seconds he fired twice through the double-glass doors at the chapel fifty yards distant, spraying glass in all directions. Stunned by the loudness of the .357 Magnum report which "sounded like a cannon" and terrified by a trickle of blood running down her neck, Woodman yelled out: "Oh, my God! I've been shot." Almost hysterically she dragged Novella Pollard, who was handcuffed to her, behind a desk for protection before rather sheepishly realizing that a glass fragment had caused a superficial wound. Still later that evening, when Estelle complied with earlier "hostile" demands by delivering three combat helmets and three walkie-talkies, which had been acquired from a local G.I. surplus store, Carrasco became furious, screaming and yelling obscenities in Spanish. Disdainfully he smashed one of the radios on the floor, describing the equipment as "Mickey Mouse" and "Boy Scout — something kids in junior high school would not use." Next he placed one of the helmets on a vacant bookshelf, stepped back, and, without warning, "blew it to smitherenes" with one shot. Together with hostage inmate Martin Quiroz he quickly sketched a helmet that looked much like a welder's mask and called Warden Husbands, demanding its immediate construction.[21]

Even though the TDC agreed to supply such daily needs as food, blankets and sheets, articles for personal hygiene, and clothing (including new suits and shoes for the three "hostiles"); even though Carrasco agreed to let Novella Pollard administer all drugs and promised that "my people are not going to take them"; and even though he was the only stabilizing influence among the captors, his periodic outbursts of malevolence and lethal threats created an ambiance of foreboding that no words or actions could erase. For instance, toward the end of negotiations that evening, Estelle flatly stated that under no circumstances would the TDC furnish the "hostiles" with rifles and bullet-proof vests. But for the release of the women hostages he would give them ammunition and, furthermore, would provide Carrasco with "a car inside the

Walls waiting for his instructions." Instead of achieving better rapport and some kind of understanding, Estelle unwittingly "struck a
raw nerve." Suddenly, Carrasco was screaming at him over the
phone, outraged by this offer of transportation. "If you think I got
into this situation without knowing how to get out, you're crazier
than I thought," he raged. "I will tell you when I'm coming out; I
will tell you how I'm coming out; I will tell you how I'm leaving."
With that he slammed down the phone.[22]

A few minutes later, however, in a calmer, more deliberate,
but still menacing tone he delivered this monologue to his attorney
Ruben Montemayor (since he vowed never to speak to Estelle
again):

> They have a weak hand; they know I have got the upper card.
> Give me everything. I will tell them how I am going to leave.
> They insult my intelligence. I don't have to have their guns be-
> cause I do not want to bluff them anymore. Now it's different.
> From now on when I tell them what time one of the three people
> at the door will die, we will open the door so you can pick them
> up . . . . When we are ready to leave, we will know how many
> people we are going to keep and how many we are going to let go.
> . . . I don't want them to make plans for me. I have already made
> them.[23]

But Jim Estelle, together with Texas law-enforcement officers,
was making plans for Carrasco, most of which for the moment
seemed futile. Upon first surveying the TDC position, he felt that
Carrasco was in complete command and control; and "in retro-
spect," he candidly admitted, "during the first thirty-six to forty-
eight hours he probably was." After all, the third-floor library complex was a "real fortress," Ranger Captain G. W. Burks grudgingly
conceded. The floor was of thick concrete, the roof of tile, and any
noise, no matter how slight, was amplified unbelievably. Because
of solid brick walls with windows plastered over completely, the
only entrance through the double-glass doors received even greater
focus, especially since a narrow ramp, three-tiered and steep,
would be a formidable obstacle course for any attacking force. And
no matter how quickly law officers could make their way to the library complex, the "hostiles" would have more than enough time
to do murder.[24]

Consequently, Estelle and Texas lawmen sought other alter-
natives. If Carrasco did kill a hostage, "we were coming in," Cap-

W. J. Estelle, Jr., TDC director

Using Warden Hal Husbands' office, TDC Director Jim Estelle talks directly with the hostiles and hostages. From left are FBI agent Bob Wiatt, TDC staff interpreter Ben Aguilar, Ruben Montemayor, TDC Public Affairs Officer Ron Taylor, and Ranger Capt. G. W. Burke.

— Courtesy Bob Wiatt

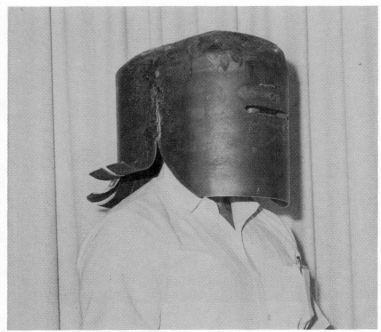

FBI agent Bob Wiatt tries on one of the three iron helmets which Carrasco demanded.

— Courtesy Bob Wiatt

Explosive charges placed at the rear of the library area, together with a rope walk from nearby building.

— Courtesy Bob Wiatt

tain Burks adamantly asserted. But how? The best possibility seemed to be through the rear of the building. So on Friday, July 26, demolition experts placed two charges at strategic locations (Dominguez heard them working) and stationed assault teams at the back of the library next to the prison laundry. Upon detonation of the explosives the assault officers would climb to the second story of the laundry, then cross over to the library on a rung-type ladder or catwalk. Of course, this means of forced entry also had its drawbacks. Moving from one building to another would take time and the assault team might be exposed to gunfire. Nor did this plan guarantee the safety of the hostages, especially since Carrasco might have them secured against the wall next to the explosives.[25]

Estelle and the men under his command therefore explored other possibilities, with their overriding concern always being to "preserve life, . . . [to] save everybody up there, and yet put an end to the situation." As a result he set up a "think tank" composed of six men other than himself: Warden Hal Husbands, Texas Ranger Captains Pete Rogers of Company A and G. W. Burks of Company B, Agent Bob Wiatt from the FBI regional office, and two members of Estelle's immediate staff, D. V. McKaskle and Jack Kyle. These daily "brainstorming sessions" were "very imaginative, very creative," Estelle fondly recollected, having a "Buck Rogers quality about them." In other words, no matter "how wild and off-the-wall" an idea was, they explored it and, at times, would take one element of a "wayout" proposal and use it. Quite logically, they first thought of using tear gas, but quickly ruled it out when TDC engineers estimated that only a tremendous volume would be effective in the library complex. Carrasco also rendered the idea useless by announcing to Hal Husbands: "If we smell gas, we will assassinate everyone." Far more intriguing, therefore, would be the application of a gaseous agent — a nerve gas — that would debilitate the "hostiles" without sounding an alarm. But in discussions with Redstone Arsenal officials in Alabama and with the assistant secretary of the army, Estelle could receive no confirmation that such a weapon even existed; hence, he concluded, "we couldn't smell it, couldn't see it, couldn't get it." Another possibility was to insert a narcotic in the food which would put the "hostiles" to sleep or dull their senses and reflexes; that is, until Estelle learned that the wily Carrasco was using Father O'Brien as a "court taster." Still another idea was to implant explosive devices in the three helmets which Carrasco was demanding, then detonate them. But again the "hostiles" might demonstrate their animal cunning and paranoia by forcing the hostages to wear them.[26]

So for the moment Estelle had to use whatever devices were readily available, to apply the enormous experience and collective training of his men in a constructive way, to work for success through conventional means and techniques. Whenever someone carried food to the library complex or collected trash, that individual was "debriefed" concerning what he had seen or heard. As a further means of obtaining information, a TDC electronics specialist placed a "spike mike" (a microphone "spaghetti-like" in appearance) in a pipe which ran up from the second floor into the "picket fence" area near the desk with the telephone. Although unable to hear everything, the TDC listeners "could piece things together" fairly well.[27]

Even more important was the psychological game between combatants. From the very beginning Estelle had firmly resolved that the "hostiles" were not going to leave the prison. "To cave in, to capitulate to that kind of violence," he steadfastly asserted, "well, the mildest thing I can say, is wrong." He was not about to knuckle under to "that kind of blackmail, that kind of brute force" and turn three killers loose on the public. He therefore followed three rules in negotiating. One that he used most often was the exchange process: "You give something and they give something." Although Carrasco was constantly setting deadlines, threatening to kill the hostages, even staging a scenario like the "Robinson shooting," Estelle was determined not to be "stampeded" into precipitous action. On a number of occasions Ranger Captains Pete Rogers and G. W. Burks had worked on cases in which people had lost their lives. Whether through voice inflection or intuition or training and experience, they ascertained that the "hostiles" had not killed anyone, because "you can't execute somebody in front of a number of people," Captain Burks stated, without "either a complete state of shock on the part of everyone or sheer bedlam occurring. . . . We didn't experience either." Estelle also realized that at some time in the negotiations the combatants would reach a critical juncture; therefore, he had a warrant sworn out for the arrest of Carrasco's beloved wife Rosa after evidence was uncovered that she had supplied the money for the smuggled-in guns. But under no circumstances was Montemayor to mention this fact because, Estelle reasoned, "one of these days soon we'll reach an impasse and I'll need to break it." About two days later Carrasco announced: "I'm not going to talk anymore." So Estelle ordered Montemayor "to tell him." After a barrage of accusations and invectives, the discussions continued.[28]

A second Estelle rule in negotiating was the tactic of delay. After the third day it became increasingly obvious that Carrasco had been "set up" and betrayed, that his planned means of escape was highly illusionary, that someone had hoped "to get rid of him" by raising false expectations for freedom. As a consequence, Carrasco lost the momentum, his edge over the TDC. No longer, in athletic terminology, was the ball in his court; Estelle could now afford to wait out the "hostiles." So, he confidently admitted, "we played stupid, stupid, stupid." In regard to the three helmets, for example, he kept asking, "What do you mean? What are you talking about?" Even with Carrasco's self-explanatory sketch as an example, TDC welders purposely managed to botch the first model, hence more delay. And although Ranger Captains Rogers and Burks wanted the "hostiles" to have those helmets (constructed out of boiler plate and weighing fifteen to twenty pounds) because, besides being cumbersome and limiting peripheral vision, "if you put a piece of steel on a man's head and hit it with a bullet, his head's going to ring for the next six months," Estelle took an excessive amount of time in making them.[29]

The third Estelle rule in negotiating was to imbue the "hostiles" with false hope. Prison psychiatrists, after studying the records and charts of Carrasco, Dominguez, and Cuevas, affirmed in their profiles what was already known, that all three were macho and desperate, having little regard for human life. Thus, under some guise, the TDC must persuade the "killers" to leave their "fortress," to believe that escape was feasible. Otherwise, a bloodbath was a real possibility, if not an absolute certainty. Toward such a convincing facade Estelle realized that he must eventually focus all the energy and talent of the TDC.[30]

At the same time a different kind of human drama was taking place inside the library complex. Since on Saturday and Sunday (July 27–28) the news media interviewed all the third-floor participants, the events during days four and five were, in comparison to the previous three, less tense, although for some they were equally traumatic. Threats, intimidation, and the ever-present specter of death reconstructed normal behavior patterns whereby some of the participants assumed different roles. Through the various stages of captivity, through moments of fear and despair, of anger and frustration, of hope and salvation, the eleven hostages faced this trial for survival in their own individual ways, with human frailties starkly obvious and acts of heroism silently appreciated.[31]

Without question the four male hostages suffered most, handcuffed singly, set apart and alone much of the time during meals and at night, and always used as a shield at the door. Twenty-seven-year-old Bobby Heard (6'2, 235 pounds), the only TDC guard held captive, received the most attention. For the first thirty-six hours he was in a most precarious position, handcuffed in a chair atop the barricade with his back to the double-glass doors, often with his eyes taped and his mouth gagged. Whenever Carrasco threatened to kill a hostage, Heard was "Numero Uno" — and he knew it. Hence, under such pressure, constantly having the unfathomable Dominguez or the sinister Cuevas thrust a gun against his temple, he understandably "broke down," at times reduced to uncontrollable sobbing.

Ron Robinson (6'2, 190 pounds) also had a difficult time. At thirty-five, having a wife and two children, he had taught with the TDC for several years while working on a Ph.D. in criminology. Yet his knowledge about inmates seemed to be limited to textbooks. for instance, he tried to ingratiate himself early-on with the "hostiles" by stating that he was writing a paper on "inmate rights" and would be happy to help them negotiate "some understanding" concerning their position, to which Carrasco replied: "Man, I'm not interested in my rights or anybody else's rights. I'm getting out of here." After Dominguez used him as a guinea pig in the orchestrated "shooting" on the second day, Robinson was no longer any trouble — except to his fellow hostages. Described by several companions as "young," which was the euphemistic way of saying he was disliked, he often carped at the "silly" and "stupid" women for laughing and joking away their tensions, for taking their ordeal "so lightly." As a consequence, his suggestions were often ignored while his presence was endured rather than accepted.

In contrast, the other male teacher, thirty-six-year-old Anthony "Jack" Branch (6'1, 185 pounds) was a low-profile person, quiet and studious-looking, especially when wearing dark, horn-rimmed glasses. Although amiable and pleasant, he was a "loner,"

Hostage Bobby Heard with back to double glass door.
— Courtesy Bob Wiatt

HOSTAGES

Bobby Heard

Ron Robinson

Anthony Branch, Jr.

Rev. Joseph O'Brien

Novella Pollard

Linda Woodman

Aline House

Glenn Johnson

Ann Fleming

Julia Standley

Elizabeth "Von" Beseda

Bertha Davis

one hostage recollected, who "kept alone and therefore was alone." Being black, he feared that the three Mexican-American "hostiles" might react unfavorably to him; then, to his sorrow, he found out. Other than Bobby Heard, he put in more time on the barricade than anyone. And on Saturday, the fourth day, he was almost slain by Carrasco and Dominguez when he unwittingly answered a question too descriptively about conditions in the library complex which Cal Thomas of Channel 2 (Houston) had put to him. After the incident he was "Numero Dos" — the second to die if the TDC stormed the library complex.

By far, the best liked and most respected hostage was Father O'-Brien. Invariably, his Irish wit supplied relief when tensions became unbearable; his ever-present faith and sage counsel gave solace and strength to those who began to doubt; and his example of inner serenity in the face of constant threats from the three "hostiles" encouraged others who at times were wavering or had lost hope.[32]

In comparison, the seven female hostages may have enjoyed better conditions, but not much better. Instead of being handcuffed singly, they were joined with someone; so at least they had a fellow hostage with whom to converse. Although Carrasco promised that no women would be raped, that "you will be treated as though you are my mother," Dominguez (along with Cuevas) threatened them continually. "We never made a move without asking [their permission]," Novella Pollard remembered, especially since Dominguez, on one occasion, evilly hissed: "You all think you are going to get out of here. But you are not . . . I'm going to kill all of you and tell Fred I'm sorry." But the mere fact of being handcuffed, of servilely having to ask permission to do something, of being frightened and then frightened all over again, played accordion-like upon their emotions. At one time or another all cried or were close to tears. Fortunately, not everyone was "down" at the same time; someone was always on hand to comfort the disconsolate.[33]

Because of the handcuff pairings, because of Carrasco's personality, and because of the effects enforced captivity had upon each individual, the women fell into certain behavorial patterns. Unquestionably, forty-six-year-old Novella Pollard, the assistant principal of the Windham TDC School District, assumed leadership and seldom did anyone, except Linda Woodman, ever question her decisions. Although not large physically or especially impressive looking (5′4, 120 pounds), she was formidable, her manner authoritative and "bossy," her voice "schoolteacherish," like "she was shaking a finger at you." Her attitude regarding their enforced captivity was extremely practical and down-to-earth. As soon as anyone else, she understood the dire circumstances of their position and was willing to cooperate as long as Carrasco protected "her people."

Linda Woodman was fashioned from an identical mold. Two years younger than Pollard, the assistant librarian could not keep a low profile, especially after determining "to be her own person." Gravelly, almost husky-voiced, also with a "schoolteacherish" tone, sturdy but not large at 5'6, 135 pounds, she achieved group prominence when Carrasco appointed her "secretary" to make his phone calls and carry out his instructions. Meticulous and fussy almost to the point of being officious, she was perfect for the job; yet her rapport with Carrasco as well as her constant criticism of his "friends" for infringing upon hostage rights imperiled her existence. On Sunday, the fifth day, both Cuevas and Dominguez, on separate occasions, vowed to kill her once outside "The Walls"; therefore, she told Carrasco not to include her as the third woman hostage. Since she was slue-footed and Pollard pigeon-toed, the two sometimes laughingly speculated that Carrasco had purposely handcuffed them together for balance. Whatever the reason, he could not have made a better selection. Together with Father O'Brien, they provided the leadership — and hope — for the hostages.[34]

A second group among the women believed in keeping a low profile. Aline House, the director of library services for the Windham School District, was the most outstanding. At age sixty-one (5'3, 150 pounds), she was the "elder statesman" among the hostages. Because of her position and the respect of fellow workers, she could have been a leader, especially since, as Linda Woodman put it, "she felt responsible for her people." But, unlike Pollard and Woodman, she was not going to volunteer for anything, to be cooperative in any way. The "hostiles" would have to do everything for themselves; that is, unless Carrasco singled her out for a specific task. Her companions, however, by nature and disposition and "handcuffs" were pleased to keep a low profile. Bertha "Bert" Davis, fifty-four (5'4½, 130 pounds), had taught at the prison for several years; in fact, Cuevas had been one of her students. Exceedingly prim and ladylike, almost to the point of being prudish, she was one of the few women who continued to wear a dress (and girdle) rather than be more comfortable in slacks. Actually, Davis was a fretter, a worrier, but never to the extent of being obnoxious; hence, she was quiet and unobtrusive, yet cooperative, wrapped up much of the time in her imagined or real problems. Ann Fleming, fifty-one, had joined the library staff less than a month before. A large woman (5'7, 190 pounds), freckle-faced and fair-complected, with fiery red hair, she was a "very stable" individual who never complained, who regularly took her turn on the barricade, and who entered in with the group when called upon or became a part of the library milieu by quietly reading a book. In looking back on those terror-filled days, several of the hostages admiringly remembered her because on the third day, when word arrived that her mother had died, she never once begged Carrasco to release her (although others did). She also volunteered unsuccessfully, and without fanfare, to be the third woman hostage after Woodman reneged on Sunday, the fifth day.[35]

The third group, because of their personalities, fluctuated between the other two. At age forty-three, Julia Standley had been hired the previous May as an assistant librarian. The mother of four children, slender, even petite at 5'1½, 119 pounds, she was quiet, in some ways distant. To all the women except her "handcuff-in-arms" Von Beseda, she was an enigma. For instance, no one knew why she adamantly decided to be the third woman hostage. Nor did she ever explain — or have a chance to. On the other hand, Von Beseda, age forty-six, was enthusiastic, vivacious, the life-of-the-party type. A bleached blonde, fair complected and petite (5'2, 120 pounds), who had recently lost fifty pounds after being under the supervision of a "fat doctor," she had an upbeat attitude, optimistically making plans for the future, outwardly confident that everything would work out. "You would have had to know Von," Novella Pollard fondly reflected. "She was a very special person" whose immediate concerns were for her teenage daughter rather than herself. To handle pressure she and Standley, who were usually handcuffed together, "joked a lot" or supplied humor for an otherwise grim situation. Because both were approximately the same size, they laughingly called themselves the "stardust twins." But Beseda was the catalyst for comedy, the one who continually lightened the onerous burden of terror from the hostages. For instance, in time of crisis she inevitably and routinely had bladder trouble. Novella Pollard recalled that on one occasion, when the "hostiles" were threatening to kill someone, Beseda, hugging her pillow, called out: "Fred, *Freeeddd* . . ." To which Carrasco replied, "I know, Mrs. Beseda. You've got to go to the bathroom" — and the tension was broken.[36]

Throughout these long days and nights the hostages as well as the "hostiles" began to settle into certain routines and fixed habits. Because of her "organizer's disposition" and position as "secretary," Linda Woodman was able to persuade Carrasco that a schedule of assignments would prove beneficial to everyone. She therefore typed up a timetable which rotated three hostages off the barricade every two hours, thereby relieving Bobby Heard and Jack Branch of such long stints. Much of the time, however, she frustratingly reworked her charts because Carrasco, in his paranoia, was continually altering the daily program. As another aspect of her secretarial duties Woodman checked with each hostage every morning for requests to Estelle and the TDC — newspapers, clothing changes, personal hygiene articles, and accessories such as cigarettes, playing cards, ice, drinks, and candy. At times she even ordered meals when Carrasco became involved in more important business. She was also expected to telephone Montemayor or anyone else with whom the "hostiles" wished to speak. At the same time Bert Davis, Julia Standley, and Von Beseda formed a "cleanup detail," their task being to tidy up the horrendous mess in the library complex. Surprisingly, even Carrasco fell into a set pattern, a constancy of action with which the hostages could begin to identify. Although moving them to different parts of the third floor whenever someone left, he inevitably assembled them in certain designated places: the "fear area" within the "picket fence" behind the barricade, the "eating area" at tables next to Novella Pollard's office on the library side, and the "sleeping area" in the front corner of the library. In between specific assignments and Carrasco's emergency meetings, they leisurely played cards or slept or solemnly discussed their future. But, for the women specifically, Father O'Brien held small "study" sessions in which he discussed how everyone should scatter if "the killing" was initiated, how each person could make a smaller target by rolling on the floor, how they might best impede the "hostiles" and yet preserve life if the TDC should attempt a rescue mission.[37]

On Monday, July 29, the hostages had good reason to believe

that they might have need of Father O'Brien's instruction; it was a horrible sixth day. At 5:30 that morning all was quiet within the library complex. Bobby Heard and Jack Branch were taking their turn atop the barricade; Henry Escamilla, one of the four inmate hostages, was acting as guard; and Aline House, as had been her custom for several nights when unable to sleep on a pallet, was trying to doze in a corner chair. Suddenly and without warning, Escamilla dove headlong into the double-glass door, bouncing off the glass with a terrific thud. As Bobby Heard yelled, "Don't do it, Henry," he tried once again, this time shattering the heavy pane, and then, cut horribly about the head and bleeding profusely, rolled down the ramp to safety. Awakened by the noise, Carrasco rushed toward the barricade with gun in hand. After learning what had happened, he reacted by saying, "Damn fool. He knew nothing was going to happen to him." But Escamilla was convinced otherwise, a few hours earlier having confided to fellow inmate hostages Steve Robertson and Martin Quiroz his fears that Carrasco believed him to be "a snitch" and was "going to kill him." Whatever the reason, the Escamilla escape intensified the situation unbelievably. Angrily, Dominguez railed at the three remaining inmate hostages: "Go on. All go. Then we get it over with." Fortunately, they refused to leave or, as Aline House reflected, "it would have been terrible for us."[38]

Yet the terror continued unbated. Carrasco ordered the three inmate hostages to strip the prison law library or "writ room" of all its contents and tape manila folders, cardboard, and other opaque materials to its glass partitions. Next he had them, and the male hostages as well, repeat this process in the library office, the noise from such demolition and destruction creating an anxiety of uncertainty, a cacophony of fear. Then he herded the eleven hostages, together with their bedding, into the library office, where they sat side by side on the floor. Whereas in the rest of the library the lights had remained on both day and night, here in this small enclosure, with the paneled walls shutting out the light, they sat in almost complete darkness, close together — and helpless — if the "killing" should begin. Ever so often, through a small space in one partition, the diabolical face of Dominguez or Cuevas would appear, thus increasing the pressure and heightening their claustrophobia.[39]

Nor did Carrasco, whom the women hostages depended upon to be their "protector," give any solace or relief. Shortly after mid-

day he first received word that Estelle had sworn out a warrant for
the arrest of his wife Rosa. And he "lost his cool," Aline House
stated, announcing: "This is the end. We're going to force the
issue." He immediately ordered Dominguez to put Bobby Heard
and Jack Branch atop the barricade, to handcuff Father O'Brien
(both wrists and ankles) near the library office with Ron Robinson
next to him, and to keep the women inside the office but handcuffed together in pairs. There they waited, expecting at any moment to hear two terrifying blasts from Dominguez's gun and the
dead bodies of Heard and Branch being rolled down the ramp. Instead, there was only silence. Several minutes went by. Then Steve
Robertson, who was told to sit at the office door, began speaking in
a soft, almost muffled voice: "I am afraid this is the end. I can't
face a gun, so I'm going to O.D. Would anyone else prefer that to
facing the guns?" To several replies of "yes," Martin Quiroz quietly announced: "If it comes to the worst, I'll pass something to
anyone who wants it." Five, ten, fifteen minutes went by and still
nothing but silence. Then Father O'Brien calmly asked if they
would like to participate in a prayer. In the darkness, huddled together, forlorn and despairing, they asked God to "stay with and
help . . . [them] meet death in a brave way."[40]

After what seemed to be an eternity, the crisis ended as quickly
as it had begun — at least for the moment. Carrasco appeared,
"looking a little more relaxed," Aline House noted, and ordered all
handcuffs be removed. He had just talked with Montemayor about
a contract to publish his life's story and he wanted House, Novella
Pollard, and Father O'Brien to look over the typed document being
sent to him. Julia Standley, who had formerly been a legal secretary, offered to type their revised version, which she promptly did,
and Carrasco, pleased with the results, sent it back to Montemayor
with his signature.[41]

Despite this brief interlude of calm, most of the hostages felt
that they were still in dire peril, that at any moment Carrasco
might revert to his previous disposition. But Aline House, whether
by accident or design, "saved our lives," both Linda Woodman
and Novella Pollard agreed. So great had been the strain, so high
the tension, that she began to "feel ill," her skin becoming clammy,
her feet and hands almost numb. Known to have high blood pressure and heart trouble, she decided to fake her condition. But at the
time no one would have believed that her symptoms were not gen-

uine — not Pollard, not Woodman, and surely not Carrasco, who rushed to her side, knelt down, and clasped her hand while asking rhetorically: "Are you all right?" As a result he immediately phoned the TDC to send some heart medicine. After a lengthy discussion in which Montemayor tried to obtain her removal, concluding that if she died "in his custody" he might be facing a murder charge, Carrasco called for a prison ambulance and stretcher (a reaction contradictory to and inconsistent with previous statements and actions). Within minutes, with Robertson and Quiroz helping at the barricade, Aline House was being carried down the ramp, almost rollercoaster style, to the prison hospital. Without question, her real or simulated heart attack proved to be an important diversion and change of pace. Consequently, ten hostages and three inmates had survived the long sixth day while two had escaped the "fortress" confines.[42]

For the next three days (July 30–August 1), both sides jockeyed to find a way out of their common dilemma — Estelle by persuading the "hostiles" to leave their "fortress" and Carrasco by selecting a suitable means of evacuation. Routinely, Estelle and TDC officers asked Carrasco to surrender, promising both to revoke the arrest warrant for his wife Rosa and to allow national television coverage if he submitted. They also complied with his requests for the three special-made helmets and three two-way radios by delivering them near the end of the sixth day. But they unequivocally rejected demands for hacksaw blades and bolt cutters which might be used to build homemade bullet-proof vests. And after much hesitation and debate in which Estelle admittedly almost made a "grievous error" in judgment, they refused an offer to swap five TDC officials, including Estelle and Warden Hal Husbands, for the ten hostages. Nor were they "stampeded" by threats to blow up Novella Pollard with a homemade bomb or led to be sympathetic to hostage pleas, obviously made under duress, that all of Carrasco's demands be met.[43]

With this "hardline" approach, Estelle began forcing the "hostiles" toward his desired objective: that of convincing them that staying in the library complex was futile, if not senseless, and that escape was feasible. Already Carrasco was preparing for his flight for freedom, his moment of glory — and dramatically so. From a suggestion by Steve Robertson he decided to construct a "Trojan Horse" (or, as the TDC officers called it, the "Trojan

Taco"), which in essence was a movable shield. The idea appealed to his flare for the grandiose, his sense of histrionics. Using as side walls two portable blackboards, approximately eight feet long and four feet high, on a two-foot stand with rollers, he nailed long pieces of wood across them as reinforcements. Next he fastened a double row of heavy law books on one side (after determining their level of impenetrability by firing bullets into them) with brightly colored, four-inch bookbinding tape "wound round and round and round." He then attached pressboard or "pegboard," obtained from the prison school art room, to the bottom part of the blackboards in order to hide anyone's legs from view. For entry and exit he designed a front hatch — the width of three bodies — which could easily be removed or set in place, while overhead and at the back he also used pegboard reinforced at intervals with wood. At several locations on the sides and front he cut small openings or gunports which could be utilized in case someone tried to stop him. But if, in fact, Estelle and the TDC were of the mind to prevent his quest for freedom, he had Martin Quiroz wire a bomb inside the "Trojan Horse" which he could detonate simply by pressing a button, thereby carrying out his repeated promise to die rather than surrender.[44]

In turn, Martin Quiroz, while helping to construct this shield, was also devising other weapons and defensive armor for the "hostiles." To Linda Woodman he confided that many of his ideas resulted from a stint in the military. Hence, from duplicator fluid, varnish, and other inflammables poured in a glass bottle wrapped with bookbinding tape, he concocted several rather crude Molotov cocktails or incendiary bombs. Together with Steve Robertson, who had found a baseball catcher's chest protector, he made a bullet-proof vest by stripping away iron and steel supports in the library complex and placing them within or on the protector; however, it was too heavy and therefore unusable. Then, rather mysteriously and secretively, he wired in the "Trojan Horse" a bomb which only Carrasco and he knew how to detonate.[45]

All participants, regardless of their situation, seemed to be arriving at the same conclusion almost simultaneously. Possibly it was a matter of exhaustion. Or it may have been the realization that each protracted day added to the possibility of murder, which would result in a no-win situation. Whatever the reason, everyone did appear to work for a quick departure from the library complex.

On Wednesday, July 31, the eighth day, Estelle once again offered a vehicle to the "hostiles," this time in exchange for all but four of the hostages. Although arrogantly rejecting this proposal, Carrasco changed his mind the next day by demanding an armored car equipped with a shortwave radio and mobile telephone; however, Estelle now balked, trying in his negotiations to obtain the release of all hostages. He wanted no human shields. At the same time the women hostages "worked on" Carrasco, praising his ingenuity and imagination. To help him beautify his creation Linda Woodman, Von Beseda, and Julia Standley agreed, at his request, to duplicate and paint four Mexican flags, then place one on each side of the "Trojan Horse." Whenever he appeared the least bit skeptical or hesitant about using the shield, they remarked how "good look-ing," how "colorful" it was, and how "great for your book" its im-plementation would be. And to counter the impasse between Es-telle and Carrasco concerning human shields, Pollard, Beseda, and Standley released a formal statement to the news media, endorsing Carrasco's plan as their "chance for survival." So the matter stood at the end of the ninth day still unresolved.[46]

Early on Friday morning, August 2, nothing seemed to go right for Linda Woodman; in fact, the tenth day began as the worst, but turned out to be the best, of her captivity. Usually a sound sleeper, even with the library lights on, she rested fitfully, unable to calm down, to keep her mind from racing. At 3:00 A.M. she was fully awake, having to take her turn atop the barricade. And what a horrible two hours it would be. Alone except for inmate hostage Florencio Vera, she at first began "talking at" a hanging light on the ramp just outside the double-glass doors, erroneously believing that she was relaying information into one of the TDC's "spike mikes." She then became aware of Vera, soon discovering that he had been taking Valium and "was stoned out of his head." In his hallucinogenic state he became amorous, to such an extent that he proposed marriage. While easily fending off his suggestive ad-vances, Woodman had to deal with one of her childhood fears. Over the past hour an electrical storm had been building up, with claps of thunder booming ever closer and lightning illuminating the darkness. And here she was, soaked to the skin by blowing rain, "sitting on a metal file cabinet, in a metal chair, with five pairs of metal handcuffs." Afraid that lightning would strike and that she "would be electrocuted," she became almost oblivious to Vera's continuing spiel of jibberish.

Then it happened. A bolt of lightning flashed through the double-glass doors, hitting a fuse box just opposite her with "a loud pop," and enveloped the library complex in darkness. Startled from their sleep and with guns in hand, Carrasco, Dominguez, and Cuevas rushed to the barricade, believing that the TDC was at last launching an attack, while Linda Woodman, "talking a blue streak," yelled above the noise: "It's just a storm! It's just a storm! The lights are out in the other building." After seeing evidences of flashlights in the darkened hospital across the way, Carrasco and his cohorts gradually began to relax somewhat.[47]

But with the electricity gone, with lights out and air-conditioning off, the hot Texas summer took over, making evacuation even more imperative. As temperatures rose, the "fortress" was like an oven, the humidity high and the heat stifling. Perspiring and miserable, "hostiles" and hostages alike "rested a lot that day," napping whenever possible. For the first time Carrasco began using a cane, noticeably limping from the gunshot wounds received the previous year, while Dominguez stealthily prowled around the complex, thrusting his gun in the face of one hostage and then another. Tensions along with the temperature increased.[48]

Under such circumstances Woodman and Pollard devised a plan of action and pursued it as vigorously as circumstances would allow. At noon, when Carrasco emerged from his resting quarters, Woodman once again mentioned the shield to him, praising not only its "beauty" but his genius in concocting it. "This will go down in history as one of the most spectacular escapes in Texas — even in the United States," she confidently predicted. "You can't afford to give it up." Despite his negative response, she and Pollard persisted throughout the afternoon with their campaign of persuasion, one approaching him and then the other, until he finally relented by saying: "O.K., call the TDC and explain it to them." Quickly, however, Woodman initiated phase two of their campaign. "Fred, it will do no good to call. You know they don't believe most of what is said over the phone." She thus suggested that he send "someone" to describe his creation, its "degree of safety" for all concerned, and explain, because of its weight and bulkiness, the need for so many hostages in guiding it down the ramp.[49]

When Carrasco replied that he would have to confer with his

"compadres" and that the hostages should choose one of their number in case the proposal was approved, another human drama in group psychology, in selecting only one out of ten for freedom, occurred. Conducting a hurriedly called meeting, Novella Pollard related to her forlorn colleagues the discussions with Carrasco over the past several hours and announced that Woodman, because of repeated threats on her life, "was going." Ron Robinson immediately offered himself to the group as a better alternative, suggesting that "a man" could explain measurements and dimensions and construction much "better than a woman." In response, Pollard once again demonstrated why Carrasco considered her "boss" and why the hostages concurred. In her best "schoolteacherish" tone she snapped back: "Linda watched this thing being built day by day. She knows exactly how it was built." Then, authoritatively settling the issue, she concluded: "And she is going."[50]

Now for Woodman the waiting began. How slowly the time went by: 4:30 P.M., 5:00 P.M., 5:30 P.M. Still no word. Unbeknown to her, Carrasco had been trying to describe to Montemayor over the telephone his plan of action and how the "Trojan Horse" would facilitate his exit. But under strict orders from Estelle, Montemayor "played very stupid," thereby forcing the conclusion that the release of one hostage "to explain how . . . [they] were coming out" was both prudent and wise. To pressure Carrasco further through delay, he apologetically stated that, because of a previous appointment in San Antonio, he must break off negotiations at 6:00 P.M. until the next afternoon at 4:00. Meanwhile, Linda Woodman was urging Novella Pollard, with whom she was handcuffed, to "try one more time." Deciding to use restroom needs as an excuse, they approached Carrasco, who had just hung up the telephone, to ask permission, then added an aside that their suggested plan "would work." In reply, Carrasco stated that they would "have to wait" until tomorrow. Then to their surprise Dominguez, who had been listening to their conversation and "who seldom ever spoke to the hostages," asked, "Mrs. Woodman, if we let you go, will you help us?" Without hesitation she responded: "I'll do everything I can to help all of us get out of here." But Carrasco asked if she would come back up. Again she truthfully answered, "I will come back up here, but you can't make this a requirement because they may not let me come back." Satisfied with these responses, Carrasco picked up the phone, hoping that Montemayor had not already departed;

and just as Jim Estelle exclaimed to his TDC colleagues, "God! If he'd only release Linda Woodman!" the telephone rang. Montemayor answered, and Carrasco said: "Linda Woodman is on her way out."[51]

The next few minutes were almost a blur to Woodman. Briefly she went to the restroom to put on some Keds or "jumping shoes" (as she called them), made sure that Novella Pollard's rings, which were given to her earlier, were secure, and returned to the "picket fence" area. Excitedly she began climbing over the several filing cabinets which constituted the barricade when Carrasco called out that they would gladly "open the door." Then, as she was ready to jump, "a real nervous feeling" enveloped her and, turning toward Dominguez, she hesitantly implored: "Rudy, you're not going to shoot me, are you?" After he assured her that he would not, she found herself zigzagging down the ramp to freedom. At 6:15 P.M. she was greeted by an exuberant Estelle and a cheering group of law-enforcement officers. The hostage count was now down to nine.[52]

Yet day ten was by no means over for the participants. In the library complex Carrasco staged a "dress rehearsal" in preparation for the morrow, ever cognizant that careful planning could be the difference between success and failure. Despite the heat, despite increasing weariness, despite the ever-lengthening day, he painstakingly "walked" everyone through their roles. At the rear of the "Trojan Horse" he assigned Father O'Brien, who would serve as a "brakeman" by facing backwards as they went forward. Next came Dominguez with Julia Standley, Carrasco in the center with Novella Pollard (except that Ann Fleming stood in for her because of the heat), and Cuevas in the front with Von Beseda. He also placed three abreast in the shield to satisfy himself that seven should be the maximum number inside. Then, because of the stifling temperature, he demonstrated outside the shield with Pollard how each "hostile" was going to control his own hostage, simply by placing his left arm around the hostage's neck from the back while using the right hand to shove a gun into her ribs. As a final detail he assigned the five remaining hostages and three inmates to specific positions on the outside, their job being to direct the course of the shield as well as to control its speed on the steep-sloping ramp. At the same time Jim Estelle and his "think tank" team, after a short-lived celebration, debriefed Linda Woodman for several hours. Because of her penchant for detail and, as Estelle noted, her "photographic memory," they learned fully about the "Trojan Horse" and the conditions in the library complex. More and more they realized that it was imperative to lure the "hostiles" from their "fortress" and that they too had much preparation to do for the morrow.[53]

At 7:00 A.M. on August 3, Estelle therefore met with the six members of his "think tank" team to decide how best to outwit and overcome the three "hostiles" in the "Trojan Horse." To coax them out, they agreed to park as "bait" an armored car, complete with a two-way radio and mobile phone, at the foot of the three-tiered ramp. But what then? What should be their strategy, their plan of attack? Someone suggested detonating the charges at the rear of the library after the "Trojan Horse" was clearly going down the ramp. They discarded this idea, however, because the wily Carrasco might anticipate their move and leave several hostages tied to the wall; besides, too much time might elapse in climbing up the back way, securing the area, and following Carrasco down the ramp. So what options were left? Under no circumstances could they allow the "hostiles" to reach the armored car because it would be "another fortress to attack." So, they agreed, "a confrontation had to come" — one that "would not be peaceful."

But where? To them the best place would be at the last turn on the ramp before entering the prison courtyard which was next to the abandoned inmates' dining hall. Again, though, with Carrasco well-fortified within the "Trojan Horse," with hostages somewhere inside, and with a bomb (supposedly consisting of gunpowder) ready to be exploded, the casualties would be high. Bob Wiatt thus proposed using high-pressure fire hoses which might, other than startle and confuse the "hostiles," effectively overturn the shield, thereby placing Carrasco, Dominguez, and Cuevas on a less than equal footing with the assault team. But if the "hostiles" should reach the armored car, the "think tank" members were all of one mind that the hostages would not be jeopardized in another fortress. As soon as the "Trojan Horse" began its descent to the inmate yard, TDC Lieutenant Willard Stewart and a squad of five men would dash to the armored car, slam shut its doors, then run up the other side of the three-tiered ramp, secure the library complex, and block off any retreat. Yet, if by some remote chance the "hostiles" should obtain entry into the armored car, Ranger Cap-

tains Rogers and Burks would immediately rush forward and dis-
able the vehicle by firing bullets into the engine, then place shields
(made of boiler plate) over the car's gunports, while the assault
team, behind shields on rollers, would force an entry and overcome
the occupants.[54]

The leader of the assault team was fifty-one-year-old Ranger
Captain Pete Rogers of Company A, selected partly because the
Huntsville area was in his boundary jurisdiction but mainly because of the man himself. At 5'11½, 170 pounds, he was lean and
lanky, even more so in boots and western garb; in looks and actions
he epitomized a Texas Ranger. During most of his adult life he had
lived with stress, having "earned his ulcers" as a fighter pilot on
sixty-eight missions mostly over Germany in World War II, as a
pilot investigator for the Department of Public Safety (DPS) late in
the 1940s and early 1950s, and as a Texas Ranger after 1952. Although quiet and soft-spoken, he seldom had to be concerned about
anyone challenging his authority, having unusual green-colored
eyes that "could stare anyone down." As his maxim for leadership,
especially in a critical situation, he "never sent one of his men to do
a job that . . . [he] would not do himself." And in the case of Carrasco, he told his wife, "I don't intend to start now."[55]

Captain G. W. Burks of Company B was of similar mind and
attitude when facing danger. Two years younger than Rogers, he
was 5'9, 160 pounds, shorter but somewhat sturdier. Having a reputation as a "tough cop" in his earlier years with the DPS, he had
mellowed only slightly during his sixteen years as a Ranger, not
necessarily looking for trouble but never running from it. Why did
he volunteer himself and some of his Company B men for the
Huntsville assignment? It was "the challenge," he candidly replied, "the same reason a man climbs a mountain — because it's
there." At the same time he also wanted "to be of service." Besides,
he prided himself in being a Texas Ranger captain; that seemed to
be explanation enough.[56]

During the morning and afternoon of August 3, the two
Ranger captains prepared for their task ahead as if it were routine,
as if day eleven held no special significance. For two hours, while
Estelle was obtaining an armored car from Houston and firetrucks
(with pressure hoses) from the Huntsville Fire Department, they
were busy at the prison machine shop, having the supervisor make
shields from boiler plate to their specifications. Next, they checked

their equipment for the final assault: army combat helmets, bullet-proof body armor, guns and ammunition. Both decided against rifles and shotguns, preferring instead two Colt .45 revolvers, which were the "best weapons" in close-quarter combat. They also selected "hard ball ammo" — 150 grain, steel-jacketed bullets — which might penetrate the "Trojan Horse" effectively. Then Rogers met with his thirteen-man assault team including Burks, Agent Bob Wiatt of the FBI (who was there as "an observer"), Agent Winston Padgett of DPS Intelligence, Ranger Sergeant Johnny Krumnow of Company A, eight officers from Company A and DPS Intelligence, and six TDC personnel who were to man the three fire hoses. Calmly he explained their plan of action, that at approximately 6:00 P.M. they would enter the inmates' dining hall through the rear windows and station themselves in readiness — and without sound or movement — at the front doors by the ramp. No one had to tell them that they "were not going to initiate lethal action," that they were giving Carrasco "the first chance" at them, that casualties would probably be high. That was understood. Yet, as Rogers and Burks strapped on their Colt .45s, they gave "everyone a sense of confidence," Jim Estelle admiringly remembered. "When you go into combat with men like that, whether people believe it or not, courage is as contagious as fear." So all was in readiness on the Texas law-enforcement side. Only one question remained unresolved: Would Carrasco show?[57]

Day eleven was miserable for the occupants on the third-floor library complex. The heat was "killing," Novella Pollard remembered. "No ventilation at all, no fans, no air, no movement, . . . we were sorta in a stupor." Weary and exhausted, everyone survived as best they could, some drinking orange juice and liquids, others wanting nothing at all. Intermittently, but in no specific order, the hostages (those who were going with Carrasco) were allowed to call their families and talk with them at length. Yet the "hostiles" still maintained a semblance of routine by keeping at least one hostage atop the barricade. For a long time Carrasco did not stir that day. But eventually he emerged from his resting quarters, visibly limping and depending heavily on a cane. To help him survive the suffocating heat and physical pain he asked Novella Pollard, who felt "deathly ill," for some Valium. Then he bided his time by resting, since Estelle had installed a "news blackout" at the prison, ever cognizant that at 4:00 P.M. negotiations with Montemayor would begin again.[58]

At the appointed time Montemayor called Carrasco, thereby initiating the final countdown of their eleven-day ordeal. He stated that, as prescribed by the "hostiles," an armored car, complete with a two-way radio and mobile phone, would be parked in front of the ramp. From the exuberant shouts over the telephone of "We've won! We've won! We're going to get the car in!" (which revealed the first chink in Carrasco's emotional armor), Montemayor knew that he "had him going . . . [Estelle's] way." He therefore agreed to let an inmate hostage have free access to the vehicle without interference. As a result, Martin Quiroz thoroughly checked out the car over the next hour, then drove it around the courtyard before transporting luggage, purses, and personal items of the departing participants down the ramp. At the same time, Carrasco permitted Novella Pollard, Von Beseda, and Julia Standley to adjourn to the women's restroom, where they changed into pant suits. In trying to bolster their flagging spirits, Von Beseda exclaimed: "We are going on a trip. We have to get pretty." But soon they became silent, lost in their own thoughts, unable to alter their prevailing mood of uncertainty. When they emerged from the restroom after an extended stay, Carrasco jolted them back to reality with: "O.K., we're ready. Let's get in the cart."[59]

Carrasco, however, continued to be unpredictable and full of surprises, indeed a worthy adversary. Although Novella Pollard and Father O'Brien entered the "Trojan Horse" immediately after his orders, he seemed to be in no hurry to regiment the other participants to his commands. Possibly he was waiting for darkness. Whatever his thinking, he continued to delay, talking on the telephone at length. After at least thirty minutes had elapsed, he allowed Pollard and Father O'Brien, upon request, to leave the sweltering confines of the shield and assemble the hostages for their last time together. And together in prayer they tried to find peace within themselves, praying in unison: "Father, if it be Thy will, take this cup from me. Let not my will, but Thine be done." Then, with darkness descending upon the library complex, Carrasco authoritatively called out: "O.K., ladies, let's go." Yet once again he surprised them. Whereas in the "dress rehearsal" on Friday Novella Pollard had been "his hostage," he now switched with Cuevas and took control over Von Beseda. Unlike the night before, he also placed handcuffs on every hostage; but for Father O'Brien, the "Trojan Horse's brakeman," he had a special treat, not only having him walk backwards but handcuffing his hands over his head and to the outside of the shield. To the astonishment of the remaining hostages and inmates — and even more unexpectedly — Carrasco wound a rope, which the women had prepared for him several days before, tightly around the outside of the "Trojan Horse," about four feet from the floor, and handcuffed them to it.[60]

With everyone in their assigned positions, and inexorably bound together, Carrasco decided to "move out." But again the unexpected occurred. Within the shield "confusion" best described their predicament, the occupants adjusting badly to their strange new environment. As the "Trojan Horse" groaned and squeaked slowly forward, the three "hostiles" stumbled in the blackness, their special-designed helmets heavy and cumbersome, causing them to lurch forward into their handcuffed partners. They also had difficulty seeing in their darkened confines, the rays from two flashlights aiding somewhat but far from satisfactory. For instance, Cuevas could not hold both a flashlight and gun, while being handcuffed to Novella Pollard, and still be responsible for steering the "Trojan Horse" down the ramp. He therefore gave her the flashlight and forgot about the handcuffs. Yet still another unforeseen obstacle had to be overcome. When building the shield (on the school side of the third floor), Carrasco had failed to anticipate how difficult it would be to move and had thus been unconcerned that it faced away from the double-glass doors. Once everyone was in position, however, he was not about to begin all over again. Consequently, they all struggled mightily, Novella Pollard asserted, just "to get it turned around." After what seemed to be an interminable length of time, with perspiration dripping freely, with oxygen expended and strength drained, they still had to bull their way through another unanticipated obstacle, the "picket fence." And by the time they pushed past the double-glass doors everyone was "extremely tired."[61]

Now the "Trojan Horse" began its descent along the ramp, its wheels squeaking eerily on the concrete base. "Our hearts [were] pounding, our fears building," Father O'Brien recollected, with "thoughts on that awful gulf that separates the living from the dead." At the front of the shield Novella Pollard "closed . . . [her] mind to everything — like I had pulled a shade in front of me," she

shuddered, letting only the noises and groans of the participants
record the next few minutes. After Cuevas yelled "go right" at the
first turn, no one made a sound inside the shield, the darkness
causing them to concentrate on maintaining their equilibrium and
the sweltering heat forcing them to conserve their strength. On the
outside, however, the hostages had to combat the weight and bulkiness of the "Trojan Horse," which careened almost uncontrollably
down the incline and threatened to crush them against the concrete
sidewalls of the three-tiered ramp. Down to the second turn and
then the next they came, Robinson and Branch and Heard pleading with or directing their comrades to "slow down" or "push
hard." After three or four minutes of strength-draining toil, they
were at last nearing the final turn of the ramp, thankful that their
journey was almost at an end.[62]

At the same time the thirteen-man assault team was also
grateful for the descent of the "Trojan Horse." For almost three
and a half hours they had suffered intolerable conditions. At a little
past 6:00 P.M. they had entered the inmates' dining hall through its
rear windows to find, as Captain Burks recollected, "maggots
crawling all over the floor" and the stench "almost unbearable"
from the "spoiled, rotten food." Even without air conditioning in
the building they stood quietly near the front doors, soaked with
perspiration from the suffocating heat, with no conversation, no
smoking, no movement. Yet "no one left; not a man flinched,"
Burks proudly asserted. Rogers "didn't have to give any pep talks
to that group . . . They were ready to go." But at 9:30 P.M., when
they finally heard the "eerie sound" of squeaking wheels on the
ramp, they were gratified, realizing that their vigil would soon be
over.[63]

Within four minutes the "Trojan Horse" creaked into view
and came to a grinding halt upon hitting a level spot on the concrete surface just opposite the dining hall. The time for waiting was
over. Out from the doors burst Pete Rogers with G. W. Burks and
FBI Agent Bob Wiatt close behind. Stepping within five or six feet
of the "Trojan Horse" or "close enough," Burks vividly recalled,
"that you felt you could reach out and touch it," Rogers announced: "Police officers! Surrender!" During the next split second
several muffled shots occurred within the shield; Rogers yelled "hit
the hoses"; and then some force knocked him sprawling into Burks
as withering gunfire erupted. Almost simultaneously, six TDC

men, manning three fire hoses at the doors, inundated the "Trojan Horse" with high-pressure water, while the eight hostages and inmates, handcuffed to the outside rope, cringed helplessly on the cement walkway. In the confusion, however, TDC Lieutenant Willard Stewart, who had already carried out his assignment of slamming shut the armored car doors and securing the library complex, suddenly decided to improvise. Impulsively, he ran down the ramp, crawled to the shield, and, with bullets "flying" in all directions, cut the rope with a pocketknife. And it was none too soon; for as the eight hostages scurried down the ramp to safety, one of the high pressure hoses ruptured and the water, which had been a partial equalizer for the assault team, dropped off to a trickle.[64]

With the antagonists within a few feet of one another, and with no further water distractions, the fighting intensified. After five minutes of returning fire from the mess hall's doors and windows, Rogers, Burks, and Wiatt, all of whom had slugs rip into their bullet-proof body armor, were pulled back safely through the doors of the inmates' dining hall. Then, for ten incredible minutes, the assault team applied their experience and ingenuity to defeat the "hostiles." While Burks and other officers kept up a steady barrage of gunfire, the six TDC men worked frantically to repair the fire hoses. In the meantime, Rogers and several officers, who had been surprised that the water pressure had not overturned the "Trojan Horse" and laid bare the occupants, decided to upend it another way. Appropriating the aluminum ladder which had been used to enter the dining hall, they waited for the pressure hoses to become operational again. Then, under the cover of water power, they used the ladder as a jousting pole, hooking the upper part of the shield at an upward angle, and sent it crashing down the ramp. At the same moment, Burks heard two muffled shots, obviously fired by the "hostiles" — and the gunfire ceased.[65]

Rushing out from the inmates' dining hall, the assault team moved swiftly to secure the area as well as to see whether anyone was alive. At first glance seven motionless bodies lay on the ramp with "blood everywhere." Burks yelled out, "Show me your hands! Show me your hands!" Father O'Brien, who had been shot in the chest and had fallen across Dominguez, suddenly felt the "hostile" move his hand "as if to bring his pistol muzzle against my body." Rolling to one side, he weakly pointed at Dominguez as Winston Padgett of DPS Intelligence ran forward and dispatched him with two bullets to the head. Farther down the ramp, Rogers and Burks found another "hostile," with a helmet still on his head, sitting propped up against the low cement wall. At first they thought him to be dead until Rogers, after removing the helmet and recognizing Cuevas, heard a low moan. The two Ranger captains quickly handcuffed him, realizing that he had gone "into a state of shock." They also examined Novella Pollard, finding her to be in the same condition, though she "was not the fainting kind," and whisked her off to the hospital. But as for the rest there was no hope. Carrasco was covered with blood, having blown away part of his head rather than surrender. Next to him was Von Beseda, with one shot through the heart. And handcuffed to the cruel Dominguez was the lifeless body of Julia Standley, with four bullets in the back.[66]

With the fighting over and the danger past, G. W. Burks relaxed and smoked a cigarette, sapped of his energy and content to let others do the "mopping up." In reflecting on his performance and that of the assault team, he regretted that people had been killed but found consolation in the fact that they had done everything humanly possible and had made "one good effort, one concerted effort." To a certain extent Pete Rogers was of like mind. Yet, even though Father O'Brien and the surviving hostages, as well as the families of Von Beseda and Julia Standley, were effusive in their praise of Jim Estelle and Texas law enforcement, one question continued to prey on his mind until his death in February 1978: "Was there something we didn't do that might have saved the ones that were killed?" But of all the statements about those eleven days with Carrasco, the most reflective came from Jim Estelle. "Everyone was in shock and very, very tired, sad at the loss of the two women," he pensively commented. "Those so-called big, tough, macho Rangers — everybody had tears in their eyes that night — and for days to come." And then, as if to summarize the futility of it all, he quietly said: "There was no joy, no victory."[67]

Third-floor library-reading room after the assault.
— Courtesy Bob Wiatt

Third-floor classroom area after the assault.
— Courtesy Bob Wiatt

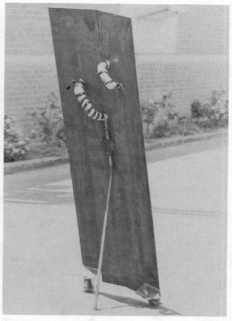

Shields manufactured in the TDC mechanical shop to afford the assault team maximum protection.

— Courtesy Bob Wiatt

Linda Woodman leaps to freedom.

— Courtesy Bob Wiatt

Inmate hostage carries hostiles' belongings down ramp to waiting armored car.

— Courtesy Bob Wiatt

Armored car that was delivered to Carrasco.

— Courtesy Bob Wiatt

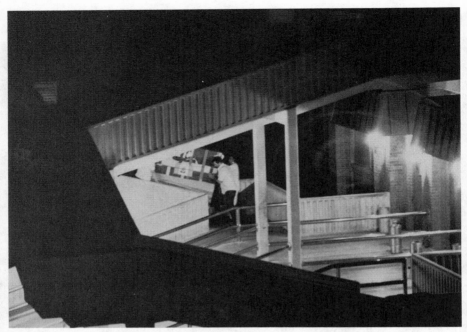

Carrasco's "Trojan Horse" at second turn on ramp with hostages manacled to it.
— Courtesy Bob Wiatt

The "Trojan Horse" after the third turn on the ramp opposite second-floor mess hall.
— Courtesy Bob Wiatt

Attacking the "Trojan Horse" with high-pressure fire hoses. Hostages are still manacled.

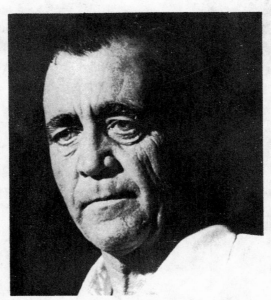

Capt. Pete Rogers

Toppling the "Trojan Horse" with aluminum ladder.
— Courtesy Bob Wiatt

The "Trojan Horse" toppled and the assault team attacking.
— Courtesy Bob Wiatt

The bodies of Dominguez (upper left) and Carrasco (lower right).
— Courtesy Bob Wiatt

The demolished "Trojan Horse."

— Courtesy Bob Wiatt

Epilogue

During the twentieth century the Texas Rangers have changed dramatically. Whereas they were basically frontier marshals prior to 1935, without training and not necessarily aware of, or concerned with, individual civil rights — as were all law-enforcement agencies in the United States before 1964 — they have adjusted to meet the demands of an urbanized state in the throes of a computerized and scientific age. Stationed at strategic locations, mainly in rural Texas counties, which are oftentimes lacking in both law-enforcement manpower and criminal investigative know-how and facilities, the Rangers are now walking police laboratories, highly mobile, well-armed, and well-trained. And by emphasizing formal as well as practical education and training, detailed written reports, cooperation with all law-enforcement groups, and a low-profile policy, they no longer reflect the image of a lone, hard-bitten frontier marshal who administered six-gun justice singularly and without mercy. Such changes are readily apparent when contrasting the lone Ranger activities of Bill McDonald at Brownsville with the actions of the Ranger organization during the Carrasco affair at Huntsville.

Yet the Rangers have retained the traits and qualities of character that Walter Prescott Webb lamented in 1935 were being lost; indeed, in many ways they appear to be cut from the same rough mold as their predecessors. Basically, they are uncomplicated men: direct, straightforward, and not especially concerned about social amenities. They use the English language simply as a tool for direct

141

communication, not as a device to trick or deceive (hence their difficulty in the 1960s with newsmen or reporters who tended toward sensationalism). In terms of grammar, they may be an English teacher's nightmare; yet they express themselves clearly, sometimes punctuating their sentences with colorful if not downright earthy expressions. Although courteous and outwardly easygoing, they are suspicious of strangers and hesitant to talk. ("You might have been one of those damn New York magazine writers.") But once a person wins their trust, they will go out of their way to be helpful.

Make no mistake about these men. They have been, and are, the scourge of those outside the law, obviously feared, sometimes hated, more often respected. They are proud men — proud of their traditions and their fellow officers' accomplishments, proud of holding a job that all other Texas lawmen envy. They have an intangible, almost unexplainable quality of toughness about them. Possibly it is the way they handle themselves. Some are no longer lean and trim; a few are wrinkled and graying; yet all exude a certain poise and rugged self-confidence. Or perhaps it is the realization that these men have confronted the worst criminals in the state, that their tradition of "One Riot, One Ranger" has steeled them toward danger and death.

Whatever the reason, the Texas Rangers do have the reputation of toughness and bravery, of dedication to law enforcement, of being the elite of Texas lawmen. Their esprit de corps is almost unbelievable. They will admit, in fact, that becoming a Ranger has completely transformed their lives. "You feel lucky to get the Ranger badge. So many want it," Captain Jim Riddles once candidly stated. "So you take an eternal vow that whatever happens you won't break your oath to uphold the law." Probably Colonel Adams, in viewing the history of the force and assessing the modern-day Rangers, put it best, however: "I contend that the Texas Rangers will always be an integral part of the DPS because they get better every year from the standpoint of training, better weaponry, better technology; and they retain what they've always had which is basically that a Texas Ranger is a highly motivated individual, courageous, well-trained, and self-disciplined."

Notes

CHAPTER I

1. Walter Prescott Webb, *The Texas Rangers: A Century of Frontier Defense*, 2d ed. (Austin: University of Texas Press, 1965), 11–15; Ben Procter, "Ben McCulloch," *Rangers of Texas* (Waco: Texian Press, 1969), 65. In Walter Prescott Webb, *The Great Plains* (Boston: Ginn and Company, 1931), 166, the author states that Ford, who was editor of the *Texas Democrat*, "probably wrote this summary statement" describing the Rangers on September 9, 1846.

2. Samuel C. Reid, Jr., *The Scouting Expeditions of McCulloch's Texas Rangers* (Austin: Steck Company, 1935), 26; John Salmon Ford, *Rip Ford's Texas*, ed. by Stephen B. Oates (Austin: University of Texas Press, 1963), xxiii; Webb, *Texas Rangers*, 78–83.

3. Webb, *Texas Rangers*, 79–80; Procter, "Ben McCulloch," 65.

4. Ford, *Rip Ford's Texas*, 229–236, 266–307; Harold B. Simpson, "John Salmon (Rip) Ford," *Rangers of Texas*, 95–97; James Kimmins Greer, *Colonel Jack Hays: Texas Frontier Leader and California Builder* (New York: E. P. Dutton and Company, Inc., 1952), 126–203; Procter, "Ben McCulloch," 70–78; James M. Day, "Samuel H. Walker," *Rangers of Texas*, 43–58; Adjutant Generals' Papers, 1875–1878, MSS, Texas State Archives, Austin, Texas; Ben Procter, "Fort Brown," *Frontier Forts of Texas* (Waco: Texian Press, 1966), 55–56; George Durham and Clyde Wantland, *Taming the Nueces Strip: The Story of McNelly's Rangers* (Austin: University of Texas Press, 1962), 34–42, 52–69; Joe B. Frantz, "Leander H. McNelly," *Rangers of Texas*, 139–140; Billy Mac Jones, "John B. Jones," *Rangers of Texas*, 151–159; Webb, *Texas Rangers*, 91–124, 151–193, 238–280, 307–342. See Julian Samora, Joe Bernal, and Albert Pena, *Gunpowder Justice* (Notre Dame: University of Notre Dame Press, 1979), 27–31, for a critical view of the Rangers during the Mexican War, which ignores the historical perspective of the nineteenth century. In turn, these authors disregard the legitimate reasons for the establishment and function of the Ranger force in frontier Texas, which was protection of Anglo-Texan life and property against intrusions by Indians and Mexicans.

5. Greer, *Hays*, 52–53; Procter, "Ben McCulloch," 76–78; William Warren Sterling, *Trails and Trials of a Texas Ranger* (Norman: University of Oklahoma Press, 1968), 523; Webb, *Texas Rangers*, x; Albert Bigelow Paine, *Captain Bill McDonald, Texas Ranger: A Story of Frontier Reform* (New York: J. J. Little & Ives Co., 1909), 353. For a differing view — "tarnishing of the Ranger image" — see Samora, Bernal, and Pena, *Gunpowder Justice*, 2–7, 39–45, and Americo Paredes,

With His Pistol in His Hand (Austin: University of Texas Press, 1958), 23–25.

6. Webb, *Texas Rangers*, 233–454; Samora, Bernal, and Pena, *Gunpowder Justice*, 47–61; Adjutant Generals' Papers, 1874–1882, 1888–1898; Jones, "John B. Jones," 154–159; James B. Gillett, *Six Years with the Texas Rangers, 1876 to 1881*, ed. by M. M. Quaife (New Haven: Yale University Press, 1925), 46–52, 58–60, 69–80, 108–128, 136–199, 213; Harold Preece, *Lone Star Man: Ira Aten, Last of the Old Texas Rangers* (New York: Hastings House, Publishers, 1960), 126–142.

7. For detailed coverage see Robert E. Quirk, *The Mexican Revolution, 1914–1915: The Convention of Aguascalientes* (Bloomington: University of Indiana Press, 1960); John Busby McClung, "Texas Rangers Along the Rio Grande, 1910–1919," Ph.D. dissertation, Texas Christian University, Fort Worth, Texas, 1981; Charles C. Cumberland, "Border Raids in the Lower Rio Grande Valley — 1915," *Southwestern Historical Quarterly*, LVII (January 1954), 285–311; Clarence C. Clendenen, *The United States and Pancho Villa: A Study in Unconventional Diplomacy* (Ithaca: Cornell University Press, 1961), 7ff; Webb, *Texas Rangers*, 473–516. See Samora, Bernal, and Pena, *Gunpowder Justice*, 63–76. Their chapter is entitled "The Most Irresponsible Officers in the State."

8. "Proceedings of the Joint Committee of the Senate and the House in the Investigation of the Texas State Ranger Force, 1919," MSS, Texas State Archives, Austin, Texas (hereafter cited as the "Canales Report"); U.S. Senate, *Investigation of Mexican Affairs*, Sen. Doc. 285, 66th Cong., 2d Sess., Ser. 7665–7666 (Washington: Government Printing Office, 1920), I, 1243ff; Webb, *Texas Rangers*, 508, 513–516.

9. "Canales Report," 3ff; *Investigation of Mexican Affairs*, I: 1205–1206, 1510–1515; Webb, *Texas Rangers*, 473–516; Clendenen, *United States and Pancho Villa*, 234–269, 296–304.

10. "Canales Report," 1479–1511, 1586–1605; Webb, *Texas Rangers*, 495–516.

11. Ben Procter, "The Modern Texas Rangers: A Law-Enforcement Dilemma in the Rio Grande Valley," *Reflections of Western Historians*, ed. by John Alexander Carroll (Tucson: University of Arizona Press, 1969), 216–217; "Canales Report," 3–5, 123–127, 144–149, 164–165, 562–563, 570–576, 1440–1449; Sterling, *Trails and Trials of a Texas Ranger*, 47; Webb, *Texas Rangers*, 504–505; James R. Ward, "The Texas Rangers, 1919–1935," Ph.D. dissertation, Texas Christian University, Fort Worth, Texas, 1972, Chapter I.

12. Ward, "The Texas Rangers, 1919–1935," Chapter I; *General Laws of the State of Texas*, 36th Legis., Reg. Sess., 1919, 263–266; *The Statesman* (Austin), January 28, 1919, 2; *Houston Post*, February 20, 1919, 1.

13. Ward, "The Texas Rangers, 1919–1935," Chapters II and III; interview with E. A. "Dogie" Wright, former Texas Ranger and sheriff of Hudspeth County, by author and James Ward, Sierra Blanca, Texas, September 26, 1969; Charles C. Alexander, *The Ku Klux Klan in the Southwest* (Lexington: University of Kentucky Press, 1965), 1–19; Sterling, *Trails and Trials of a Texas Ranger*, 97–114, 129–133, 227–241; Charles C. Alexander, *Crusade for Conformity: The Ku Klux Klan in 1920–1930* (Houston: Texas Gulf Coast Historical Association, 1962), 1–13; Brownson Malsch, *Captain M. T. Gonzaullas, Lone Wolf: The Only Texas Ranger Captain of Spanish Descent* (Austin: Shoal Creek Publishers, Inc., 1980), 57–127; Norman Brown, *Hood, Bonnet, and Little Brown Jug: Texas Politics, 1921–1928* (College Station: Texas

A&M University Press, 1984), 49–88, 95ff.

14. Wright interview; Sterling, *Trails and Trials of a Texas Ranger*, 397–416; Webb, *Texas Rangers*, 509–513, 552–554, 556–557.

15. Stephen W. Schuster, IV, "The Modernization of the Texas Rangers, 1930–1936," M.A. thesis, Texas Christian University, Fort Worth, Texas, 1965, 12, 38–39; Webb, *Texas Rangers*, 549–550; Ward, "The Texas Rangers, 1919–1935," 154–156; C. L. Douglas, *The Gentlemen in White Hats: Dramatic Episodes in the History of the Texas Rangers* (Dallas: South-West Press, 1934), 181–188; Sterling, *Trails and Trials of a Texas Ranger*, 107–128, 202, 221–231; Malsch, *Lone Wolf*, 65.

16. Webb, *Texas Rangers*, 519–545; John H. Jenkins and H. Gordon Frost, *"I'm Frank Hamer": The Life of a Texas Peace Officer* (Austin: Pemberton Press, 1968), 5–112; interview with Captain Manuel T. "Lone Wolf" Gonzaullas by author, Dallas, Texas, October 27, 1969.

17. Texas Ranger Roster Rolls, 1920–1930, MSS, Texas Department of Public Safety Files, Austin, Texas; John Toland, *The Dillinger Days* (New York: Random House, 1963), 36–37; Schuster, "Modernization of the Texas Rangers," 7–10; Ward, "The Texas Rangers, 1919–1935," Chapter VII.

18. Ward, "The Texas Rangers, 1919–1935," Chapter VII; Texas Ranger Records, 1930–1932, MSS, Texas Department of Public Safety, Austin, Texas; Schuster, "Modernization of the Texas Rangers," 10–16.

19. Procter, "The Modern Texas Rangers," 214–215; Ward, "The Texas Rangers, 1919–1935," Chapter VIII; Schuster, "Modernization of the Texas Rangers," 17–25; Special Ranger Rosters, 1933–34, MSS, Texas Department of Public Safety, Austin, Texas; Sterling, *Trails and Trials of a Texas Ranger*, 277, 517–519; Jenkins and Frost, *"I'm Frank Hamer,"* 174; *Report of the Adjutant General of the State of Texas: January, 1933 to December, 1934* (Austin: Knape Printing Co., 1934), 46–52; *Report and Recommendations of the Senate Committee Investigating Crime*, 43d Texas Legis., 1933–1934, 58, 63–64; *Austin American*, February 28, 1935, 1–2.

20. Procter, "The Modern Texas Rangers," 214–215; Sterling, *Trails and Trials of a Texas Ranger*, 277, 517–519; Schuster, "Modernization of the Texas Rangers," 25–33; Ward, "The Texas Rangers, 1919–1935," Chapter VIII; Jenkins and Frost, *"I'm Frank Hamer,"* 179.

21. *General and Special Laws of the State of Texas*, 44th Legis., Reg. Sess., 1935, 444–454; Schuster, "Modernization of the Texas Rangers," Chapter II; Ward, "The Texas Rangers, 1919–1935," Chapter VIII; Procter, "The Modern Texas Rangers," 215; William E. Atkinson, "The Texas Gubernatorial Campaign of 1934," M.A. thesis, Texas Christian University, Fort Worth, Texas, 1965, 52ff; Webb, *Texas Rangers*, 567. In 1961–1962 Webb revised his conclusion of "Farewell to the Texas Rangers." In the chapter revision that remained unpublished, entitled "The Texas Rangers in the Modern World, 1935–1960," he told of the reorganization of the Rangers and sketched "in broad outlines its functions and activities for the past century." See Llerena B. Friend, "W. P. Webb's Texas Rangers," *Southwestern Historical Quarterly*, LXXIV (January 1971), 319–320.

22. "Rules and Regulations Regarding Appointments, Transfers, and Promotions of Employees, January 21, 1936," MSS, Texas Department of Public Safety, Austin, Texas; Procter, "The Modern Texas Rangers," 215–216; Schuster, "Modernization of the Texas Rangers," 53–56; Ward, "The Texas Rangers, 1919–1935," Chapter VIII; Douglas, *Gentlemen in White Hats*, 201. On February 1,

1934, Lee Simmons, the superintendent of the state penitentiary at Huntsville, persuaded Hamer to accept a commission as a state highway patrolman (specifically to track down Clyde Barrow and Bonnie Parker). Hamer was still recognized as the foremost Texas Ranger, having held a commission for twenty-six years before submitting his resignation to Governor Miriam A. "Ma" Ferguson on November 1, 1932. See Jenkins and Frost, *"I'm Frank Hamer,"* 174, 201–210; Webb, *Texas Rangers,* 538–544.

23. *Department of Public Safety, August 10, 1935–December 1, 1936* (Austin: Department of Public Safety, 1936), 1–9; *General and Special Laws of the State of Texas,* 45th Legis., Reg. Sess., 1937, 772ff; Schuster, "Modernization of the Texas Rangers," 55–61, 65–66; Thomas Lee Charlton, "The Texas Department of Public Safety, 1935–1957," M.A. thesis, University of Texas, Austin, Texas, 1961, 39–62.

24. Schuster, "Modernization of the Texas Rangers," 61–65; Charlton, "Department of Public Safety," 42, 54–61, 65–70, 96; Ward, "The Texas Rangers, 1919–1935," Chapter VIII; Webb, *Texas Rangers,* 567; Sterling, *Trails and Trials of a Texas Ranger,* 520–521; Samora, Bernal, and Pena, *Gunpowder Justice,* 80–82.

25. *Dallas Morning News,* September 28, 1938; *American-Statesman* (Austin), May 7, 1950; October 21, 1956; interview with Colonel Wilson E. Speir, director of the Department of Public Safety, by author, Austin, Texas, August 4, 1974; Charlton, "Department of Public Safety," 97–99.

26. "Texas Ranger Strength — Authorized," MSS, Department of Public Safety, Austin, Texas, 1, 6, 8, 10; *General and Special Laws of the State of Texas,* 46th Legis., Reg. Sess., 1939, II: 184–199; *Annual Report, Texas Department of Public Safety, Fiscal Year Ending August 31, 1939,* 3; Charlton, "Department of Public Safety," 103–105, 113, 115–116.

27. Allen Z. Gammage, "The Texas Department of Public Safety and Its Administration of War Duties," M.A. thesis, University of Texas, Austin, Texas, 1945, 102ff; "Texas Ranger Strength," 9–10; Charlton, "Department of Public Safety," 112–141, 142–146, 159–163; Samora, Bernal, and Pena, *Gunpowder Justice,* 82–83; Jenkins and Frost, *"I'm Frank Hamer,"* 169.

28. *Department of Public Safety, Biennial Report, 1947–1948 Fiscal Years, January 1, 1949,* 41–44; *General and Special Laws,* 49th Legis., Reg. Sess., 1945, 907–914; *General and Special Laws of the State of Texas,* 51st Legis., Reg. Sess., 1949, 1308–1314; "Texas Ranger Strength," 18; Charlton, "Department of Public Safety," 142–146, 159–163.

29. Interview with Senior Captain Clint Peoples by author, Waco, Texas, July 13, 1970; interview with Captain Bob Crowder by author, Dallas, Texas, February 24, 1969; interview with Captain A. Y. Allee by author, Carrizo Springs, Texas, November 15, 1969; interview with Ranger Lewis Rigler by author, Gainesville, Texas, October 2, 1970; Charlton, "Department of Public Safety," 166–170; James M. Day, *Captain Clint Peoples, Texas Ranger: Fifty Years a Lawman* (Waco: Texian Press, 1980), 108–110.

30. Rigler interview; "Texas Ranger Strength," 1; Charlton, "Department of Public Safety," 175–177, 184–185, 189–190; Procter, "The Modern Texas Rangers," 220–225; Allee interview. In Samora, Bernal, and Pena, *Gunpowder Justice,* 131–156, the authors have presented a sympathetic account of "La huelga," entitling their chapter "John Connally's Strikebreakers." Two of the authors, State

Senator Joe Bernal of San Antonio and Bexar County Commissioner Albert Pena, were indirectly involved, and their account is emotional and lacking in objectivity.

31. *Houston Chronicle,* January 9, 1968, February 6, 1969, May 21, 1978; *San Antonio Express,* July 8, 1968; *Houston Post,* January 5, 1969, August 20, 1972; *Dallas Times Herald,* April 26, July 11, 1968.

32. Procter, "Modern Texas Rangers," 230–231; Speir interview, August 4, 1974; "Texas Ranger Strength," 1; interview with Senior Captain Clint Peoples by author, Austin, Texas, November 4, 1971; Day, *Peoples,* 154–158.

33. Interview with Lieutenant Colonel Leo Gossett by author, Austin, Texas, November 11, 1971; interview with Colonel Wilson E. Speir by author, Austin, Texas, November 11, 1971; interviews with Senior Captain Bill Wilson by author, Austin, Texas, August 4 and August 11, 1974.

34. Wilson interviews, August 4 and August 11, 1974; Samora, Bernal, and Pena, *Gunpowder Justice,* 159–161. The authors fail to understand the basic investigative role of the modern Ranger force and its vital function of providing assistance to underequipped and inexperienced rural law-enforcement organizations in major felony cases.

35. Interview with Captain H. R. "Lefty" Block and Captain Maurice Cook by author, Austin, Texas, July 23, 1985.

36. *Ibid.;* Interview with Captain H. R. "Lefty" Block by author, Austin, Texas, January 15, 1986.

37. Block and Cook interview; Block interview.

38. Interview with Colonel James Adams by author, Austin, Texas, July 23, 1985; Block and Cook interview.

39. Block and Cook interview; Block interview; Adams interview.

40. Adams interview; Block and Cook interview; Block interview.

41. *Dallas News,* July 18, 1987, January 14, April 20, July 29, 1988; *Austin American-Statesman,* January 13, 14, 29, April 19, July 29, 1988; *Corpus Christi Caller,* April 29, 1988; *Dallas Times Herald,* July 29, 1988; interview with Captain H. R. "Lefty" Block by author, Austin, Texas, June 5, 1989. See also "Texas Ranger" file, Legislative Library, Capitol, Austin, Texas.

42. Block and Cook interview; Adams interview.

CHAPTER II

1. Paine, *McDonald,* 79, 160–161, 210–211, 215–220, 262–264; Webb, *Texas Rangers,* 459–460.

2. Paine, *McDonald,* 151–153, 190, 194–198, 219–220, 273–289; Webb, *Texas Rangers,* 446–447, 458–460.

3. Paine, *McDonald,* 16–18, 113, 190.

4. *Ibid.,* 19–22.

5. *Ibid.,* 22–30.

6. *Ibid.,* 30–31.

7. *Ibid.,* 33–35.

8. *Ibid.,* 35–38.

9. *Ibid.,* 43–47, 53–86.

10. *Ibid.,* 13–14, 75, 86.

11. *Ibid.,* 79, 87, 172–174; Tyler Mason, *Riding for Texas: The True Adventures*

of Captain Bill McDonald of the Texas Rangers (New York: Reynal and Hitchcock, 1936), 92–99.

12. Paine, *McDonald,* 139–145; Mason, *Riding for Texas,* 1–12.

13. Paine, *McDonald,* 151–158, 199–220, 260–264; Mason, *Riding for Texas,* 142–156.

14. Procter, "Fort Brown," 43–52; Webb, *Texas Rangers,* 93–94, 175–193.

15. U.S. Congress, Senate, *Companies B, C, and D, Twenty-fifth United States Infantry. Report of the Proceedings of the Court of Inquiry Relative to the Shooting Affray at Brownsville, Texas, August 13–14, 1906 by Soldiers of Companies B, C, and D Twenty-fifth United States Infantry.* Sen. Doc. 701, 61st Cong., 3d Sess., Ser. 5889, 1390 (hereafter cited as *Court of Inquiry*); Ann J. Lane, *The Brownsville Affair: National Crisis and Black Reaction* (Port Washington, New York: Kennikat Press, Inc., 1971), 5; John D. Weaver, *The Brownsville Raid* (New York: W. W. Norton & Company, Inc., 1970), 18–19; Henry F. Pringle, *Theodore Roosevelt: A Biography* (New York: Harcourt, Brace and Company, 1931), 458; James Aubrey Tinsley, "The Brownsville Affray," M.A. thesis, University of North Carolina, Chapel Hill, North Carolina, 1948, 8–12; John M. Carroll, ed., *The Black Military Experience in the American West* (New York: Liveright, 1971), 424–425, 471–492; Paine, *McDonald,* 316–318; Webb, *Texas Rangers,* 466.

16. U.S. Congress, Senate, *Affray at Brownsville, Tex. Hearings Before the Committee on Military Affairs United States Senate Concerning the Affray at Brownsville, Tex. on the Night of August 13 and 14, 1906.* Sen. Doc. 402, 60th Cong., 1st Sess., Ser. 5254, 765–776; Ser. 5255, 1100, 1117, 1185, 1192, 1497, 1552, 1787, 1945–1946; Ser. 5256, 2381, 2484, 2486, 2501–2502, 2525–2528, 2540–2543, 2941–2942, 2949, 2974 (hereafter cited as *Hearings Before Senate Military Affairs Committee*); U.S. Congress, Senate, *Affray at Brownsville, Tex. August 13 and 14, 1906. Proceedings of a General Court-Martial Convened at Headquarters Department of Texas, San Antonio, Tex., February 4, 1907 in the Case of Major Charles W. Penrose, Twenty-fifth United States Infantry.* Sen. Doc. 402, 60th Cong., 1st Sess., Ser. 5253, 1090, 1146–1147 (hereafter cited as *Penrose Court-Martial*); U.S. Congress, Senate, *Summary Discharge or Mustering Out of Regiments or Companies. Message from the President of the United States, Transmitting a Report from the Secretary of War, Together with Several Documents, Including a Letter of General Nettleton, and Memoranda as to Precedents for the Summary Discharge or Mustering Out of Regiments or Companies.* Sen. Doc. 155, 59th Cong., 2d Sess., Pt. 1, Ser. 5078, 88, 241, 301, 479, 506–508 (hereafter cited as *Summary Discharge,* Pt. 1); *Court of Inquiry,* Ser. 5888, 724; Ser. 5890, 1610, 1655–1667; Ser. 5891, 2116–2121, 2317–2321; Weaver, *Brownsville Raid,* 20–25; Lane, *The Brownsville Affair,* 12–15; Paine, *McDonald,* 316–317; Tinsley, "The Brownsville Affray," 9, 13–17.

17. U.S. Congress, Senate, *Affray at Brownsville, Tex. August 13 and 14, 1906. Proceedings of a General Court-Martial Convened at Headquarters Department of Texas, San Antonio, Tex., April 15, 1907 in the Case of Capt. Edgar A. Macklin, Twenty-fifth United States Infantry.* Sen. Doc. 402, 60th Cong., 1st Sess., Ser. 5254, Pt. 3, 179 (hereafter cited as *Macklin Court-Martial*); Weaver, *The Brownsville Raid,* 25–32; Lane, *The Brownsville Affair,* 15–17; Tinsley, "The Brownsville Affray," 17–21; Paine, *McDonald,* 317–318; *Summary Discharge,* Pt. 1, 61–62; *Hearings Before Senate Military Affairs Committee,* Ser. 5256, 2370–2372, 2381, 2958–2962; Ser. 5255, 1784–1787; U.S. Congress, Senate, *The Brownsville Affray. Report of the Inspector-General of the Army; Order of the President Discharging Enlisted Men of Companies B, C, and D Twenty-*

fifth Infantry; Messages of the President to the Senate; and Majority and Minority Reports of the Senate Committee on Military Affairs. Sen. Doc. 389, 60th Cong., 1st Sess., Ser. 5252, 143–144 (hereafter cited as *Inspector General's Report*); U.S. Congress, Senate, *Summary Discharge or Mustering Out of Regiments or Companies. Message from the President of the United States, Transmitting a Letter from the Secretary of War Containing Additional Testimony in the Brownsville Case.* Sen. Doc. 155, 59th Cong., 2d Sess., Pt. 2, Ser. 5078, 118 (hereafter cited as *Summary Discharge*, Pt. 2); *Penrose Court-Martial*, 542–543, 1146–1148.

18. *Macklin Court-Martial*, 66, 178, 196, 226–227; *Penrose Court-Martial*, 824, 1058, 1152; *Hearings Before Senate Military Affairs Committee*, Ser. 5256, 2382ff; Tinsley, "The Brownsville Affray," 1–3; Paine, *McDonald*, 318–319; Weaver, *The Brownsville Raid*, 32–43; Lane, *The Brownsville Affair*, 17–18; Webb, *Texas Rangers*, 466.

19. *Penrose Court-Martial*, 395, 1058, 1152–1153, 1156; *Hearings Before Senate Military Affairs Committee*, Ser. 5254, 799; Ser. 5256, 2245, 2384–2386; *Court of Inquiry*, Ser. 5891, 2026–2032; Tinsley, "The Brownsville Affray," 3–6; Weaver, *The Brownsville Raid*, 43–63; Lane, *The Brownsville Affair*, 17–19.

20. *Penrose Court-Martial*, 1058, 1152–1153, 1156; *Hearings Before Senate Military Affairs Committee*, Ser. 5254, 59–62, 323, 332, 437, 530, 792; Ser. 5256, 2389ff; *Court of Inquiry*, Ser. 5889, 1300; Ser. 5891, 2031; *Inspector General's Report*, 87–94, 96ff; Tinsley, "The Brownsville Affray," 6–7, 22–26; Weaver, *The Brownsville Raid*, 61–63; Lane, *The Brownsville Affair*, 18; Paine, *McDonald*, 320.

21. *Hearings Before Senate Military Affairs Committee*, Ser. 5256, 2105, 2140, 2250–2255, 2393ff, 2533; *Summary Discharge*, Pt. 1, 20–21, 26–28, 34, 38–39, 45, 52–53, 78, 81–84, 87; Tinsley, "The Brownsville Affray," 7–8; Weaver, *The Brownsville Raid*, 64–79; Lane, *The Brownsville Affair*, 18–19; Paine, *McDonald*, 320–322.

22. Paine, *McDonald*, 323–324; Weaver, *The Brownsville Raid*, 79–80.

23. Paine, *McDonald*, 324–325; Weaver, *The Brownsville Raid*, 81–82; *Hearings Before Senate Military Affairs Committee*, Ser. 5256, 2397–2398; *Court of Inquiry*, Ser. 5891, 2323; *Summary Discharge*, Pt. 1, 84, 208, 449.

24. Paine, *McDonald*, 326–327; Weaver, *The Brownsville Raid*, 81–83; *Summary Discharge*, Pt. 1, 88; Webb, *Texas Rangers*, 467.

25. *Hearings Before Senate Military Affairs Committee*, Ser. 5256, 2397–2398, 2431, 2532–2533, 2544–2545; Paine, *McDonald*, 327–328; Weaver, *The Brownsville Raid*, 82–84; Webb, *Texas Rangers*, 467.

26. Paine, *McDonald*, 329–338; Weaver, *The Brownsville Raid*, 82–83; *Inspector General's Report*, 3–62; *Hearings Before Senate Military Affairs Committee*, Ser. 5254, 560; Ser. 5256, 2431.

27. Paine, *McDonald*, 336–337; Weaver, *The Brownsville Raid*, 83–85; *Hearings Before Senate Military Affairs Committee*, Ser. 5256, 2397–2398, 2431.

28. Paine, *McDonald*, 338–340; Weaver, *The Brownsville Raid*, 83–85; Lane, *The Brownsville Affair*, 30; Webb, *Texas Rangers*, 467–468.

29. *Summary Discharge*, Pt. 1, 50–51, 103–104; Paine, *McDonald*, 341–343; Weaver, *The Brownsville Raid*, 83–85; Lane, *The Brownsville Affair*, 20–21; Webb, *Texas Rangers*, 467–468.

30. Paine, *McDonald*, 343–346; *Summary Discharge*, Pt. 1, 103–104; Weaver, *The Brownsville Raid*, 84–86; Webb, *Texas Rangers*, 468.

31. Paine, *McDonald,* 346–349; *Summary Discharge,* Pt. 1, 103–104; Weaver, *The Brownsville Raid,* 84–86; Webb, *Texas Rangers,* 468–469; Tinsley, "The Brownsville Affray," 28–29.

32. Paine, *McDonald,* 350–353; Weaver, *The Brownsville Raid,* 485–486; Webb, *Texas Rangers,* 469; Tinsley, "The Brownsville Affray," 28–29.

33. Paine, *McDonald,* 353–355; Weaver, *The Brownsville Raid,* 86–88; Webb, *Texas Rangers,* 469.

34. Lane, *The Brownsville Affair,* 20–23; Pringle, *Roosevelt,* 459–464; Weaver, *The Brownsville Raid,* 86–87, 91, 93, 95, 97; Tinsley, "The Brownsville Affray," 25–41. See also chapters III-VII for a discussion of the political and legal controversies.

35. Paine, *McDonald,* 373–396; Webb, *Texas Rangers,* 469; Weaver, *The Brownsville Raid,* 80, 82; Walter Prescott Webb, "The Texas Rangers," MSS, Walter Prescott Webb Papers, University of Texas at Austin Archives, Austin, Texas.

CHAPTER III

1. Alexander, *The Klan in the Southwest,* 1–35; Alexander, *Crusade for Conformity: The Ku Klux Klan in 1920–1930,* 8, 43–53; Brown, *Hood, Bonnet, and Little Brown Jug,* 49–87; David M. Chalmers, *Hooded Americanism: The First Century of the Ku Klux Klan, 1865–1965* (Garden City, New York: Doubleday & Co., 1965), 28–38; Stanley Frost, *The Challenge of the Klan* (Indianapolis: Bobbs-Merrill Co., 1924), 79–115; Kenneth T. Jackson, *The Ku Klux Klan in the City, 1915–1930* (New York: Oxford University Press, 1967), 9–15; John M. Mecklin, *The Ku Klux Klan: A Study of the American Mind* (New York: Harcourt, Brace and Co., 1924), 8, 13, 29, 38, 86–87, 123–124, 127–128; Arnold Rice, *The Ku Klux Klan in American Politics* (Washington, D.C.: Public Affairs Press, 1962), 1–29.

2. Frederick Lewis Allen, *Only Yesterday: An Informal History of the Nineteen-Twenties* (New York: Harper & Row, Publishers, 1931), 54–57, 73–101, 209–212, 215–223; William Eugene Atkinson, "James V. Allred: A Political Biography, 1899–1935," Ph.D. dissertation, Texas Christian University, Fort Worth, Texas, 1978, 51–55; Brown, *Hood, Bonnet, and Little Brown Jug,* 49–87; Alexander, *The Klan in the Southwest,* 25–27, 29–33; Rice, *KKK in American Politics,* 15–17.

3. Allen, *Only Yesterday,* 29–30, 38–62; Alexander, *The Klan in the Southwest,* 11–19, 21–28, 33–35; Chalmers, *Hooded Americanism,* 110; John D. Hicks, *Republican Ascendancy, 1921–1933* (New York: Harper & Brothers Publishers, 1960), 3, 16, 82, 93–94, 168, 183, 185.

4. Mecklin, *Ku Klux Klan,* 232; Alexander, *The Klan in the Southwest,* 36–54; Jackson, *KKK in the City, 1915–1930,* 66–80, 83–85; Rice, *KKK in American Politics,* 14–15, 20; Henry P. Fry, *The Modern Ku Klux Klan* (Boston: Small, Maynard, & Company Publishers, 1922), 97–98; Brown, *Hood, Bonnet, and Little Brown Jug,* 51–68.

5. Interviews with Red Burton by author, Waco, Texas, February 4, 5, 1967; April 6, 7, 1968.

6. *Ibid.*

7. *Ibid.*

8. *Ibid.*

9. *Ibid.*

10. *Ibid.*

11. *Ibid.*

12. *Ibid.;* interview with Mr. and Mrs. Tilley Buchanan, Margrett Curton, and Mary Dollins by author, Waco, Texas, November 19, 1969.

13. Burton interviews, February 4, 5, 1967; April 6, 7, 1968.

14. *Ibid.*

15. *Ibid.;* interview with Red Burton by author, Waco, Texas, September 18, November 6, 1969; *Texas Almanac and State Industrial Guide, 1914* (Dallas: Galveston-Dallas News, 1914), 309–310; *Texas Almanac and State Industrial Guide, 1925* (Dallas: A. H. Belo & Company, 1925), 62, 319–320.

16. Burton interviews, February 4, 5, 1967; April 6, 7, 1968; *Waco Tribune-Herald*, October 2, 1921.

17. Buchanan, *et al.* interview; Burton interviews, February 4, 5, 1967; April 6, 7, 1968.

18. Burton interviews, February 4, 5, 1967; April 6, 7, 1968; September 18, 1969.

19. *Ibid.*

20. Buchanan, *et al.* interview; Burton interviews, February 4, 5, 1967; April 6, 7, 1968; September 18, 1969.

21. Buchanan, *et al.* interview; Burton interviews, February 4, 5, 1967; April 6, 7, 1968; September 18, 1969; *Waco Tribune-Herald*, October 2, 1921.

22. Burton interviews, February 4, 5, 1967; April 6, 7, 1968; September 18, November 6, 1969.

23. *Ibid.; Waco Tribune-Herald*, October 2, 1921.

24. Burton interviews, February 4, 5, 1967; April 6, 7, 1968; September 18, November 6, 1969.

25. *Ibid.; Waco Tribune-Herald*, October 2–6, 1921.

26. Burton interviews, February 4, 5, 1967; April 6, 7, 1968; September 18, November 6, 1969.

27. Buchanan, *et al.* interview; Burton interviews, February 4, 5, 1967; April 6, 7, 1968; November 6, 1969; *Waco Tribune-Herald*, October 2, 1921.

28. Burton interviews, February 4, 5, 1967; April 6, 7, 1968; November 6, 1969. See *Waco Tribune-Herald*, October 2–12, 1921, for reactions to the Lorena affair.

29. Burton interviews, February 4, 5, 1967; April 6, 7, 1968; November 6, 1969.

30. *Ibid.*

31. *Ibid.; Waco Tribune-Herald*, October 10, 11, 1921.

32. Burton interviews, February 4, 5, 1967; April 6, 7, 1968; November 6, 1969.

33. *Ibid.*

34. *Ibid.; Waco Tribune-Herald*, October 2–12, 1921; Brown, *Hood, Bonnet, and Little Brown Jug*, 62, 68; Alexander, *The Klan in the Southwest*, 50.

35. Buchanan, *et al.* interview.

36. Burton interviews, February 4, 5, 1967; April 6, 7, 1968; November 6, 1969; speech by Red Burton, May 1, 1956, Waco Heritage Society, Waco, Texas; Brown, *Hood, Bonnet, and Little Brown Jug*, 450, n. 45.

CHAPTER IV

1. Interviews with Leo Bishop by author, Carta Valley, Texas, September 12, 1968 and November 15, 1969.

2. *Ibid.*

3. *Ibid.*

4. *Ibid.*

5. *Ibid.*

6. *Ibid.;* Webb, *Texas Rangers,* 551–560.

7. Bishop interviews, September 12, 1968; November 15, 1969.

8. *Ibid.;* Sterling, *Trails and Trials of a Texas Ranger,* 264–266; Schuster, "Modernization of the Texas Rangers," 17–22; Procter, "The Modern Texas Rangers," 214–215; Webb, *Texas Rangers,* 551–560; Malsch, *Lone Wolf,* 116–120.

9. Bishop interviews, September 12, 1968, November 15, 1969; Robert W. Stephens, *Lone Wolf: The Story of Texas Ranger Captain M. T. Gonzaullas* (Dallas: Taylor Publishing Company, [1979?]), 60–61; Malsch, *Lone Wolf,* 120.

10. Bishop interviews, September 12, 1968, November 15, 1969; Malsch, *Lone Wolf,* 120–122.

11. Malsch, *Lone Wolf,* 103–118, 192, 195.

12. Bishop interviews, September 12, 1968, November 15, 1969.

13. *Ibid.;* Schuster, "Modernization of the Texas Rangers," 34–49; Malsch, *Lone Wolf,* 120, 122; Webb, *Texas Rangers,* 567; Atkinson, "The Texas Gubernatorial Campaign of 1934," 47–49.

14. Bishop interviews, September 12, 1968, November 15, 1969; interview with former Lieutenant Governor Ben Ramsey by author, San Augustine, Texas, August 4, 1976; interview with Judge Wardlow Lane by author, Dallas, Texas, August 26, 1976; *Texas Almanac and State Industrial Guide, 1936* (Dallas: A. H. Belo Corporation, 1936), 442.

15. *Texas Almanac, 1936,* 442; Ramsey interview, August 4, 1976; interview with Arlan Hays by author, San Augustine, Texas, August 3, 1976; closed interview with a prominent San Augustine citizen, San Augustine, Texas, August 4, 1976. On August 3–4, 1976, several prominent citizens escorted the author to the sites where the events of this story occurred. As these citizens readily admitted, San Augustine had changed very little since 1935.

16. Bishop interviews, September 12, 1968, November 15, 1969; Ramsey interview, August 4, 1976; Hays interview, August 3, 1976; closed interview, August 4, 1976; *San Augustine Tribune,* December 22, 1934, to January 10, 1935.

17. Bishop interviews, September 12, 1968, November 15, 1969; Ramsey interview, August 4, 1976; Hays interview, August 3, 1976; closed interview, August 4, 1976.

18. Bishop interviews, September 12, 1968, November 15, 1969; closed interview, August 4, 1976; Ramsey interview, August 4, 1976; Hays interview, August 3, 1976; Malsch, *Lone Wolf,* 103–120.

19. Bishop interviews, September 12, 1968, November 15, 1969; closed interview, August 4, 1976.

20. Bishop interviews, September 12, 1968, November 15, 1969; Lane interview, August 26, 1976; Hays interview, August 3, 1976; closed interview, August 4, 1976; *San Augustine Tribune,* March 1935.

21. Bishop interviews, September 12, 1968, November 15, 1969.

22. *Ibid.*

23. *Ibid.*; closed interview, August 4, 1976.

24. Bishop interviews, September 12, 1968, November 15, 1969; closed interview, August 4, 1976; Hays interview, August 3, 1976; Lane interview, August 26, 1976; *San Augustine Tribune,* February–March, 1935.

25. Lane interview, August 26, 1976; Bishop interviews, September 12, 1968, and November 15, 1969.

26. Lane interview, August 26, 1976; Bishop interviews, September 12, 1968, and November 15, 1969; *San Augustine Tribune,* March 1935.

27. Bishop interviews, September 12, 1968, November 15, 1969; Hays interview, August 3, 1976; Ramsey interview, August 4, 1976; closed interview, August 4, 1976; *San Augustine Tribune,* March 22–23, 1935.

28. Bishop interviews, September 12, 1968, November 15, 1969.

CHAPTER V

1. Interviews with Captain Clint Peoples by author, Waco, Texas, September 3, 1968, September 18, 1969; James M. Day, *Captain Clint Peoples, Texas Ranger: Fifty Years a Lawman* (Waco: Texian Press, 1980), 1.

2. Peoples interviews, September 3, 1968, September 18, 1969; Day, *Peoples,* 1–2.

3. *Texas Almanac and State Industrial Guide, 1925* (Dallas: A. H. Belo Corporation, 1925), 66, 323–324; Peoples interviews, September 3, 1968, September 18, 1969; Day, *Peoples,* 2–3; Leon Charles Hallman, "A Geographic Study of Montgomery County, Texas," M.A. thesis, Southern Methodist University, Dallas, Texas, 1966, 7–19ff. For more information on Montgomery County, see Robin Montgomery, *The History of Montgomery County* (Austin: Pemberton Press, 1975); William Harley Gandy, "A History of Montgomery County, Texas," M.A. thesis, University of Houston, Houston, Texas, 1952.

4. Peoples interviews, September 3, 1968, September 18, 1969; Day, *Peoples,* 5–7.

5. Peoples interviews, September 3, 1968, September 18, 1969; Day, *Peoples,* 8–9.

6. Peoples interviews, September 3, 1968, September 18, 1969; Day, *Peoples,* 9–10.

7. Peoples interviews, September 3, 1968, September 18, 1969; Day, *Peoples,* 10–15.

8. Peoples interviews, September 3, 1968, September 18, 1969; Day, *Peoples,* 11, 14–16; *Texas Almanac and State Industrial Guide, 1931* (Dallas: A. H. Belo Corporation, 1931), 347.

9. Peoples interviews, September 3, 1968, September 18, 1969; Day, *Peoples,* 16–18; *Texas Almanac and State Industrial Guide, 1933* (Dallas: A. H. Belo Corporation, 1933), 206, 349. In 1931 the oil production in Montgomery County was 1 barrel; in 1932, it was 2,525 barrels.

10. Peoples interviews, September 3, 1968, September 18, 1969; Day, *Peoples,* 16–20.

11. Peoples interviews, September 3, 1968, September 18, 1969; Day, *Peoples,* 26–51ff.

12. Peoples interviews, September 3, 1968, September 18, 1969; Day, *Peoples,*

52–99ff; newspaper articles in Texas Ranger Scrapbooks, Texas Department of Public Safety, Austin, Texas.

13. Peoples interviews, September 3, 1968, September 18, 1969; Day, *Peoples,* 99, 101–102; Ranger Scrapbooks.

14. Peoples interviews, September 3, 1968, September 18, November 5, 1969, July 12, 1970; Day, *Peoples,* 108.

15. On two occasions Captain Clint Peoples escorted the author on a tour of the area, pointing out where the events occurred. See pictures and newspaper accounts in Ranger Scrapbooks. Peoples interviews, September 3, 1968, September 18, November 5, 1969, July 12, 1970; interview with inspector J. L. Rogers of the Department of Public Safety by author, Austin, Texas, July 20, 1970; Day, *Peoples,* 108–109.

16. Rogers interview, July 20, 1970; Peoples interviews, September 3, 1968, September 18, November 15, 1969, July 12, 1970; Ranger Scrapbooks; Day, *Peoples,* 109.

17. Peoples interviews, September 3, 1968, September 18, November 15, 1969, July 12, 1970; Rogers interview, July 20, 1970; interview with Ranger Trenton Horton by author, Temple, Texas, July 20, 1970; Ranger Scrapbooks; Day, *Peoples,* 109.

18. Peoples interviews, September 3, 1968, September 18, November 15, 1969, July 12, 1970; Rogers interview, July 20, 1970; Ranger Scrapbooks; Day, *Peoples,* 109.

19. Peoples interviews, September 3, 1968, September 18, November 15, 1969, July 12, 1970, November 4, 1971; Rogers interview, July 20, 1970; interview with Captain Bob Crowder by author, Dallas, Texas, December 31, 1969; Ranger Scrapbooks; Day, *Peoples,* 109–110.

20. Peoples interviews, September 3, 1968, September 18, 1969; Crowder interview, December 31, 1969. On May 15, 1974, Clint Peoples retired from Ranger service; that same day he took the oath of office as a federal marshal (stationed in Dallas, Texas). Day, *Peoples,* 162.

CHAPTER VI

1. Richard Hofstadter, *The Age of Reform: From Bryan to F. D. R.* (New York: Vintage Books, 1960), 23–46, discusses the Agrarian Myth. John D. Hicks, in a luncheon address to the Western History Association, San Francisco, California, October 1967, refuted the Agrarian Myth.

2. Interviews with Bob Crowder by author, February 24, October 24, 1969, Dallas, Texas.

3. *Ibid.*

4. *Ibid.*

5. *Ibid.*

6. *Ibid.*

7. *Ibid.*

8. *Ibid.;* see Walter Prescott Webb, "The Texas Rangers in the Modern World," MSS, University of Texas at Austin Archives, Austin, Texas, 1–7, concerning the Griffenhagen Report of 1933, which studied the State Highway Patrol and the Texas Rangers.

9. Crowder interviews, February 24, October 24, 1969. For more informa-

tion on creating the Department of Public Safety, see Charlton, "The Department of Public Safety, 1935–1957," 8–15ff; Malsch, *Lone Wolf,* 119–120.

10. A discrepancy arises as to dates. In Crowder interviews, February 24, October 24, 1969, Crowder stated that he became a Texas Ranger in 1937, while "Texas Ranger Strength — Authorized," Ranger File, Department of Public Safety, Austin, Texas, 6, 8, first listed Crowder as a Ranger beginning in January 1939, and Gonzaullas as a Ranger in February 1940. Malsch, *Lone Wolf,* 122, 140, corroborates the DPS files.

11. Crowder interviews, February 24, October 24, 1969; newspaper articles in Ranger Scrapbooks.

12. Crowder interviews, February 24, October 24, 1969. In conversations with the author, Crowder colleagues verified the information in this paragraph.

13. *Ibid.;* "Texas Ranger Strength — Authorized," 6, 8; Malsch, *Lone Wolf,* 5–6, 192.

14. Crowder interviews, February 24, October 24, 1969; newspaper articles in the Ranger Scrapbooks.

15. Mary Patterson, "April 16, 1955 Revisited — A Look at the Riot in Maximum Security Unit," *Rusk Cherokeean,* January 9, 1975; interview with Emmett Whitehead, publisher and editor of the *Rusk Cherokeean,* Rusk, Texas, July 19, 1981; Emmett Whitehead Scrapbooks, Rusk, Texas. Whitehead escorted the author on a tour of the Rusk State Hospital, pointing out where the events occurred.

16. Patterson, "April 16, 1955 Revisited"; Whitehead interview, July 19, 1981.

17. Crowder interviews, December 31, 1969; January 11, 1970; Patterson, "April 16, 1955 Revisited"; Whitehead interview, July 19, 1981; Whitehead Scrapbooks.

18. Whitehead interview, July 19, 1981; Patterson, "April 16, 1955 Revisited"; Whitehead Scrapbooks.

19. *Ibid.*

20. *Ibid.*

21. Crowder interviews, December 31, 1969; January 11, 1970; *Texas Almanac, 1956–1957: The Encyclopedia of Texas* (Dallas: A. H. Belo Corporation, 1957), 615–616, 701. In July 1981 the author retraced Crowder's route.

22. Crowder interviews, December 31, 1969, January 11, 1970; Patterson, "April 16, 1955 Revisited."

23. Crowder interviews, December 31, 1969, January 11, 1970; Whitehead interview, July 19, 1981; Whitehead Scrapbooks.

24. Crowder interviews, December 31, 1969, January 11, 1970; Whitehead interview, July 19, 1981.

25. Crowder interviews, December 31, 1969, January 11, 1970; Whitehead interview, July 19, 1981; Whitehead Scrapbooks; Patterson, "April 16, 1955 Revisited."

26. Crowder interviews, December 31, 1969, January 11, 1970.

CHAPTER VII

1. Jim Estelle, director of the Texas Department of Corrections, escorted the author through Huntsville Prison and pointed out where every episode during the siege took place. Interview with Jim Estelle by author, Huntsville, Texas, Sep-

tember 11, 1981; interviews with Linda Woodman by author, Gatesville, Texas, August 3, September 6, 1981; Aline House, *The Carrasco Tragedy: Eleven Days of Terror in the Huntsville Prison* (Waco: Texian Press, 1975), x–xii; *Huntsville Item,* July 24, 1974, extra section, 1–2; *Houston Chronicle,* July 25, 1974, 1, 4.

2. Woodman interviews, August 3, September 6, 1981; interview with Jim Estelle by author, Dallas, Texas, August 11, 1981; House, *The Carrasco Tragedy,* 1–2. See Linda Woodman Scrapbooks, Gatesville, Texas, for numerous newspaper accounts of the siege and of the participants.

3. Woodman interviews, August 3, September 6, 1981; Estelle interview, August 11, 1981; House, *The Carrasco Tragedy,* 1–2; Woodman Scrapbooks; *Houston Chronicle,* July 25, 1974, 1, 4.

4. Woodman interviews, August 3, September 6, 1981; interview with Novella Pollard by author, Sugarland, Texas, August 26, 1981; House, *The Carrasco Tragedy,* 2–3; Woodman Scrapbooks; *San Antonio Express-News,* August 11, 1974, 3.

5. See the eight-part interview of Father Joseph J. O'Brien as told to Tom McGowan in the *San Antonio Light,* September 2–9, 1974 (hereafter cited as O'Brien interview); Wilson McKinney, *Fred Carrasco: The Heroin Merchant* (Austin: Heidelberg Publishers, Inc., 1975), 13–211. See Wilson McKinney, "Carrasco, Merchant of Death and Drugs," *San Antonio Express-News,* April 6–17, 1975; see *San Antonio Light,* July 25, 27, 1974; *San Antonio News,* July 25, 26, 1974; Woodman Scrapbooks.

6. Biographical materials in TDC files, Huntsville Unit, Huntsville, Texas; Woodman interviews, August 3, September 6, 1981; Estelle interview, August 11, 1981; O'Brien interview, September 4, 1974.

7. Woodman interviews, August 3, September 6, 1981; Estelle interviews, August 11, September 11, 1981; O'Brien interview, September 5, 1974; "Report by Warden Hal Husbands," Huntsville Unit, TDC files, Huntsville, Texas (hereafter cited as Husbands Report); House, *The Carrasco Tragedy,* 3–4; *Huntsville Item,* July 24, 1974, extra section, 1–2; *Houston Post,* July 25, 1974, 1; *San Antonio Express-News,* August 11, 1974, 3; *San Antonio Express,* July 25, 1974, 1; *Dallas Morning News,* July 26, 1974, 1.

8. Estelle interviews, August 11, September 11, 1981; Woodman interviews, August 3, September 6, 1981; *San Antonio Light,* July 25, 1974; Woodman Scrapbooks.

9. Estelle interviews, August 11, September 11, 1981.

10. *Ibid.;* Woodman interviews, August 3, September 6, 1981; House, *The Carrasco Tragedy,* 4–5; *San Antonio News,* July 25, 1974, 1, 3; *San Antonio Express-News,* August 11, 1974, 3; O'Brien interview, September 5, 1974.

11. Estelle interview, August 11, 1981; Husbands Report; House, *The Carrasco Tragedy,* 9–10; O'Brien interview, September 6, 1974; *San Antonio Express,* July 26, 1974, 1; *Dallas Morning News,* July 26, 1974, 1.

12. Woodman interviews, August 3, September 6, 1981; Estelle interview, August 11, 1981; House, *The Carrasco Tragedy,* 8.

13. Woodman interviews, August 3, September 6, 1981; Estelle interview, August 11, 1981; House, *The Carrasco Tragedy,* 4; Woodman Scrapbooks.

14. Woodman interviews, August 3, September 6, 1981; Estelle interview, August 11, 1981; House, *The Carrasco Tragedy,* 5; O'Brien interview, September 5,

1974; "O'Brien 'Tough' Little Irishman," newspaper article in Woodman Scrapbooks.

15. Woodman interviews, August 3, September 6, 1981; Estelle interview, August 11, 1981; House, *The Carrasco Tragedy,* 6; biographical materials in TDC files; O'Brien interview, September 3, 1974; *San Antonio News,* August 12, 1974, 1; *Daily Courier* (Conroe), August 8, 1974, 1.

16. Woodman interviews, August 3, September 6, 1981; biographical materials in TDC files; O'Brien interview, September 3, 1974; Pollard interview, August 26, 1981; House, *The Carrasco Tragedy,* 5–6; *San Antonio News,* August 12, 1974, 1; *Daily Courier* (Conroe), August 8, 1, August 11, 1974, 1.

17. Woodman interviews, August 3, September 6, 1981; House, *The Carrasco Tragedy,* 8–9; Pollard interview, August 26, 1981; Estelle interviews, August 11, September 11, 1981; O'Brien interview, September 6, 1974; *Huntsville Item,* March 19, 1975, in Woodman Scrapbooks; *Houston Chronicle,* March 19, 1975, 18.

18. Woodman interviews, August 3, September 6, 1981; Estelle interviews, August 11, September 11, 1981; House, *The Carrasco Tragedy,* 9–11; *Houston Post,* August 20, 1974, in Woodman Scrapbooks; Husbands Report.

19. Woodman interviews, August 3, September 6, 1981; House, *The Carrasco Tragedy,* 13–14; McKinney, *Carrasco,* 269–270.

20. Woodman interviews, August 3, September 6, 1981; Pollard interview, August 26, 1981; *Huntsville Item,* March 19, 1975, 1, 11; *San Antonio News,* August 13, 1974, 1; *San Antonio Express-News,* August 11, 1974, 3; House, *The Carrasco Tragedy,* 17; McKinney, *Carrasco,* 270.

21. Woodman interviews, August 3, September 6, 1981; House, *The Carrasco Tragedy,* 15–17; Pollard interview, August 26, 1981; Estelle interviews, August 11, September 11, 1981; Husbands Report; *San Antonio Light,* July 27, 1974, 1, 3, 4. See newspaper articles dated July 27, 1974, and March 21–22, 1975, in Woodman Scrapbooks.

22. Woodman interviews, August 3, September 6, 1981; Estelle interviews, August 11, September 11, 1981; Pollard interview, August 26, 1981; House, *The Carrasco Tragedy,* 17. See similar newspaper articles such as the *San Antonio Light,* July 27, 1974, 1, in Woodman Scrapbooks.

23. Estelle interview, August 11, 1981.

24. *Ibid.;* interview with Ranger Captain G. W. Burks by author, Dallas, Texas, August 12, 1981.

25. Burks interview, August 12, 1981; Estelle interviews, August 11, September 11, 1981.

26. Estelle interview, August 11, 1981; Burks interview, August 12, 1981; Husbands Report.

27. Estelle interview, August 11, 1981; Burks interview, August 12, 1981; Husbands Report; O'Brien interview, September 7, 1974.

28. Estelle interview, August 11, 1981; see the *Houston Chronicle,* July 27, 1974, and the *Houston Post,* July 27, 1974, in Woodman Scrapbooks; *Dallas Morning News,* July 28, 1974, 20; July 29, 1974, 1; O'Brien interview, September 6, 1974.

29. Estelle interview, August 11, 1981; Burks interview, August 12, 1981; *Dallas Morning News,* July 28, 1974, 20.

30. Estelle interview, August 11, 1981.

31. See numerous newspaper accounts in which reporters interviewed Car-

rasco and the hostages such as the *Huntsville Item,* July 28, 1974; *San Antonio Express-News,* July 28, 1974; *Houston Post,* July 28, 1974; and *Houston Chronicle,* July 28, 1974.

32. Woodman interviews, August 3, September 6, 1981; Pollard interview, August 26, 1981; Estelle interview, August 11, 1981; *Dallas Morning News,* July 28, 20; July 29, 1974, 1; *Dallas Times Herald,* July 28, 1974, 4B, 5B; biographical materials in TDC files; "Carrasco Says Teacher Now First To Die," newspaper account dated July 29, 1974, in Woodman Scrapbooks; House, *The Carrasco Tragedy,* 43–45; *San Antonio News,* August 15, 1974, 1; *Huntsville Item,* August 7, 1974, 4.

33. Woodman interviews, August 3, September 6, 1981; Pollard interview, August 26, 1981; articles in *Houston Post,* March 20, 1975, and *Houston Chronicle,* March 19, 1975, in Woodman Scrapbooks; *San Antonio Express-News,* August 11, 1974, 3.

34. Woodman interviews, August 3, September 6, 1981; Pollard interview, August 26, 1981; Estelle interview, August 11, 1981; biographical materials in TDC files; *Daily Courier* (Conroe), August 11, 1974, 1; *Dallas Times Herald,* July 28, 1974, 4B; House, *The Carrasco Tragedy,* 62.

35. Woodman interviews, August 3, September 6, 1981; Pollard interview, August 26, 1981; House, *The Carrasco Tragedy,* 18, 39; biographical materials, in TDC files; *Dallas Times Herald,* July 28, 1974, 4B.

36. Woodman interviews, August 3, September 6, 1981; Pollard interview, August 26, 1981; House, *The Carrasco Tragedy,* 46–47; biographical materials in TDC files; *Dallas Times Herald,* July 28, 1974, 4B.

37. Woodman interviews, August 3, September 6, 1981; Pollard interview, August 26, 1981; Estelle interview, September 11, 1981; *Daily Courier* (Conroe), August 11, 1974, 1.

38. Woodman interviews, August 3, September 6, 1981; Estelle interviews, August 11, September 11, 1981; House, *The Carrasco Tragedy,* 57–59; *San Antonio Express,* August 5, 1974, 3; *San Antonio News,* July 29, 1974, 1; *Houston Chronicle,* July 29, 1974, 1; *Daily Courier* (Conroe), July 29, 1974, 1; *Dallas Times Herald,* July 29, 1974, 1.

39. Woodman interviews, August 3, September 6, 1981; Pollard interview, August 26, 1981; House, *The Carrasco Tragedy,* 59–62.

40. Woodman interviews, August 3, September 6, 1981; Pollard interview, August 26, 1981; House, *The Carrasco Tragedy,* 62–63; Estelle interview, August 11, 1981; *San Antonio Light,* August 1, 1974, 1; *San Antonio News,* August 1, 1974, 4.

41. Woodman interviews, August 3, September 6, 1981; Estelle interview, August 11, 1981; House, *The Carrasco Tragedy,* 63.

42. House, *The Carrasco Tragedy,* 61, 64–65; Woodman interviews, August 3, September 6, 1981; Pollard interview, August 26, 1981; Estelle interview, August 11, 1981; Husbands Report; *San Antonio News,* July 30, 1974, 1, 6; *Houston Post,* July 30, 1974, 1; *Daily Courier* (Conroe), July 30, 1974, in Woodman Scrapbooks; *Huntsville Item,* July 31, 1974, 2.

43. Estelle interview, August 11, 1981; Woodman interviews, August 3, September 6, 1981; House, *The Carrasco Tragedy,* 67–68; *San Antonio News,* July 30, 1974, 1; *Dallas Times Herald,* July 30, 1974, 1; August 1, 1974, 1; *San Antonio Light,* July 31, 1974, 1; *Huntsville Item,* July 31, 1974, 2.

44. Estelle interview, August 11, 1981; Burks interview, August 12, 1981;

Woodman interviews, August 3, September 6, 1981; Pollard interview, August 26, 1981; House, *The Carrasco Tragedy*, 68–70ff; O'Brien interview, September 7, 1974; McKinney, *Carrasco*, 275.

45. Woodman interviews, August 3, September 6, 1981; McKinney, *Carrasco*, 274; House, *The Carrasco Tragedy*, 68; Estelle interview, August 11, 1981.

46. Estelle interview, August 11, 1981; Woodman interviews, August 3, September 6, 1981; Pollard interview, August 26, 1981; House, *The Carrasco Tragedy*, 70–72; *San Antonio Light*, August 1, 1974, 1; *San Antonio Express*, August 1, 1974, 1; *Houston Post*, August 1, 1974, 1; August 2, 1974, 1; *Houston Chronicle*, August 1, 1981, 1; *San Antonio News*, August 2, 1974, 1.

47. Woodman interviews, August 3, September 6, 1981; House, *The Carrasco Tragedy*, 74–75; *Daily Courier* (Conroe), August 11, 1974, 1; McKinney, *Carrasco*, 278.

48. Woodman interviews, August 3, September 6, 1981; Pollard interview, August 26, 1981.

49. Woodman interviews, August 3, September 6, 1981; Pollard interview, August 26, 1981; House, *The Carrasco Tragedy*, 75–76.

50. Pollard interview, August 26, 1981; Woodman interviews, August 3, September 6, 1981; House, *The Carrasco Tragedy*, 76.

51. Estelle interview, August 11, 1981; Pollard interview, August 26, 1981; Woodman interviews, August 3, September 6, 1981; House, *The Carrasco Tragedy*, 76; McKinney, *Carrasco*, 279.

52. Woodman interviews, August 3, September 6, 1981; Pollard interview, August 26, 1981; Estelle interview, August 11, 1981; Husbands Report; House, *The Carrasco Tragedy*, 76–77; *Dallas Morning News*, August 3, 1974, 1; *San Antonio Express-News*, August 3, 1974, 1; *Houston Chronicle*, August 3, 1974, 1; *Houston Post*, August 3, 1974, 1; *San Antonio Light*, August 3, 1974, 1.

53. Pollard interview, August 26, 1981; Estelle interview, August 11, 1981; Woodman interviews, August 3, September 6, 1981; O'Brien interviews, September 2, 7, 1974; McKinney, *Carrasco*, 280–281; House, *The Carrasco Tragedy*, 77; *Houston Post*, March 21, 1975, 1, 19.

54. Estelle interviews, August 11, September 11, 1981; Burks interview, August 12, 1981; Woodman interviews, August 3, September 6, 1981; Husbands Report.

55. Interview with Mrs. Pete Rogers by author, Silsbee, Texas, August 18, 1981; Burks interview, August 12, 1981; "Grim-Faced Ranger Narrates Breakout Film," newspaper article [March 23, 1975?] in Woodman Scrapbooks; *Houston Post*, March 25, 1975, 1, 15.

56. Burks interview, August 12, 1981; Estelle interview, August 11, 1981.

57. Burks interview, August 12, 1981; Estelle interviews, August 11, September 11, 1981; Husbands Report.

58. Pollard interview, August 26, 1981; McKinney, *Carrasco*, 280; *Daily Courier* (Conroe), August 2, 1974, 1; *Dallas Times Herald*, August 4, 1974, 23; *Dallas Morning News*, August 5, 1974, 25.

59. McKinney, *Carrasco*, 280–282; Estelle interview, August 11, 1981; Pollard interview, August 26, 1981; *Dallas Morning News*, August 4, 1974, 1; *Dallas Times Herald*, August 4, 1974, 21.

60. Pollard interview, August 26, 1981; House, *The Carrasco Tragedy*, 79–80;

McKinney, *Carrasco*, 281; O'Brien interviews, September 2, 9, 1974; *Dallas Times Herald*, August 4, 1974, 21.

61. Pollard interview, August 26, 1981; Estelle interview, September 11, 1981; O'Brien interview, September 9, 1974.

62. Interview with Ronald Robinson by Mike Bryan and Carter Pettit of *Daily Courier* (Conroe), [August 4, 1974?], Woodman Scrapbooks; O'Brien interviews, September 2, 9, 1974; McKinney, *Carrasco*, 281–283; *Houston Chronicle*, September 8, 1974, 2.

63. Burks interview, August 12, 1981; Estelle interviews, August 11, September 11, 1981.

64. Burks interview, August 12, 1981; Estelle interviews, August 11, September 11, 1981; *Dallas Times Herald*, August 4, 1974, 5; McKinney, *Carrasco*, 283–284. See the videotapes of August 3, 1974, recording this action, TDC, Huntsville, Texas. See also on August 4, 1974, the *Huntsville Item, Daily Courier* (Conroe), *Houston Post, Houston Chronicle, Dallas Times Herald,* and *Dallas Morning News* for front-page coverage of the final hours.

65. Burks interview, August 12, 1981; Estelle interviews, August 11, September 11, 1981; Husbands Report; McKinney, *Carrasco*, 284–285; *Houston Post*, March 25, 1975, 1; O'Brien interview, September 9, 1974; *Dallas Morning News*, August 5, 1974, 1; *Dallas Times Herald*, August 4, 1974, 5; TDC videotapes.

66. Burks interview, August 12, 1981; O'Brien interview, September 9, 1974; Pollard interview, August 26, 1981; TDC videotapes; *Houston Post*, March 25, 1975, 1; McKinney, *Carrasco*, 285–286; *Houston Chronicle*, March 22, 1975; Woodman Scrapbooks; *Huntsville Item*, March 21, 1975, 1; *Houston Chronicle*, September 8, 1974, sec. 2; *Dallas Morning News*, August 5, 1974, 1; *Dallas Times Herald*, August 4, 1974, 5; McKinney, *Carrasco*, 285–286.

67. Burks interview, August 12, 1981; Rogers interview, August 18, 1981; Estelle interview, August 11, 1981; House, *The Carrasco Tragedy*, 81–82; McKinney, *Carrasco*, 286–287; *Dallas Morning News*, August 5, 1974, 1.

Bibliography

I. THE TEXAS RANGERS: INTO THE TWENTIETH CENTURY

Primary Sources

Government Documents

National

U.S. Senate. *Investigation of Mexican Affairs.* Sen. Doc. 285, 66th Cong., 2d Sess., Ser. 7665–7666. Washington, D.C.: GPO, 1920.

State

General and Special Laws of the State of Texas. 44th Legis., Reg. Sess., 1935.
General and Special Laws of the State of Texas. 45th Legis., Reg. Sess., 1937.
General and Special Laws of the State of Texas. 46th Legis., Reg. Sess., 1939.
General and Special Laws of the State of Texas. 49th Legis., Reg. Sess., 1945.
General and Special Laws of the State of Texas. 51st Legis., Reg. Sess., 1949.
General Laws of the State of Texas, 36th Legis., Reg. Sess., 1919.
Report and Recommendations of the Senate Committee Investigating Crime. 43d Legis., 1933–1934.
Report of the Adjutant General of the State of Texas: January, 1933 to December, 1934. Austin: Knape Printing Co., 1934.
Texas. Department of Public Safety. *Annual Report, Texas Department of Public Safety, Fiscal Year Ending August 31, 1939.*
———. *Biennial Report, 1947–1948 Fiscal Years, January 1, 1949.*
———. *Department of Public Safety, August 10, 1935–December 1, 1936.* Austin: Department of Public Safety, 1936.

Manuscripts

Adjutant Generals' Papers, 1874–1898. Texas State Archives, Austin, Texas.
"Proceedings of the Joint Committee of the Senate and House in the Investigation of the Texas State Ranger Force, 1919." Texas State Archives, Austin, Texas.
Texas. Department of Public Safety. Austin, Texas. Ranger Scrapbooks.
Texas. Department of Public Safety. Austin, Texas. "Rules and Regulations Re-

garding Appointments, Transfers, and Promotions of Employees, January 21, 1936."

Texas. Department of Public Safety. Austin, Texas. Special Ranger Rosters, 1933–1934.

Texas. Department of Public Safety. Austin, Texas. Texas Ranger Records, 1930–1932.

Texas. Department of Public Safety. Austin, Texas. Texas Ranger Roster Rolls, 1920–1930.

Texas. Department of Public Safety. Austin, Texas. "Texas Ranger Strength — Authorized."

Interviews

Interview with Colonel James B. Adams, director of the DPS, by author. Austin, Texas, July 23, 1985.

Interview with Captain A. Y. Allee by author. Carrizo Springs, Texas, November 15, 1969.

Interview with Senior Captain H. R. "Lefty" Block by author. Austin, Texas, January 15, 1986.

Interview with Senior Captain H. R. "Lefty" Block and Assistant Supervisor Maurice Cook by author. Austin, Texas, July 23, 1985.

Interview with Captain Bob Crowder by author. Dallas, Texas, February 24, 1969.

Interview with Manuel T. "Lone Wolf" Gonzaullas by author. Dallas, Texas, October 27, 1969.

Interview with Lieutenant Colonel Leo Gossett by author. Austin, Texas, November 11, 1971.

Interviews with Captain Clint Peoples by author. Waco, Texas, July 13, 1970; Austin, Texas, November 4, 1971.

Interview with Sergeant Jim Riddles and Ranger Bill Wilson by author. Austin, Texas, September 10, 1966.

Interview with Ranger Lewis Rigler by author. Gainesville, Texas, October 2, 1970.

Interviews with Colonel Wilson E. Speir, director of the Department of Public Safety, by author. Austin, Texas, November 11, 1971; August 4, 1974.

Interviews with Senior Captain Bill Wilson by author. Austin, Texas, August 4 and 11, 1974.

Interview with E. A. "Dogie" Wright by James Ward and author. Sierra Blanca, Texas, September 26, 1969.

Books

Ford, John Salmon. *Rip Ford's Texas.* Edited by Stephen B. Oates. Austin: University of Texas Press, 1963.

Gillett, James B. *Six Years with the Texas Rangers, 1876–1881.* Edited by M. M. Quaife. New Haven: Yale University Press, 1925.

Reid, Samuel C., Jr. *The Scouting Expeditions of McCulloch's Texas Rangers.* Austin: Steck Company, 1935.

Sterling, William Warren. *Trails and Trials of a Texas Ranger.* Norman: University of Oklahoma Press, 1968.

Newspapers

Austin American. February 28, 1935.
American-Statesman (Austin). May 7, 1950; October 21, 1956.
Dallas Morning News. September 28, 1938.
Houston Post. February 20, 1919.
The Statesman (Austin). January 28, 1919.

Secondary Sources

Books

Alexander, Charles C. *Crusade for Conformity: The Ku Klux Klan in 1920–1930.* Houston: Texas Gulf Coast Historical Association, 1962.
———. *The Ku Klux Klan in the Southwest.* Lexington: University of Kentucky Press, 1965.
Brown, Norman. *Hood, Bonnet, and Little Brown Jug: Texas Politics, 1921–1928.* College Station: Texas A&M University Press, 1984.
Clendenen, Clarence C. *The United States and Pancho Villa: A Study in Unconventional Diplomacy.* Ithaca: Cornell University Press, 1961.
Day, James M. *Captain Clint Peoples, Texas Ranger: Fifty Years a Lawman.* Waco: Texian Press, 1980.
Douglas, C. L. *The Gentlemen in White Hats: Dramatic Episodes in the History of the Texas Rangers.* Dallas: South-West Press, 1934.
Durham, George, and Clyde Wantland. *Taming the Nueces Strip: The Story of McNelly's Rangers.* Austin: University of Texas Press, 1962.
Greer, James Kimmins. *Colonel Jack Hays: Texas Frontier Leader and California Builder.* New York: E. P. Dutton and Company, Inc., 1952.
Jenkins, John H., and Gordon Frost. *"I'm Frank Hamer": The Life of a Texas Peace Officer.* Austin: Pemberton Press, 1968.
Kilgore, D. E. *A Ranger Legacy: 150 Years of Service to Texas.* Austin: Madrona Press, Inc., 1973.
Malsch, Brownson. *Captain M. T. Gonzaullas, Lone Wolf: The Only Texas Ranger Captain of Spanish Descent.* Austin: Shoal Creek Publishers, Inc., 1980.
Paine, Albert Bigelow. *Captain Bill McDonald Texas Ranger: A Story of Frontier Reform.* New York: J. J. Little & Ives Co., 1909.
Paredes, Americo. *With His Pistol in His Hand.* Austin: University of Texas Press, 1958.
Preece, Harold. *Lone Star Man: Ira Aten, Last of the Old Texas Rangers.* New York: Hastings House, Publishers, 1960.
Quirk, Robert E. *The Mexican Revolution, 1914–1915: The Convention of Aguascalientes.* Bloomington: University of Indiana Press, 1960.
Rigler, Lewis C., and Judyth Wagner Rigler. *In the Line of Duty: Reflections of a Texas Ranger Private.* Houston: Larksdale, 1984.
Samora, Julian, Joe Bernal, and Albert Pena. *Gunpowder Justice.* Notre Dame: University of Notre Dame Press, 1979.
Toland, John. *The Dillinger Days.* New York: Random House, 1963.
Webb, Walter Prescott. *The Great Plains.* Boston: Ginn and Company, 1931.
———. *The Texas Rangers: A Century of Frontier Defense.* 2nd ed. Austin: University of Texas Press, 1965.

Articles

Cumberland, Charles C. "Border Raids in the Lower Rio Grande Valley — 1915."
    Southwestern Historical Quarterly, LVII (January 1954), 285–311.
Day, James M. "Samuel H. Walker." *Rangers of Texas.* Waco: Texian Press, 1969.
Frantz, Joe B. "Leander H. McNelly." *Rangers of Texas.* Waco: Texian Press, 1969.
Friend, Llerena B. "W. P. Webb's Texas Rangers," *Southwestern Historical Quarterly,*
    LXXIV (January 1971), 293–323.
Jones, Billy Mac. "John B. Jones." *Rangers of Texas.* Waco: Texian Press, 1969.
Procter, Ben. "Ben McCulloch." *Rangers of Texas.* Waco: Texian Press, 1969.
———. "Fort Brown." *Frontier Forts of Texas.* Waco: Texian Press, 1966.
———. "The Modern Texas Rangers: A Law-Enforcement Dilemma in the Rio
    Grande Valley." *Reflections of Western Historians.* Edited by John Alexander
    Carroll. Tucson: University of Arizona Press, 1969.
Simpson, Harold. "John Salmon (Rip) Ford." *Rangers of Texas.* Waco: Texian
    Press, 1969.

Theses and Dissertations

Atkinson, William E. "The Texas Gubernatorial Campaign of 1934." M.A. thesis,
    Texas Christian University, Fort Worth, Texas, 1965.
Charlton, Thomas Lee. "The Texas Department of Public Safety, 1935–1957."
    M.A. thesis, University of Texas at Austin, Austin, Texas, 1961.
Gammage, Allen Z. "The Texas Department of Public Safety and Its Administra-
    tion of War Duties." M.A. thesis, University of Texas at Austin, Austin,
    Texas, 1945.
McClung, John Busby. "Texas Rangers Along the Rio Grande, 1910–1919."
    Ph.D. dissertation, Texas Christian University, Fort Worth, Texas, 1981.
Schuster, Stephen W., IV. "The Modernization of the Texas Rangers, 1930–
    1936." M.A. thesis, Texas Christian University, Fort Worth, Texas, 1965.
Ward, James R. "The Texas Rangers, 1919–1935." Ph.D. dissertation, Texas
    Christian University, Fort Worth, Texas, 1972.

II.   BILL McDONALD AND THE BROWNSVILLE AFFRAY

Primary Sources

Government Documents

U.S. Congress. Senate. *Preliminary Report of the Commission of the Constitution League of
    the United States on Affray at Brownsville, Texas, August 13 and 14, 1906, and the Dis-
    charging "Without Honor" of the Third Battalion, Twenty-fifth Infantry, United States
    Army, at Fort Reno, Oklahoma, in November, 1906.* Sen. Doc. 107, 59th Cong., 2d
    Sess. Washington, D.C.: GPO, 1906. Ser. 5070.
———. *Summary Discharge or Mustering Out of Regiments or Companies. Message from the
    President of the United States, Transmitting a Report from the Secretary of War, Together
    With Several Documents, Including a Letter of General Nettleton, and Memoranda as to
    Precedents for the Summary Discharge or Mustering Out of Regiments or Companies.*
    Sen. Doc. 155, 59th Cong., 2d Sess. Washington, D.C.: GPO, 1907. Part One.
    Ser. 5078.

————. *Summary Discharge or Mustering Out of Regiments or Companies. Message from the President of the United States, Transmitting a Letter from the Secretary of War Containing Additional Testimony in the Brownsville Case.* Sen. Doc. 155, 59th Cong., 2d Sess. Washington, D.C.: GPO, 1908. Part Two. Ser. 5078.

————. *Summary Discharge or Mustering Out of Regiments of Companies; Message from the President of the United States Transmitting a Report from the Secretary of War Together with General Documents, Including a Letter of General Nettleton, and Memoranda as to Precedents for the Summary Discharge or Mustering Out of Regiments or Companies.* Sen. Doc. 402, 60th Cong., 1st Sess. Washington, D.C.: GPO, 1908. Ser. 5252.

————. *Affray at Brownsville, Tex. August 13 and 14, 1906. Proceedings of a General Court-Martial Convened at Headquarters Department of Texas, San Antonio, Tex., February 4, 1907 in the Case of Major Charles W. Penrose, Twenty-fifth United States Infantry.* Sen. Doc. 402, 60th Cong., 1st Sess. Washington, D.C.: GPO, 1908. Ser. 5253.

————. *Affray at Brownsville, Tex. August 13 and 14, 1906. Proceedings of a General Court-Martial Convened at Headquarters Department of Texas, San Antonio, Tex., April 15, 1907 in the Case of Capt. Edgar A. Macklin, Twenty-fifth United States Infantry.* Sen. Doc. 402, 60th Cong., 1st Sess. Washington, D.C.: GPO, 1908. Ser. 5254.

————. *Affray at Brownsville, Tex. Hearings Before the Committee on Military Affairs United States Senate Concerning the Affray at Brownsville, Tex. on the Night of August 13 and 14, 1906. Vols. I–III.* Sen. Doc. 402, 60th Cong., 1st Sess. Washington, D.C.: GPO, 1908. Ser. 5254–5256.

————. *The Brownsville Affray. Report of the Inspector-General of the Army; Order of the President Discharging Enlisted Men of Companies B, C, and D, Twenty-fifth Infantry; Messages of the President to the Senate; and Majority and Minority Reports of the Senate Committee on Military Affairs.* Sen. Doc. 389, 60th Cong., 1st Sess. Washington, D.C.: GPO, 1908. Ser. 5252.

————. *Summary Discharge or Mustering Out of Regiments or Companies; Message from the President of the United States Transmitting a Report from the Secretary of War Together With Several Documents, Including a Letter of General Nettleton, and Memoranda as to Precedents for the Summary Discharge or Mustering Out of Regiments or Companies. Appendix I. Affray at Brownsville, Texas, August 13 and 14, 1906. Investigation of the Conduct of United States Troops (Companies B, C, and D, Twenty-fifth Infantry) Stationed at Fort Brown, Texas; Reports of Major Augustus P. Blocksom, Inspector-General's Department, Lieutenant Colonel Leonard A. Lovering, Fourth Infantry, Acting Inspector-General, Brigadier General Ernest A. Garlington, Inspector-General, United States Army.* Sen. Doc. 402, 60th Cong., 1st Sess. Washington, D.C.: GPO, 1908. Ser. 5252.

————. *Names of Enlisted Men Discharged on Account of Brownsville Affray, with Applications for Reenlistment. Letter from the Acting Secretary of War, Transmitting, Pursuant to a Senate Resolution of April 6, 1908, the Names of the Enlisted Men of the Twenty-fifth Infantry Discharged Without Honor on Account of the Brownsville, Texas, Shooting Affray, who Have Applied for Reenlistment Under the Order of the Secretary of War, and the Statements Submitted by Them.* Sen. Doc. 430, 60th Cong., 1st Sess. Washington, D.C.: GPO, 1908. Ser. 5256.

————. *Special Message of the President of the United States Communicated to the Senate on*

December 14, 1908. Sen. Doc. 587, 60th Cong., 2d Sess. Washington, D.C.: GPO, 1908. Ser. 5407.

————. *Companies B, C, and D, Twenty-fifth United States Infantry. Report of the Proceedings of the Court of Inquiry Relative to the Shooting Affray at Brownsville, Tex., August 13–14, 1906 by Soldiers of Companies B, C, and D, Twenty-fifth United States Infantry.* Sen. Doc. 701, 61st Cong., 3d Sess. Washington, D.C.: GPO, 1910. Ser. 5889–5891.

Manuscripts

Webb, Walter Prescott. Papers. University of Texas at Austin Archives. Austin, Texas.

Secondary Sources

Carroll, John M., ed. *The Black Military Experience in the American West.* New York: Liveright, 1971.

Lane, Ann J. *The Brownsville Affair: National Crisis and Black Reaction.* Port Washington, New York: Kennikat Press, Inc., 1971.

Mason, Tyler. *Riding for Texas: The True Adventures of Captain Bill McDonald of the Texas Rangers.* New York: Reynal and Hitchcock, 1936.

Paine, Albert Bigelow. *Captain Bill McDonald, Texas Ranger: A Story of Frontier Reform.* New York: J. J. Little & Ives Co., 1909.

Pringle, Henry F. *Theodore Roosevelt: A Biography.* New York: Harcourt, Brace and Company, 1931.

Procter, Ben. "Fort Brown." *Frontier Forts of Texas.* Waco: Texian Press, 1966.

Tinsley, James A. "The Brownsville Affray." M.A. thesis, University of North Carolina, Chapel Hill, North Carolina, 1948.

Weaver, John D. *The Brownsville Raid.* New York: W. W. Norton & Company, Inc., 1970.

Webb, Walter Prescott. *The Texas Rangers: A Century of Frontier Defense.* New York: Houghton Mifflin, 1935.

III.   RED BURTON AND THE KLAN

Primary Sources

Interview with Mr. and Mrs. Tilley Buchanan, Margrett Curton, and Mary Dollins by author. Waco, Texas, November 19, 1969.

Interviews with Red Burton by author. Waco, Texas, February 4, 5, 1967; April 6, 7, 1968; September 18 and November 6, 1969.

Speech by Red Burton. Waco Heritage Society. Waco, Texas, May 1, 1956.

Texas. Department of Public Safety. Austin, Texas. MSS. Ranger Files.

Waco Tribune-Herald. October 2–12, 1921; May 17, 1970.

Secondary Sources

Alexander, Charles C. *Crusade for Conformity: The Ku Klux Klan in 1920–1930.* Houston: Texas Gulf Coast Historical Association, 1962.

————. *The Ku Klux Klan in the Southwest.* Lexington: University of Kentucky Press, 1965.

Allen, Frederick Lewis. *Only Yesterday: An Informal History of the Nineteen-Twenties.* New York: Harper & Row, Publishers, 1931.

Atkinson, William Eugene. "James V. Allred: A Political Biography, 1899–1935." Ph.D. dissertation, Texas Christian University, Fort Worth, Texas, 1978.

Brown, Norman. *Hood, Bonnet, and Little Brown Jug: Texas Politics, 1921–1928.* College Station: Texas A&M University Press, 1984.

Chalmers, David M. *Hooded Americanism: The First Century of the Ku Klux Klan, 1865–1965.* Garden City, New York: Doubleday & Co., 1965.

Frost, Stanley. *The Challenge of the Klan.* Indianapolis: Bobbs-Merrill, Co., 1924.

Fry, Henry P. *The Modern Ku Klux Klan.* Boston: Small, Maynard, & Company, Publishers, 1922.

Hicks, John D. *Republican Ascendancy, 1921–1933.* New York: Harper & Brothers, Publishers, 1960.

Jackson, Kenneth T. *The Ku Klux Klan in the City, 1915–1930.* New York: Oxford University Press, 1967.

Mecklin, John M. *The Ku Klux Klan: A Study of the American Mind.* New York: Harcourt, Brace and Co., 1924.

Rice, Arnold. *The Ku Klux Klan in American Politics.* Washington, D.C.: Public Affairs Press, 1962.

Texas Almanac and State Industrial Guide, 1914. Dallas: Galveston-Dallas News, 1914.

Texas Almanac and State Industrial Guide, 1925. Dallas: A. H. Belo & Company, 1925.

IV.   LEO BISHOP AND THE SAN AUGUSTINE CRIME WAVE

Primary Sources

Interviews with Leo Bishop by author. Carta Valley, Texas, September 12, 1968; November 15, 1969.

Interview with Arlan Hays, editor of the *San Augustine Tribune,* by author. San Augustine, Texas, August 3, 1976.

Interview with Judge Wardlow Lane by author. Dallas, Texas, August 26, 1976.

Interview with former Lieutenant Governor Ben Ramsey by author. San Augustine, Texas, August 4, 1976.

San Augustine Tribune. December 1934–June 1935.

Sterling, William Warren. *Trails and Trials of a Texas Ranger.* Norman: University of Oklahoma Press, 1968.

Secondary Sources

Malsch, Brownson. *Captain M. T. Gonzaullas: Lone Wolf, The Only Texas Ranger of Spanish Descent.* Austin: Shoal Creek Publishers, Inc., 1980.

Schuster, Stephen W., IV. "The Modernization of the Texas Rangers, 1930–1936." M.A. thesis, Texas Christian University, Fort Worth, Texas, 1965.

Stephens, Robert W. *Lone Wolf: The Story of Texas Ranger Captain M. T. Gonzaullas.* Dallas: Taylor Publishing Company, [1979?].

Texas Almanac and State Industrial Guide, 1936. Dallas: A. H. Belo Corporation, 1936.

Webb, Walter Prescott. *The Texas Rangers: A Century of Frontier Defense.* 2d ed. Austin: University of Texas Press, 1965.

V.   CLINT PEOPLES AND THE CRAZED MAN

Primary Sources

Interview with Captain Bob Crowder by author. Dallas, Texas, December 31,
    1969.
Interview with Ranger Trenton Horton by author. Temple, Texas, July 20, 1970.
Interviews with Captain Clint Peoples by author. Waco, Texas, September 3,
    1968; September 18, November 5, 1969; Austin, Texas, July 12, 1970.
Interview with Clint Peoples (telephone) by author, Austin, Texas, November 4,
    1971.
Interview with Inspector J. L. Rogers of the Texas Department of Public Safety by
    author. Austin, Texas, July 20, 1970.
Texas. Department of Public Safety. Austin, Texas. Ranger Scrapbooks.

Secondary Sources

Day, James M. *Captain Clint Peoples, Texas Ranger: Fifty Years a Lawman*. Waco:
    Texian Press, 1980.
Gandy, William Harley. "A History of Montgomery County, Texas." M.A. thesis,
    University of Houston, Houston, Texas, 1952.
Hallman, Leon Charles. "A Geographic Study of Montgomery County, Texas."
    M.A. thesis, Southern Methodist University, Dallas, Texas, 1966.
Montgomery, Robin. *The History of Montgomery County*. Austin: Pemberton Press,
    1975.
Texas Almanac and State Industrial Guide, 1925. Dallas: A. H. Belo Corporation, 1925.
Texas Almanac and State Industrial Guide, 1931. Dallas: A. H. Belo Corporation, 1931.
Texas Almanac and State Industrial Guide, 1933. Dallas: A. H. Belo Corporation, 1933.

VI.   BOB CROWDER AND THE RUSK HOSPITAL RIOT

Primary Sources

Interviews with Senior Ranger Captain Bob Crowder by author. Dallas, Texas,
    February 24, October 24, December 31, 1969; January 11, 1970.
Interview with Emmett Whitehead, publisher and editor of the *Rusk Cherokeean*, by
    author. Rusk, Texas, July 19, 1970.
Texas. Department of Public Safety. Austin, Texas. Ranger Scrapbooks.
Texas. Department of Public Safety. Austin, Texas. "Texas Ranger Strength —
    Authorized." Ranger File.
Whitehead, Emmett. Scrapbooks. Rusk, Texas.

Secondary Sources

Charlton, Thomas Lee. "The Texas Department of Public Safety, 1935–1957."
    M.A. thesis, University of Texas at Austin, Austin, Texas, 1961.
Hicks, John D. Luncheon address, Western History Association. San Francisco,
    California, October 1967.

Hofstadter, Richard. *The Age of Reform: From Bryan to F. D. R.* New York: Vintage Books, 1960.

Malsch, Brownson. *Captain M. T. Gonzaullas: Lone Wolf, The Only Texas Ranger Captain of Spanish Descent.* Austin: Shoal Creek Publishers, Inc., 1980.

Patterson, Mary. "April 16, 1955 Revisited — A Look at the Riot in Maximum Security Unit," *Rusk Cherokeean,* January 9, 1975.

Texas Almanac, 1956–1957: The Encyclopedia of Texas. Dallas: A. H. Belo Corporation, 1957.

Webb, Walter Prescott. Papers. University of Texas at Austin Archives. Austin, Texas.

VII. FRED GOMEZ CARRASCO vs. TEXAS LAW ENFORCEMENT

Primary Sources

House, Aline. *The Carrasco Tragedy: Eleven Days of Terror in Huntsville Prison.* Waco: Texian Press, 1978.

Interview with Ranger Captain G. W. Burks, Company B, by author. Dallas, Texas, August 12, 1981.

Interviews with Jim Estelle, director of the Texas Department of Corrections, by author. Dallas, Texas, August 11, 1981; Huntsville, Texas, September 11, 1981.

Interviews with Father Joseph J. O'Brien by Tom McGowan, in the *San Antonio Light,* September 2–9, 1974.

Interview with Novella Pollard, principal of Jester III Unit, by author. Sugarland, Texas, August 26, 1981.

Interview with Ronald Robinson by Mike Bryan and Carter Pettit, in *Daily Courier* (Conroe), August 4, 1974.

Interview with Mrs. Pete Rogers by author. Silsbee, Texas, August 18, 1981.

Interviews with Linda Woodman, warden at Gatesville TDC Facility, by author. Gatesville, Texas, August 3, and September 6, 1981.

Texas. Department of Corrections. Huntsville Unit. Biography materials in TDC files.

Texas. Department of Corrections. Huntsville Unit. "Report by Warden Hal Husbands."

Texas. Department of Corrections. Huntsville Unit. Videotapes, August 3, 1974.

Woodman, Linda. Scrapbooks. Gatesville, Texas.

Newspapers

Daily Courier (Conroe). July–August, 1974.
Dallas Morning News. July–August, 1974.
Dallas Times Herald. July–August, 1974.
Huntsville Item. July–August, 1974; March 1975.
Houston Chronicle. July–September, 1974; March 1975.
Houston Post. July–August, 1974; March 1975.
San Antonio Express. July–August, 1974.

San Antonio Express-News. July–August, 1974.
San Antonio Light. July–September, 1974.
San Antonio News. July–August, 1974.

Secondary Sources

McKinney, Wilson. "Carrasco, Merchant of Death and Drugs." *San Antonio Express-News.* April 6–17, 1975.
————. *Fred Carrasco: The Heroin Merchant.* Austin: Heidelberg Publishers, Inc., 1975.

Index

171

TEXAS RANGERS — 1989

First row left to right: *Maurice C. Cook, Capt., Asst. Cmdr., Warren Yeager, Lt., Co. "D," David Byrnes, Lt., Co. "B," Bruce Casteel, Capt., Co. "C," George Powell, Capt., Co. "E," Bobby Prince, Capt., Co. "A," Joe Wilie, Lt., Co. "F," H. R. Block, Sr. Rgr. Capt.* Second row left to right: *Kasey King, Co. "D," Doyle Holdridge, Co. "D," Bobby Connell, Co. "F," Jim Miller, Co. "F," Haskell Taylor, Co. "A," Lee Young, Co. "B," Joe Sanders, Co. "E," Al Cuellar, Co. "D."* Third row left to right: *Bill Walk, Co. "A," Ray Coffman, Co. "F," Ray Nutt, Co. "F," Bob Steele, Co. "D," Don Anderson, Co. "B," Ron Stewart, "HQ," Robert Madeira, Co. "A," Charlie Brune, Co. "D," George Turner, Co. "F."* Fourth row left to right: *Tommy Ratliff, "HQ," Joe Hunt, Co. "C," L. C. Wilson, Co. "A," James Ray, Co. "F," Marshall Brown, Co. "C," Earl Pearson, Co. "A," Barry Caver, Co. "A," Gary De Los Santos, Co. "C," John Allen, Co. "E."* Fifth row left to right: *Richard Bennie, Co. "D," David Dunaway, Co. "B," Howard Dunham, Co. "B," Joe Haralson, Co. "A," Lane Akin, Co. "A," Billy Peterson, Co. "C," Ronnie Brownlow, Co. "F," Jim Gillespie, Co. "C," Larry Gilbreath, Co. "C."* Sixth row left to right: *George Frasier, Co. "E," Danny Rhea, Co. "E," Ronnie Griffith, Co. "B," Brantley Foster, Co. "B," Gene Kea, Co. "E," Robert Garza, Co. "D," Calvin Collins, Co. "E," Charlie Havrda, Co. "E."*

— Courtesy Department of Public Safety